Aspects of modern sociology

The social structure of modern Britain

GENERAL EDITORS

John Barron Mays
Eleanor Rathbone Professor of Sociology, University of Liverpool

Maurice Craft
Senior Lecturer in Education, University of Exeter

The Legal Structure

M. D. A. Freeman, LL.M.

Lecturer in English Law,
University College London

Longman

Longman
1724-1974

LONGMAN GROUP LIMITED
London

*Associated companies, branches and representatives
throughout the world*

© Longman Group Limited 1974

First published 1974

ISBN 0582 48761·7 Cased
          48762·5 Paper

*Printed in Hong Kong
by Dai Nippon Printing Co., (H.K.) Ltd.*

Contents

Editors' Preface

British higher education is now witnessing a very rapid expansion of teaching and research in the social sciences, and, in particular, in sociology. This new series has been designed for courses offered by universities, colleges of education, colleges of technology, and colleges of further education to meet the needs of students training for social work, teaching and a wide variety of other professions. It does not attempt a comprehensive treatment of the whole field of sociology, but concentrates on the social structure of modern Britain which forms a central feature of most university and college sociology courses in this country. Its purpose is to offer an analysis of our contemporary society through the study of basic demographic, ideological and structural features, and through the study of such major social institutions as the family, education, the economic and political structure, and so on.

The aim has been to produce a series of introductory texts which will in combination form the basis for a sustained course of study, but each volume has been designed as a single whole and can be read in its own right.

We hope that the topics covered in the series will prove attractive to a wide reading public and that, in addition to students, others who wish to know more than is readily available about the nature and structure of their own society will find them of interest.

JOHN BARRON MAYS
MAURICE CRAFT

Foreword

To confine the treatment of law and lawyers in contemporary English society to 50,000 words means necessarily that many questions and perspectives have had to be ignored. What the reader will find is a treatment of some of what the author regards as key problems in this area. He will not find any discussion of such key sociological concepts as power, order or class, and only incidental treatment of sociological classics such as those by Marx, Weber or Durkheim. Nor will he find any account of legal institutions such as is presented in standard works on the English legal system.

The sociology of law and sociological treatment of legal problems are growth areas, and it is hoped that this modest treatise will stimulate study of the discipline in universities and polytechnics.

It is only fair to point out to readers north of Berwick or in Northern Ireland that although this book is in a series subtitled *The social structure of modern Britain* no attempt is made to assess the distinctive contributions of the Scots and Irish legal systems. References, though, to England embrace, of course, the principality of Wales.

This book was finished in the spring of 1972. There are, however, selective references to events and publications since then. The travails of the Industrial Relations Act get scant treatment: some of the sociolegal problems of the implementation of the Act deserve, and are bound to get, books in their own right.

It remains for me to thank all of those who have assisted in any way in the preparation of this book. Dan Prentice's perceptive comments and innumerable suggestions of improvements have been invaluable. Winnie Holland and Colin Low read individual sections and made helpful comments. Miss Gillian Hoxley and her typing pool coped goodhumouredly with my manuscript. My wife, Vivien, is responsible for many stylistic improvements. Her tact, patience and love through the year of gestation of the book are much appreciated. Needless to say I am responsible for the faults and errors that remain.

M.D.A. FREEMAN

Introduction

Fiction provides us with numerous examples of utopian societies where congruence of norm and ideal is such that there is perfect social harmony and no need for law or lawyers to emerge. History teaches us the unhappy truth that no such society has ever existed. In all societies socialisation is an unequal process; there is always deviance and conflict, and law can be seen to emerge as a norm-asserting authority with the coercive power to sanction those guilty of violating the norm. It is difficult to escape the fact that law is necessary. If a society should ever come about where it is not, it may be predicted with certainty that it will be a society different from anything we have known.

So all-pervasive is the concept of law that few of us ever stop to question its existence. It is 'there', a 'brooding omnipresence in the sky'. It is symbolised by the policeman, the judge, the solicitor's office. There is no doubt that this belief has a tranquillising effect. Equality before the law, freedom under it, the rule of law, are noble ideals. It is important for the underprivileged to believe that the law recognises their yearnings, in the same way as it is vital for the repositories of power to believe that law is behind and above them, giving them authority and permanence. Thurman Arnold put it well when he said that, 'law is . . . a great reservoir of emotionally important social symbols'.[1]

This unquestioning faith in law and legal process is largely a legacy of nineteenth-century positivism. The jurist's concern was with that which was *positum*, laid down. Law and social policy were strictly demarcated. The law was there and needed but a skilled technician to find and apply it. Problems dissolved under the heat of legal logic. The pure science of law had not to be contaminated with alien disciplines. The reaction came but slowly. Law, arcane and archaic, was foreboding to sociologists. The lawyer was both temperamentally unsuited to, and professionally untrained for, placing himself and his institutions under a microscope.

It was the lawyers' defences which were breached first. Legal sociology owes its birth to sociological jurists such as Ihering, Ehrlich, Duguit and Pound. This is not to say that sociologists have not made an important contribution. Durkheim's *The Division of Labour in Society*, itself an important influence on the work of Duguit, and Weber's *Wirtschaft und Gesellschaft* are seminal studies of the social matrix within which the legal structure is rooted.

This book is an analysis of the structure, function, workings and impact of law and lawyers in contemporary England. As such it owes much both to sociological jurisprudence and legal sociology. References to the writings of some of those mentioned in the last paragraph will be scattered throughout this volume, though none of them has written on law and lawyers in this country today. It is they who provide much of our grand theory. Field studies on particular questions are few. Socio-legal research in this country is in its infancy, and without it much that is presented in this book is speculative. This is not an excuse but a plea for the development of legal sociology in this country.

A start has been made. More research into the workings of law and lawyers in this country has been carried out in the last five years than in the previous fifty. The establishment of an Institute of Judicial Administration in Birmingham, and the setting up of a centre for socio-legal studies in Oxford are symptomatic of a new-found realisation of the necessity to examine the social underpinnings of the legal system.

But, in default of research, much of this book remains on the theoretical, rather than empirical, level. Where research is lacking, reference is sometimes made to investigations carried out in the United States or other countries. One must exercise care in handling this material. The United States, for example, has a common tradition with this country, but its legal institutions are far from replicas of an English model. It has a unified legal profession: its division is one of social stratification. Many of its judges are elected. The provision of free legal services for the underprivileged is less advanced than in this country. Conclusions from American research are thus likely to be more suggestive, than conclusive. References are made to American materials in the belief that a few crumbs are better than no bread at all.

The book is in two parts: the first is concerned with the craft of law; the second with its craftsmen and their relationship with the public. The paucity of research materials affects one's consideration of the role of 'law men' less acutely than the role of law. The feeling in the last decade that 'something was wrong with the law' led to a number of studies of legal institutions. But attention has not been focused to the same extent on law itself. One's hope must be that, as socio-legal research stands on the threshold of a new era, more attention is devoted to the mechanics of law, whilst the level of research into legal institutions is maintained and strengthened.

Part One:

The craft of law

Legal structure and social structure   1

Law is only one means of social control: it cannot impose a social order but can confirm and support one. In Bohannan's words: 'Some customs, in some societies, are *re*institutionalised at another level: they are restated for the more precise purposes of legal institutions.'[1] Law then develops with social organisation: it depends for its effectiveness on correspondence with the social matrix. This view claims a large measure of acceptance. But less sympathy is accorded today to the theses of Durkheim and Maine among others who claimed that law was *the* measuring rod of any society. Durkheim wrote: 'Since law reproduces the principal forms of social solidarity, we have only to classify the different types of social solidarity which correspond to it.'[2] Durkheim's view that punitive law and repressive sanctions were reflections of mechanical solidarity (the earlier stage of social evolution when symbolic order and group identity were the order of the day); and restitutive law, contract, cooperation the keynotes of organic solidarity (the division of labour in modern society), is oversimplified. But a survey of the law of a society will undoubtedly give a vivid and accurate picture of the tensions and values, the institutions and interests of that society.

Durkheim's thesis is comparatively modern. When Montesquieu wrote, the prevailing naturalist assumption was that ideal law was a constant through age and society. He argued that human laws were the resultant of cultural factors and physical environment. Different societies fathered different laws. Sociological jurisprudence followed Montesquieu's lead. Modern anthropological studies, moreover, have demonstrated that the core of universal law is hardly sizeable. Margaret Mead has shown that the only norms universally found are some limitation on killing, some right to private property (if only minimally to one's name), and the incest taboo, variously defined.[3] Of course, the mere discovery of these concepts universally in no way implies immutability or moral rectitude. H.L.A. Hart's view that a society which lacks a minimal code would be a suicide club is readily acceptable.[4] Every society must impose certain common restraints. But apart from these, law differs from society to society. This chapter is a survey of contemporary English society seen through the problems and workings of three areas of law: contract, family law and company law. But to understand the *limits* of this approach *three* characteristics of law must first be described.

Legal concept : stability and change

Legal concepts have a peculiar tenacity, an ability to achieve stability within changing social and economic conditions. The illusion is of conservatism and uniformity. The standard form contract in contemporary England (for example, the contract of hire purchase or insurance) bears little resemblance to the nineteenth-century ideal of a contract being an agreement freely reached between two equal parties each looking after his own interests. Nor is it the administrative arrangement imposed on two industrial enterprises in Soviet Russia. Legal stability is the source of both strength and weakness. It enables the legal order to adapt itself smoothly and efficiently to varied circumstances. But there is the danger that it does this by excessive limitation to a narrow range of policies, divorced from the living context in which the concept arose.[5]

Thus the observer of the social structure must penetrate into the economic and social base of a legal concept. Perhaps the finest study along these lines is by the Austrian Marxist, Karl Renner, whose *Institutions of Private Law and Their Social Functions* demonstrates that the legal conception of ownership formulated for a homestead economy had profound effects when

8

continued as an institution of nineteenth-century industrial society.[6]

Legal change and social change

The other two characteristics may be stated under one heading for each is the converse of the other. 'The controversy between those who believe that law should essentially follow, not lead, and that it should do so slowly, in response to clearly formulated social sentiment – and those who believe that the law should be a determined agent in the creation of new norms, is one of the recurrent themes of the history of legal thought.'[7] Yet, in spite of the persistence of the dispute, 'the role law plays in initiating – or reflecting – social change has never been fully explicated, either in theory or through research'.[8]

One model set up to explain the relationship between legal and social change is Ogburn's concept of cultural lag. He had looked at nineteenth-century American industrial society and noted the impotence of the law in the face of the massive problem of industrial accidents. How could one account for the fact that the law remained static for over half a century while accidents became more numerous, more prevalent and more serious? His explanation was that during this period (roughly from 1850 until 1915 when workmen's compensation laws were passed), 'the old adaptive culture, the common law of employers' liability, hung over after the material conditions had changed': there had been 'maladjustment' consequent on a change in culture.[9]

What makes Ogburn's thesis particularly interesting in an English context is that seemingly the same phenomenon existed here. We too had rapid industrial expansion and our common law adopted a similarly myopic response (in both cases the development of the so-called doctrine of common employment, which exempted an employer from liability for an employee's injury where this resulted from the negligence of a fellow employee, was the biggest obstacle): with us also several decades elapsed before the legal machinery caught up with material conditions.

But, though plausible, Ogburn's thesis is an over simplification of the problem, for, as Friedman and Ladinsky point out, resistance to change may only be characterised as 'lag' where there is only 'one "true" definition of a problem – and one "true" solution'. This, there clearly was not: instead a socio-historical analysis shows, not fumbling with the problem, as Ogburn suggested, but compromise and constant adjustment, experiments as new ideas were tried and retried. To quote Friedman and Ladinsky,

> the fellow-servant rule could not be replaced until economic affluence, business conditions and the state of safety technology made feasible a more social solution. Labour unions of the mid-nineteenth century did not call for a compensation plan; they were concerned with more basic (and practical) issues such as wages and hours. . . . What appears to some as an era of 'lag' was actually a period in which issues were collectively defined and alternative solutions posed, and during which interest groups bargained for favorable formulations of law. It was a period of 'false-starts' – unstable compromise formulations by decision makers armed with few facts, lacking organisational machinery, and facing great, often contradictory, demands from many publics.[10]

The legal process is part of the total culture and in the normal case *can only*, and *will*, respond to demands levelled at it. There are occasions when an enlightened legislator or corpus of the judiciary will lead and mould public sentiment. This, the converse situation, will be considered. But only an authoritarian régime can totally ignore popular feeling. What Friedman and Ladinsky are suggesting is that the history of the common employment doctrine reflects the bargaining and compromises effected by different interest groups in society. The English picture is remarkably similar.

While this is meant to cast some doubt on Ogburn's 'cultural lag', it is not disputed that there is often a certain difference between the behaviour demanded by a legal norm and what Ehrlich has described as 'living law'.[11] Legal history is replete with examples of cultural mores being translated into legal norm. The business community in the eighteenth century accepted cheques, much as today it accepts credit cards, long before the concepts were clothed with legal vestment. Children were 'adopted' many years before English law belatedly accepted the institution. Why is it that legal change is somewhat in arrears of social change?

It is all too easy to point to areas where there has been a mismatch between social change and legal development: marital disorganisation, female inequality, racial discrimination, the urban underprivileged. But what is often glossed over is the fact that in the vast majority of areas the law has developed and is constantly developing. A comparison of company law or commercial law or the law of torts in 1800 and subsequently at fifty-year intervals would amply demonstrate this. This is not to say that this development is necessarily a reflection of developing social and economic forces, though it usually is. So why are there exceptions to the rule?

That the speed of change and inadequate learning systems are to blame does not commend itself. The way in which business organises itself has undergone rapid change second to none, yet the legal mechanism has kept pace.

Much more significant is the power structure. Dicey, a leading English constitutional lawyer at the turn of this century and an apostle of the then dying faith in *laissez-faire*, wrote, in his classic account of law and public opinion in England, that:

> Men legislate. . . not in accordance with their opinion as to what is a good law, but in accordance with their interest, and this . . . is emphatically true of classes as contrasted with individuals, and therefore of a country like England, where classes exert a far more potent control over the making of laws than can any single person. . . . So true is this, that from the inspection of the laws of a country it is often possible to conjecture . . . what is the class which holds, or has held, predominant power at a given time.[12]

This would suggest that the law remains static in those areas where the status quo favours the 'power élite', who wish to retain what they already have or to increase their share. This in turn would explain the underdevelopment of certain areas of law, why company law in balancing the interests of management and shareholders cannot accommodate the interests of employees, why traditional concepts of real property law cannot cope with town planning, 'slumlordism' or squatting, why public law techniques have failed to make an impression on social welfare law, why this, indeed, has not developed at all. Similarly, the development of the law of divorce in this country was forestalled by the power of the Church, though of late this trend has been reversed and *Putting Asunder*, the result of a Church commission, led to the introduction of marital breakdown as the sole ground of divorce.

This leads to another factor which should be considered: the composition of our law-making agencies. It is said that a two-party system is a useful mechanism of change. 'The government formed by the victorious party almost invariably controls a safe majority for a number of years, and is therefore usually able to push through important legislative measures.'[13] But law reform, at least until the setting up of the Law Commission in 1965, assumed very minor significance in legislative programmes, and even today the initiative rests very often with the private member. This is not to say that the problems of multi-party states and federal systems are not greater. But, even assuming a law-reforming impulse in the government of the day or a private member, Dicey reminds us that 'law-making in England is the work of men often well advanced in life [who] . . . retain the prejudices or modes of thinking which they acquired in their youth . . . and . . . legislate in accordance with the doctrines which were current . . . in the days of their early manhood'.[14]

This is equally true of our other main agency of legal reform – the judiciary. But here an additional obstacle to legal reorientation presents itself; the tenacity of what Roscoe Pound has called, 'the taught tradition'. 'What stands out', he noted in an article attacking the economic interpretation of law, 'in the history of

Anglo-American law is the resistance of the taught tradition in the hands of judges drawn from any class you like, . . . against all manner of economically or politically powerful interests.'[15] Lawyers have an instinctive tendency to refer every case back to some general principle. When an English judge innovates he strives to follow such analogies as are to be found in existing legal principle. Nevertheless the courts do innovate. And this is frequently recognised by Parliament. So Parliament never defined the old matrimonial offence of cruelty but left it to the judges to evolve the concept taking account of developments in society. Using judicial guidelines of 'injury to health' and 'grave and weighty conduct' they fashioned the concept to take account not only of different cultures and different ages but even the spouses themselves. The courts are endowed with similar powers when they are left to decide what is 'just and equitable', 'fair in all the circumstances', or what is 'grave financial hardship'. Another judicial invention, 'the reasonable man' is but a measuring rod of current morality and opinion.

Legal change may also come about tacitly. Statutes, no longer in tune with current morality, are allowed to fall into disuse. Nobody was fined in this century for failing to attend communion, though the offence remained on the statute book. Suicide ceased to be a crime in 1961, though from a practical point of view its criminality had been removed by 'an all but universal practice of regarding suicide *ipso facto* as committed "while of unsound mind".'[16] Statutory rape, particularly where the man is not much older than the girl, is rarely prosecuted and seldom sanctioned by more than an absolute discharge. None of this improves the image of law.

Finally, the inability of the law to keep pace with social change may be explained by lack of knowledge of this change and of the law wanted by the consumer. Unless it is an area of high public sensitivity and pressure and unless, even in such a case, there is scandal or confrontation, there is unlikely to be any demand for change.

One of the few, perhaps the only, attempt that has been made to assess public sentiment on an area of law was undertaken by a lawyer and two sociologists in Nebraska.[17] Their survey showed a wide divergence between community ethic and legal norm on the question of parental authority. There was disagreement on twice as many issues as there was concurrence. Nor was there any discrepancy between different social groupings. The most surprising finding was that the majority wanted greater restrictions on parental authority, but the questionnaire was not posed so as to elicit what type of legal control was desired. The survey was received critically. Why, one sceptic asked, did the authors not question their respondents' behaviour, rather than their attitudes? It was obvious, commented another, that 'the respondents had not the slightest awareness of the practical implications of their answers', for how else could one explain such enthusiasm for Big Brother?[18]

The Nebraska survey may be crude in its technique and faulty in its conclusions, but it does point the way. Its authors stopped short of suggesting that Nebraskan law should be brought into line with community attitudes. 'It is not possible in a democratic system to impose a law on an utterly hostile community. But, a strong social ground swell sooner or later compels legal action. Between these two extremes, there is a great variety of the patterns of challenge and response.'[19] A survey, such as that conducted by Cohen, Robson and Bates provides information for the challenge by the media, by pressure groups, and by professional associations.

Law as ideology

Law may also be out of step with society because lawmakers have taken positive steps to mould social development along a predetermined line. This problem has come into focus more recently. At the turn of the century both Western and Marxian ideology countered any suggestion that this was feasible. Classical Marxian theory denied that law was anything more than superstructure geared to the economic base. Western sociology and jurisprudence were still wedded to Savigny's *Volksgeist*, the belief that law resided in the common consciousness of the people and that its growth was dictated by that society's organism. Savigny's spirit, demystified, lived on in the writings of the Austrian jurist, Eugen Ehrlich, and the American sociologist, W.G. Sumner who, in 1906, in his classic *Folkways*, wrote: 'Vain attempts have been made to control the new order by legislation. The only result is the proof that legislation cannot make mores.'[20]

But the tide had already turned upon these Canutes. The nineteenth century had already seen reforming legislation in the wake of Benthamite philosophy. Public health legislation, Factories Acts, the prohibition of cruelty to animals and, some sixty years later, to children. By the First World War the reaction to Marxian and Sumnerian determinism had set in. Lester Ward advocated 'attractive legislation' to achieve his vision of 'social telesis'.[21] Roscoe Pound pressed the case of the lawyer as 'social engineer'.[22]

Increasingly, the issue became not whether law is a significant vehicle of social change but rather how it so functions and what special problems it causes. Why the need for such 'progressive' law-making? Would behaviour be affected or would there be a 'lack of phase' between norm and 'living law'? Would attitudes change along with conformity or would they lag? How could resistance, if encountered, be overcome? A later chapter surveys the problems of behavioural and attitudinal responses to new legislation. Some of these other problems are surveyed here.

Two outstanding, well documented examples of law as ideology illustrate the problems explicitly. Prohibition in the United States was a complete failure and the legislature had to recant.[23] But, more recently, the Supreme Court ruling in *Brown* v. *Board of Education*[24] ordering desegregation of schools 'with all deliberate speed' has met with gradual, though not total, success. Prohibition was the action of Congress, *Brown* that of the highest court in the United States. Is this to suggest anything of the relative competence of the legislative and judicial arms of government? Judicial innovation is incremental, the novel is slotted into received systems of rules and concepts. 'It can safeguard a precarious consensus by avoiding radical or sweeping change and by relying on studied indirection rather than unambiguous confrontation.'[25] But *Brown* was 'radical change' and 'unambiguous confrontation'. The success of *Brown* may rather be attributed to the formation of a well-organised group of deeply committed people with clear objectives, the dramatic demonstration of the evils of segregation and the gradual neutralisation of the power of the entrenched opposition. Judicious enforcement can gradually demonstrate the evils and difficulties of the old value system until surrender is seen as honourable 'because it is into the hands of impersonal but respected powers such as "the court" and "the law of the land".'[26] So the Race Relations Board, in its first annual report, was able to postulate 'that in a society that is basically law-abiding the mere passage of a law would produce positive results. Our experience before and since the Race Relations Act came into force confirms us in our view. We have evidence of firms that have ceased to discriminate unlawfully as a result of the legislation.'[27] Why then was Prohibition such a monumental failure? No one factor is responsible, but a number are significant. There was never any serious attempt to enforce the law until it was more than a decade old. It is doubted whether it could have been adequately enforced at any time, but such piecemeal enforcement as there was in the 1920s, the bribery, the wire-tapping, the killing, together with judicial anarchy and administrative stupidity, led to complete alienation of the vast majority of Americans. Law and legal institutions suffered and the machinery of justice was cheapened. But Prohibition also failed because of the excesses of the moral reformers. Prohibition was seen as the thin end of the wedge. There were movements to outlaw cigarette smoking, dancing and jazz.

A conclusion often drawn from the failure of Prohibition is that it is impossible to 'legislate' morality. But success in the field of civil rights has cast doubt on this. The difference may be that 'laws which affect both the public arena and concern victimisation will be most effective in changing the existing moral order'. This places civil rights legislation 'at the exact opposite pole of discussions about moral legislation on prostitution and drug addiction'.[28] The ability of the law to control externally the behaviour of consenting homosexuals is minimal. But the ability of the law to control externally the behaviour of the discriminator is maximal. By passing the Sexual Offences Act of 1967 and the two Race Relations Acts of 1965 and 1968 English law has recognised its limits and its powers.

In spite of these reservations, no legal system could long survive if it failed to maintain a viable relationship with the society it served. The vast bulk of English law is intimately related to contemporary British social structure, which we will now exemplify.

The family, society and the law

The family is the smallest, and yet the most significant, grouping in our society. This is reflected in English law, one of the primary objectives of which is the reinforcement of the family unit. But not every family unit is accorded the law's full protection. Thus, English law distinguishes the monogamous marriage from polygamy on the one hand and concubinage on the other. The former is discouraged by penal sanctions, the latter in a number of ways. A mistress is not a wife: her children are illegitimate. She has no right to be maintained, no right to a roof over her head, little or no protection upon breakdown of the unit. Further such a unit is denied the tax benefits which marriage usually accords. Marriage is thus encouraged not through the application of criminal sanctions (neither fornication nor adultery are crimes, as they are in many American states) but through the withdrawal of benefits. Property-wise English wives and mistresses are barely distinguished, since English law clings to the institution of separate property (its grasp has been weakened by recent inroads), a system which fits the propertied classes for whom, in 1882, it was designed. Similarly, the distinction between legitimate and illegitimate children has been attenuated by the virtual assimilation of succession rights. Further, the concept of being 'treated' as a 'child of the family', introduced in 1970, means that the father in a stable unmarried unit will usually be obligated to maintain an illegitimate child.

Marriage is a relatively easy relationship into which to enter: divorce is proportionately more difficult. To encourage a particular type of union English law thus provides facilities: to keep that type of union intact it provides barriers. English law thus uses penal, regulatory benefit-conferring and facultative techniques to promote family cohesion. It accepts the need to loosen bonds where these become intolerable. Divorce in England today is very much easier, and accords with reality far more, than a generation ago. A change in social philosophy has seen the rejection of the concept of indissolubility, of the sacramental approach to marriage which viewed marital unhappiness as a God-ordained status to be borne with equanimity, and its replacement by an emphasis on autonomy of the individual, with power to determine the course of his own life. The evils of dissolution are now recognised to follow marital breakdown. The wife suffers when her husband leaves her, and when his new 'wife' has immediate access to the one wage packet: not when he divorces her. The law has become more realistic. A couple who want a divorce need no longer resort to the subterfuge of hotel adultery. A wife whose husband left her more than five years ago can no longer cling to the shadow of her status. The philosophy underlying the Divorce Reform Act 1969 is the strengthening of marital stability (hence the emphasis on reconciliation wherever possible) but concomitantly it is the decent burial of empty legal shells, of marriages that were failures, with 'maximum fairness, and the minimum bitterness, distress and humiliation'.[29] The defended divorce suit may well become a relic of the past, rather as enticement suits and actions for breach of promise of marriage have, as a climate of opinion prevails under which property and financial adjustment upon breakdown and arrangements over children are conducted in a rational manner by civilised people making the best of a bad job and not assuming the warring postures that the law, until recently, required of them.

A similar pattern is discernible in the law's approach to child protection and succour. Thus, whilst there is a common law duty, now reinforced by statute, not to ill-treat or neglect a child, the criminal law remains very much in the background. Since 1948 the objective of social policy has been to give every support to the family as the primary agency for the care and socialisation of children. With this in mind the administrative-regulatory has supplanted the penal as the primary legal machinery for helping children. Thus, section 1 of the Children and Young Persons Act of 1933 proclaimed: 'It shall be the duty of every local authority to make available such advice, guidance and assistance as may promote the welfare of children by diminishing the need to receive children into or keep them in care . . . or to bring children before a juvenile court.' Increasing awareness of the causes of child neglect and ill-treatment and of juvenile delinquency has led to a recognition that criminal sanctions are blunt instruments to promote family cohesion. Instead, the welfare of the child, stated explicitly as the paramount consideration, is promoted through state supportive measures. Financial assistance (family allowances, family income supplement benefits, social security, though not, as yet, a 'fatherless families' allowance) tax relief, health, education and welfare services, all in their respective ways support the child in his home environment. Increasingly, also, has come the recognition that therapy is better than surgery, prevention than cure, and measures have been adopted to relieve pressures on families at risk while enabling children to be brought up by their parents. So local authorities have devoted more resources to prophylactic work, including subsidisation of families: meanwhile fostering, day nurseries and child-minding have been developed and regularised. Assistance and supervision of the child in the family unit is seen as preferable to severing his links with his family. At the same time has come the acknowledgement that there is a close interrelationship between deprivation and social depravity, and with it gradual withdrawal of criminal sanctions from the young offender.

Contemporary family law reflects in its various ways many of the keynotes of modern British society: the importance of the family but at the same time the recognition that the state must provide services which in pre-industrial society were provided by the family; the emphasis on individual autonomy; the decline in religious faith; and the acceptance that the tensions of family life do not have purely legal solutions.

Contract, consumer protection and the law

The law is often seen by laymen as cutting down freedom, imposing duties to do or abstain from doing certain activities. To a limited extent this is correct, but it excludes a whole vista of legal experience. Most law sets up a framework of powers by means of which the individual can lead a fuller, albeit a law-regulated, life. He can acquire property, marry, bequeath his possessions, and enter into contracts. In a static society the need for contract is not great. Feudal England had little need for such an institution, and contract as we know it developed comparatively late. To a mobile, complex society it is an indispensable provision, enabling freedom of movement for labour and goods.

The law thus confers on the individual the power to make contracts. He lacks complete freedom: he cannot make certain contracts which are classified by the law as illegal, for example, to hire a room for the purpose of prostitution. But, generally, there is facilitation of freedom of will. Thus contracts are easily entered into: there is no need to draw up formal documents in the majority of cases and hence little cause to seek legal advice. Thus far English law reflects a free enterprise society, a classical capitalist model. This comes out further in the English concept of consideration, for not any agreement entered into is a contract but only those in which something of value passes from each party to the other. The theory of contract enunciated here presumes equality of the contracting parties, each being free to look after his own interests. So Romer L.J. was able to say in 1954 that 'courts of equity have never interfered with contracts merely by reason of their being improvident. . . . If a man made a foolish or improvident one so much the worse for him.'[30] Formal equality has a hollow ring where one party is a giant corporation or a mono-poly, the other an individual. Freedom of contract may here mean 'take it or leave it'; do not work, do not travel, do not buy a car or a packet of sugar. Contract in contemporary England reflects this antinomy of freedom and lack of equality.

In this type of contract one party inevitably has long experience and is supported by expert advice. The other has little opportunity to do more than scrutinise cursorily contract terms presented to him in the manner of parliamentary legislation. And if he does not like the terms of the finance company or life insurance society there is not much point his going elsewhere as he will get the same conditions. Standardisation of contract 'is an inevitable aspect of the mechanisation of modern life'.[31] In certain areas, notably labour relations, some equalisation has been secured by group pressure and contract has become a battle between, what Galbraith has called, 'countervailing powers'.[32] Consumers' associations have less power: they do not bargain collectively and can only bring indirect pressure to bear upon manufacturers. Social control is inadequate and legal control inevitable.

There has been some judicial and legislative mitigation of un-equal bargaining strength. Parliament passed Truck Acts as early as 1831 ensuring that a worker be paid in cash and not kind, and the courts for a long time have struck down restrictive covenants by which an employee engages not to use his skill and labour elsewhere on leaving his current employment. 'If these covenants were given full force, they would tend to reduce [the worker's] freedom to seek better conditions, even by asking for a rise in wages; because if he is not allowed to get work elsewhere, he is very much at the mercy of his employer.'[33] Both of these examples are in the area of labour relations. Interventions in consumer transactions have been as common but their success more frag-mentary. The Sale of Goods Act 1893, imposing certain obliga-tions on the seller with respect to quality of goods etc., restricts his freedom in theory. However, the effectiveness of these pro-visions is weakened by the fact that he can exclude his common law liability by contract. Many so-called guarantees put the purchaser into a weaker position than he was before he signed it. The courts have struggled to counter this practice but have only demonstrated their impotence. The judges did develop the concept of 'fundamental breach' of contract but this was found to be conceptually faulty and has now been laid to rest. There is little doubt, even if only vague inference, that relief will be granted when, for example, 'a *de facto* monopoly of supply is unfairly exploited'.[34] So, in *D and C Builders* v *Rees*[35] the Court of Appeal treated as void an agreement by a creditor in financial difficulties to accept part of a debt in satisfaction of the whole: the bargain was unreal because of economic pressure. The Sale of Goods Act contrasts unfavourably with the Hire-Purchase Act 1965 where conditions of liability cannot be excluded. Both the Molony Committee on Consumer Protection and the Law Commission have commented on the anomaly, the latter recommending that contracting out be outlawed in all consumer sales.[36] If this is implemented, the result would probably be an increase in prices: the consumer would pay the seller's insurance premiums.

English law thus represents an uneasy compromise. Freedom of contract, though based on outmoded economic theories, still retains the upper hand. The economically weaker party, particularly one who, like the consumer, relies on individual bargaining, provides the fuel to help light the funeral pyre of laissez-faire.

Corporate control, shareholders and the national interest

In a totalitarian state the freedom to form social groups within the State is frowned upon: competition to state hegemony cannot be tolerated. But there are dangers in a society such as England where formation of social groups is tolerated, even encouraged, that some large highly organised groups may take over the substance of sovereignty. How does English law balance these conflicting interests? This section looks at just one social grouping.

The limited liability company is a nineteenth-century creation which developed to meet the needs of entrepreneurs and investors in the free economy of the later industrial revolution. The spreading of profit and loss enables enterprises to be undertaken which would be impossible without the institution of the company. The theory is well illustrated by the leading case of *Salomon* v. *Salomon*:[37] by incorporation, the company is accorded an identity separate and distinct from the shareholders who own the assets of the company. In *Salomon*, the House of Lords refused to hold the sole beneficiary shareholder liable for the debts of the company on the grounds that the company was an entity separate and distinct from its shareholders. Occasionally, however, the courts will investigate the underlying economic realities of a company, for example where the corporate form is being used for the purposes of fraud.

The legal model of the company is that the directors manage the affairs of the company on behalf of the shareholder-owners. This in no way corresponds to reality. Shareholders, theoretically the owners, have lost control to management. The classic description of this is Berle and Means's *The Modern Corporation and Private Property*.[38]

In general, shareholders have no effective control over management. The reasons for this are partly legal. Even where there are legislative attempts to boost shareholders' power, their success is limited. The Companies Act 1948 (s. 184) gives power to an ordinary majority to dismiss any director. But, as Wedderburn points out, the shareholders 'are interested not in section 184, but in their dividends'.[39] Further, the decline in the doctrine of *ultra vires*, under which company purposes were strictly limited and management's hands tied, has further exempted managerial discretion from shareholders' control and judicial review. On occasions also the courts have strongly asserted managerial independence. Thus, in *Shaw and Sons Ltd* v. *Shaw*[40] it was held that once shareholders have delegated powers of management they cannot interfere with the directors' exercise of those functions. All told, management, particularly senior management, has a remarkably free hand.

But the reasons for this are not entirely legal. There are pragmatic ones as well. Shareholders in large public companies are widely dispersed and normally lack the expertise to evaluate the efficiency of managerial performance. The result is that share-holders tend to vote by selling their interests rather than by exercising internal corporate disciplinary action.

In spite of this legal model, as Shenfield remarks in *Company Boards*, 'the commonest explanation of company board decision-making is to describe it as a balancing of interests in which the board takes into account the interests of the various groups, such as employees, customers and the general public as well as share-holders'.[41] But this is not recognised by the legal norm. So in *Parke* v. *Daily News*, where the directors of the company owning the *News Chronicle* had negotiated the sale of the paper's goodwill to close it down, and proposed to pay the bulk of the sale price to employees as a gift to ease their redundancies (redundancy payments having not yet been introduced), a shareholder success-fully challenged the implementation of this plan. Plowman J. remarked: 'The defendants were prompted by motives which however laudable, and however enlightened from the point of view of industrial relations were such as the law does not re-cognise as sufficient justification'.[42] In considering 'the best in-terests of the shareholders', which the law demands of directors, it is the long-term interests of the shareholders which remain paramount.

Recent American jurisprudence, however, recognises the legi-timacy of corporate objectives other than that of the profit motive. In *A.P. Smith Manufacturing Co.* v. *Barlow*, the Supreme Court of New Jersey recognised the responsibility of business to the community, in this case to higher education. 'Modern conditions require', said the court, 'that corporations acknowledge and discharge social as well as private responsibilities as members of the communities within which they operate.'[43] To uphold a similar donation in England would require proof that the long-term benefits of the company would be promoted by, for example, the provision of potential skilled employees trained in that in-stitute of learning. Yet the argument that large corporations should, aside from taxation, help to solve problems, such as pollution, which they have created, is almost unanswerable.

English company law has thus encountered severe difficulties in adjusting to the contemporary business structure: the divorce between ownership and control, the tension between profit maximisation and the public interest, the struggle for employees' rights all illustrate these difficulties.

Conclusion

In these three areas the intimate relationship between English law and English society has been described. Other areas could have been selected. Thus, the importance of administrative law[44] as the key to many of the mysteries of society (its political and economic structure, type of government, the values enshrined in the system) has been omitted. So too has criminal law. This is dealt with in the next chapter.

Legal control and social control 2

There is a tendency for lawyers to exaggerate the part law plays in controlling society. They fail to see that law is but one technique of social control. This chapter describes two areas of legal activity, the regulation of deviance and conflict resolution, and relates each to a wider social context. The two selected areas throw light on different aspects of law in contemporary England: the first says something about criminal law relating this to the structure of society; the second describes and relates the different procedures for resolving conflict into peace, the inference being that these differences are due, in part, to social variances.

Social control

The concept of social control has nineteenth-century roots. It was popularised by the American sociologist, Ross, and became part of the currency of lawyers when adopted by Roscoe Pound. It grew out of rejection of the utilitarian image of society as one of natural harmony of self-interests. Social Darwinism, on the other hand, saw conflict between the individual and society as inevitable: man's animal spirits needed taming, without restraint men were prone to violence and disruption. Ross hypothesised that forces of sympathy, sociability, a sense of justice and of resentment which could maintain a 'natural social order' without law are insufficient in an industrial, urbanised society.[1] For a concrete illustration of this the reader may be referred to Cain's comparison of the work of city and country policemen.[2]

The development of legal control

Legal control emerges, according to Simmel, with growth in population size. Small groups can exist on custom, but the greater freedom, mobility and individualisation that larger groups offer brings concomitantly the need for 'rigorous and objective norm which is crystallised in law'.[3] It is the small, homogeneous and stable community which has the highest level of social control and in which resort to official and formal agencies is minimal. Thus, 'most tribal societies have no police forces, prisons, or mental hospitals: they are small enough to look after their own deviants'.[4]

Research by Schwartz into two Israeli collective communities provides some evidence for this hypothesis.[5] He compared the *kvutza*, which was entirely collective, with the *moshav*, in which the family was the economic unit. In other respects both settlements were similar. The *kvutza* lacked distinctively legal institutions, though these had developed in the *moshav*. He attributed this difference to the fact that in the *kvutza* informal controls were extremely sensitive, as they formed the basis of a closely integrated group life, with continuous interaction and public observation. The influence of public opinion and peers' sentiment was pervasive. In the *moshav,* however, norms were less explicit, uniformly applied or generally agreed. *Moshav* conditions did not permit the degree of public observation encountered in a *kvutza,* with the result that the *moshav* developed special agencies to regulate deviance and resolve conflict.

In further research Schwartz and Miller demonstrated that different techniques of legal control develop at different stages of societal complexity.[6] Contrary to Durkheim's hypothesis[7] that restitutive sanctions (civil law) replaced repressive ones (criminal law) as a result of growth of division of labour and corresponding move from mechanical to organic solidarity, they found that the simplest of societies tended to award damages and use mediation for conflict resolution, whereas the presence of police was associated with considerable technological complexity: viz., use of money, a substantial degree of specialisation, even full-time government officials. Similarly, another agency of legal control, legal counsel, developed only in the most complex of societies surveyed. Lawyers emerged only in relatively urbanised societies, with a division of labour, an understanding of advantages of specialisation, and achievement of literacy.

Legal control

The role of legal control is twofold. It provides an authoritative statement of the contours of acceptable conduct. The dominant section of a society will endeavour to have its perceptions of proper behaviour encoded in this way. But legalisation does not ensure legitimisation: 'substantial sections of the population may prefer, or even demand, to behave according to their own cultural standards, thus withdrawing their consent to the legal code'.[8] This, as a source of deviance, is considered later in this chapter.

Secondly, legal control acts as a mechanism for the resolution of conflict. This may arise from genuine differences of interpretation of the legal code. No code is complete or absolutely certain and courts thus act as authoritative agencies for the restatement, application and development of legalised definitions. In criminal law situations the emphasis rests here, but in the area of civil law the courts take on the additional function of harmonisation and adjustment. Conflict resolution is discussed later in this chapter. At this juncture it is important to appreciate the interrelationship between the dual functions of legal control.

Deviance

Deviance is not a simple quality: it is not 'a property *inherent* in certain forms of behaviour'.[9] It is false to treat it as a static condition. There is no such thing as deviance *per se*: there can only be deviance from someone's expectations of one's role within a social grouping. The ideal is a society where role expectations are so integrated and stable that there is complete conformity.

No complex, heterogeneous society could *by definition* satisfy such a utopian model.

The source of deviance has been variously described. For long it was believed that deviants were a particular type of person, different from normal people. They were defective in some way: to some they were physiologically misshapen;[10] to others they suffered mental disability; to some sociologists the fault lay not in the deviants themselves but in their environment, their family background, or delinquent gangs with which they associated. Thus stated the problem of deviance is oversimplified. As Box points out,[11] it is to assume that those in penal institutions (*official deviants*) are the equivalents of *deviants*, who are the people who engage in *deviance*. The errors in such a 'holy trinity' will become apparent in this chapter.

The functionalist school of sociology sees deviance as infraction of the normative order. Thus to Merton deviant behaviour 'must be related to the norms that are socially defined as appropriate and morally binding for people occupying various statuses'. His thesis assumes that society has certain goals and legitimate means of realising them. Aberrant conduct is thus seen 'as a symptom of dissociation between culturally defined aspirations and socially structured means'.[12] The theory presumes a value consensus in society. But most societies, ours being typical, have a plurality of cultures, with moral relativism being the keynote. Further, the theory identifies the legalised and legitimised culture, whereas the two are by no means coincident. The assumption is also that society's rules are clear and unambiguous, whereas they may be vague or novel and unfamiliar. Further, as Lemert has argued, the individual is not, as Merton claimed, a free agent making adaptation pointed toward a consistent value order, but is ' "captured" by the claims of various groups to which he has given his allegiance. . . . Overt behaviour . . . frequently reflects contingent ordering of values and compromised positioning, and their unresolved dilemmas.'[13] The individual thus becomes aware of alternatives and sees the norms of his society as compromises rather than statements of sacred values.

Labelling

More light is thrown on deviance by the interactionist school of sociologists. To them deviance is 'the product of some sort of transaction that takes place between the rule breaker and the rest of society'. It is not a fixed and given condition but 'the perception and definition by certain people that this condition poses a threat which is against their interests'.[14] In a society composed of heterogeneous groups some of them will have more power than others. Deviance is thus the description of conduct (or its appearance) of which powerful groups or their agencies of control disapprove. A lucid exponent of this thesis is Becker. He writes:

> *Social groups create deviance by making the rules whose infraction constitutes deviance*, and by applying those rules to particular people and labelling them as outsiders. From this point of view, deviance is *not* a quality of the act the person commits, but rather a consequence of the application by others of rules and sanctions to an 'offender'. The deviant is one to whom that label has successfully been applied; deviant behaviour is behaviour that people so label.[15]

Deviance thus depends on reaction. Crime rates are hence not absolutes but reflect such factors as whether the act is so perceived by potential reporters, the police ratio to the population, the 'meaning' a policemen attaches to peripheral conduct, the degree to which one's life is acted out in the public arena, and selectivity in the enforcement of certain crimes. There is considerable evidence of a bias in law enforcement against lower socio-economic classes. Thus, Sutherland showed in his study of *White Collar Crime* that major companies regularly defied the law but were seldom prosecuted, and Carson's recent studies demonstrate the Factory Inspectorate's reluctance to use prosecution as a method of social control.[16]

Deviance and control are integrally related. Whether an act is labelled rule-breaking depends on a number of variables. Responses change over a period of time. An act may be perceived as a danger which passed unnoticed a year earlier. Moral panics, as Cohen[17] has recently demonstrated, can be created by the mass media. The degree to which an act will be treated as deviant depends also on who commits it and who feels his interests are threatened by it. Further it may not be the acts to which 'significant others' respond, but the consequences of those acts. Unlawful sexual intercourse with a girl under sixteen is more likely to be prosecuted, and more likely to attract a stiffer penalty where the girl becomes pregnant. One may be labelled as a deviant not because one has committed the rule infraction in question but because one looks like, or associates with, those who commit such an offence. A student with long hair is more likely to be 'frisked' for drugs than a bank clerk.

An understanding of deviance thus requires its placing within social context. The act of rule-breaking has no finite quality, but depends on interpretations others make of behaviour.

The control of deviance

Deviance can be controlled both at the level of social relations and through formal agencies, such as the police, the courts and social workers. In spite of the discretion exercised by formal agencies, it is legalised culture they enforce. Society as a whole supports them in this, if only often through indifference. But individuals may also belong to one or more overlapping groups with their own concepts of legitimate behaviour. Thus control at different levels is not necessarily directed towards the same behaviour. Two further points need emphasising.

Firstly, total elimination of deviance may not be desirable. It may be, as Durkheim and Simmel hypothesised, that deviance is fundamental in promoting social cohesion, that is it may act as a boundary-maintaining device. In Schur's words, 'deviance defining is seen . . . not merely as a process affecting social structure but . . . almost as a functional prerequisite of such structure'.[18]

Secondly, in controlling deviance one is helping to create it. Ian Taylor's essay on soccer hooliganism is a telling illustration of this spiral process. He points to the escalation of social control that has led to an awareness of football crowds as a social problem. He reasons that as

> the scale of control increases, that is, as magistrates become more ready to sentence offenders and police become more willing to act (knowing they will obtain convictions), then by definition there develops an 'objective' demonstration of the scale of the problems . . . More and more soccer hooligans appear in the criminal statistics and the need for further control is emphasised.[19]

Mob squads are then introduced, and committees of enquiry set up, and the process of reaction spirals further. It is a syndrome that can only be broken by an analysis and understanding of the problem that delves deeper than stereotypes and labels.

Social control

Society possesses a number of devices which reduce the incidence of deviance. Most important is the *education system,* for not only does this impart knowledge and technical skills, but it is also geared towards socialisation of the individual into internalisation of role expectations of the legalised culture. Conformity is further reinforced by *ritualistic situations.* Thus, a barrister learns the ethics of the Bar during the ritual associated with dining. This institution is used to make the lawyer and novice feel part of 'an all-enveloping group that shares his attitudes and with which he can think of himself as standing in a primary-type relationship'. His status in the group depends on his 'continued commitment to the symbolic system evoked by the ritual'.[20]

There are, further, *institutional arrangements* which forestall the desire to deviate by allowing regressive behaviour in specific isolated situations. An example is the 'party' at which behaviour is tolerated which would be frowned on outside this particular institutional setting.

Mechanisms also exist which enable the individual to know what conformity is being reinforced, for there may be ambiguity in its content. This may arise from genuine doubts as to what the acceptable norms and values are, but may also develop from an individual's own definition of a situation. In the first instance *clarification* is needed, and this may come at one level from an official agency's restatement of what constitutes authoritative norm. At the level of social relations this may be done less precisely. Where doubt arises from an individual's definition, both society as a whole and authoritative agencies have techniques for the *reinforcement* of encoded behaviour. Recidivism among shoplifters is relatively low, for though they may rationalise their activity as less than theft, arrest, trauma and degradation make them realise that they are in danger of being identified by society as criminals. The shoplifter who receives a severe jolt may subsequently conform or accept redefinition as a criminal. If he or she accepts such designation it may lead to what Lemert has called secondary deviation, 'deviant behaviour, or social roles based on it, which becomes a means of defence, attack or adaptation to the overt and covert problems created by the social reaction to primary deviation'.[21] For the middle classes particularly, the administration of justice, with the trappings of police and courts, the stigma and publicity, is one of the most effective means of reinforcing societal norms and values.

Legal control

Law, in Hart's useful classification,[22] is of two types: that which is duty-imposing, laying down standards of behaviour to be observed; and that which confers powers, including powers to officials to introduce a sanctioning process against those who do not observe primary obligations. The duty-imposing, as well as the power-conferring, rules are, of course, made by authority. How this is constituted is outside the scope of this book.[23]

The two types of rule correspond to a dual role played by law and legal institutions: the *creation* of deviance by encoding certain behaviour as non-acceptable (as such the law is primarily responsible for creating criminals!); and its *control* by formal agencies.

One such agency, the police, is considered in a later chapter. This section concentrates largely on the first problem.

Legal standards are based at a minimum. Although the state has a monopoly of legal force, it plays a relatively minor role in reinforcing standards of conduct by sanctioning procedures. Of course, with the increase in mobility and the decrease in the strength of traditional status groups, class and family, informal sanctioning procedures are in relative decline. Nonetheless, the fear of losing one's reputation with one's status group still acts as an effective mechanism of social control, particularly at the upper end of social stratification where numbers are smaller and there is a high rate of social interaction. Social sanctions, Max Weber wrote, can be 'a more severe punishment than any legal penalty'.[24] Their effectiveness hinges, not only on the pervasiveness of their incidence and impact, but on the fact that even the deviant is usually motivated to retain group membership.

Legal standards mirror the society. A property-owning society will define deviance with reference to its property concepts, a religious society will label certain behaviour as heresy. Ideally, the definitions written into the legal system will be common elements in characterisations of society. But inevitably powerful groups will succeed in legalising what they regard as legitimate and outlawing that of which they disapprove. This leads to tension and conflict. Where legal definitions 'deviate' too far from popular definitions there is the danger that it will meet outright opposition. Prohibition in the United States and street betting in this country are paradigm examples.

There is also a tendency for behaviour to retain its classification as deviance long after the social reasons for so categorising it have vanished. The law then becomes a frame into which dominant interest groups can fit their perceptions of dysfunction. Chambliss[25] has pointed to one such striking hangover in his socio-historical analysis of the English vagrancy laws. Passed originally in the fourteenth century to serve the economic interests of the Church, they had served their purpose and lay dormant when revised and repassed in the Elizabethan era for the interest of landowners.

Similarly, Hall's study[26] of the relationship between theft and society shows how it was only with the rise of commerce and increased demands by merchants for the protection of their goods that the judges were pressured into extending by fiction the law of larceny.

The formal agencies of criminal law play a secondary role to that of primary groups. Nonetheless their role cannot be under-estimated. Two considerations of their use and application need surveying.

Firstly, there is no doubt of the relative importance of reliability of sanctions over their severity.[27] The more certain it is that one will be caught and punished, the less likely it is that the offence will be committed. Stepping up the punishment for a particular offence has less effect on the incidence of crime than the certainty that one will be caught. This is an argument for improving police techniques and mechanisms. But our society has values higher than the elimination of deviance: the maxim that it is better for one hundred guilty men to go free than one innocent man be imprisoned encapsulates this hierarchy. The role of the lawyer is an important one: he has developed codes of evidence and safe-guarding procedures, such as the Judges' Rules, to curb any possible 'police justice'.[28] A seemingly guilty man may thus go free on, what seems to laymen, a technicality. The effect of this on different sections of the public has never been studied, but it is assumed that the logic of this appeals to the middles classes to a greater extent than the respectable working sections of the population. To the former 'fair play' is an important consideration; whilst the latter's own conformist tendencies are shaken by the spectacle of the 'deviant' going free. It may be added that Schwartz and Skolnick's research suggests, that even on acquittal, the consequences of legal accusation on job opportunities (and doubt-less in other areas as well) are damaging.[29]

There are, secondly, types of deviance to which the criminal sanction is more appropriate than others. Herbert Packer, in *The Limits of the Criminal Sanction*, describes some criteria for the optimal use of the criminal sanction. These are:

1. The conduct is prominent in most people's views of socially threatening behaviour, and is not condoned by any significant segment of society.
2. Subjecting it to the criminal sanction is not inconsistent with the goals of punishment.
3. Suppressing it will not inhibit socially desirable conduct.
4. It may be dealt with through even-handed and non-discriminatory enforcement.
5. Controlling it through the criminal process will not expose that process to sever qualitative or quantitative strains.
6. There are no reasonable alternatives to the criminal sanction for dealing with it.[30]

Clearly, some offences meet these criteria better than others. Murder, robbery and rape may be considered typical examples of offences for which criminal sanctions are apposite. The opposite pole is reached when morals offences are considered. Some of the problems of the legal enforcement of a dominant morality are discussed in the next chapter. Space prevents a fuller discussion of Packer's criteria, for which the reader may consult the book itself.

The deviant reaction

Packer's criteria view the problem from the lawmaker's perspective. But the reaction of the 'labelled' is also a pertinent consideration in assessing the viability of control. Reference has been made to secondary deviance, or deviance amplification in Wilkins's terminology; a few further comments are called for.

A significant effect of control is to confirm the deviant in his self-identity. Wilkins hypothesises 'that it is possible for a society to operate in such a way that its social sanctions systems become devalued'.[31] There is, he believes, a 'feedback mechanism' in which initial deviation from valued norms leads to punitive reaction by the community, a concomitant of which is often segregation of deviants into groups: that this leads to development of a new identity on the part of the deviant and behaviour fitting this identity, which in its turn stimulates further punitive reaction and the amplifying sequence continues. Recent studies by Young on drugtakers in Notting Hill[32] and Cohen on 'mods and rockers' and the seaside 'invasions' of the 1960s[33] confirm the accuracy of Wilkins's theoretical model.

This is not to argue for total elimination of criminal sanctions, but it is a timely reminder of the need to reconsider social policy behind certain criminal offences, particularly moral offences where legalised culture is not acceptable to large minority groups. Wilkins, writing in 1964 of the virtues of tolerance, gives a concrete illustration of a danger which later events have vindicated:

> In the United States drug addiction is treated as a most serious crime and convicted offenders are sentenced to very long terms of imprisonment, whereas in Great Britain the drug addict is dealt with as a sick person and treated with sympathy, if not with tolerance. . . . It is possible, or even probable, that any attempt to tighten up the British regulations with a view of making a minor problem even less of a problem may be a disturbance of the generating system of perceptions which could produce a more serious problem.[34]

Legal control : the resolution of conflict

The second function of law as a system of social control is to provide a mechanism by which conflicts between individuals, or between individuals and the state, may be resolved. The statement in normative form of societal standards is an important preventative of conflict. It enables most conflict to be resolved by compromise, rather than judicial decree, though this is less true of conflict between individual and state. But this is because in criminal cases the settlement of conflict plays second fiddle to the task of upholding conformity with the law. Even in the area of criminal law, the institution of 'plea-bargaining' is accepted, at any rate as part of the living law.

Conflict may be resolved in three ways: by negotiation; by mediation; and by adjudication. Clearly, some conflictual situations lend themselves more readily to one form of resolution than another.

Thus a distinction may be drawn between occasional and inter-mittent relationships, such as that between business organisations, and social relations involving a permanent organism, as in in-dustry or between members of a family.

Writing of labour relations, before the volte-face produced by the Industrial Relations Act of 1971 Kahn-Freund wrote: 'It is almost axiomatic that such social relationships are incompatible with the intervention of the law as long as they endure. The law can either intervene at the point of their termination or else, by intervening, produce that termination.'[35] Where parties are in a continuous state of social propinquity, resolution by adjudication is inconsistent with continuing viable social interaction.

Nor must the selection of labour and family relations on the one hand, and those of business on the other, blind us to the fact that such intimacy and congruence of goal can also exist in business organisations. Thus, Macaulay, in *Law and the Balance of Power*,[36] has shown how resort to 'other-than-legal dispute settlement systems' by dealers and manufacturers of cars enables a meaningful and trusting legal working relationship to continue, where the seeking of judicial resolution would jeopardise such relationships. Further, such firms may not even enter into formal, legal relation-ships. Macaulay produces empirical evidence to substantiate Thomas Schelling's remark that 'tacit negotiation of unenforceable agreements can sometimes be more efficacious than explicit verbal negotiation of agreements that purport to carry some sanction'.[37] His study of a number of Wisconsin companies demonstrates the relative lack of recourse to the formal system of contract. 'Businessmen', he reported, 'often prefer to rely on "a man's word" in a brief letter, a handshake, or "common honesty and decency" – even when the transaction involves exposure to serious risks.' And he quotes the following 'common business attitude': 'One doesn't run to lawyers if he wants to stay in business because one must behave decently.'[38]

Even where relationships have broken down, there are actions which no amount of legal compulsion can accomplish. This applies with particular force to areas of family and labour relations.

It was, indeed, recently recognised with the abolition of the quaint remedy of restitution of conjugal rights: no court could compel a spouse to resume a marital relationship. Yet, paradoxically, a year later, the law moved into an equally sensitive area and, contrary to almost unanimous academic and professional opinion, and against the advice of a Royal Commission, imposed regulations on the relationship between employers and employees which had not been consensually arrived at. These relations, like marital relations, rest upon the social assumption that parties are ready and willing to accept and deal with each other: no amount of legal intervention can secure such a social basis.

Industrial disputes are a paradigm of what Aubert, in his stimulating essay 'Competition and dissensus: two types of conflict and of conflict resolution', calls a conflict of interest. There are not enough goods to go round: each party demands too much. Conflict is resolved when each party concedes to reduce his demands until an agreement is reached. The agreement is not to be interpreted as an ethical commitment to the terms embodied in the agreement, but rather as an expression of what the parties find it in their own interests to do. Conflicts of interest are thus susceptible to bargaining or compromise. But place this same dispute in a judicial arena, and the basic interaction process is complicated by the addition of a third party, and, more significantly, the parties are polarised by having to state an issue. What has started as a conflict of interests is metamorphosed, in Aubert's terminology, into a conflict of values. One consequence is that compromise is now wellnigh impossible, and that 'the law' in its legalistic manner can prescribe only an all-or-nothing solution. The problem is objectivised, becomes public property. The court's decision not only solves the conflict in issue but 'permits others, in advance and abstractly, to determine how certain conflicts are to be solved'.[39] The court's decision affects the normative order: an out-of-court compromise does not. The parties' freedom is restricted, for there are the interests of society to consider.

It may be asked in the light of what has been said why parties ever seek court resolution to their disputes. One reason is articulated in the very fact that court decisions have an impact on the normative order. Large corporations, public bodies, insurance companies are often eager to test conflict in the courts in order to obtain certainty with regard to their rights and duties. Nor is a test case merely a way of discovering what the law is. It 'may also be viewed as an attempt to create new law, to change and modify the existing law, thereby establishing different conditions for what may become rational behaviour in the future'. The fact that legal aid cannot be obtained to argue a test case is of peculiar significance in understanding the poverty of our law in certain areas, notably social welfare law.

Curial resolution of conflict is thus seen to have a number of important drawbacks: polarisation of the parties eliminating compromise as a solution; the inability of the legal process, except in rare instances, to apportion liability; objectivisation of the problem, placing it in a wider social frame. These considerations are aside from the obvious burden of legal costs and the inconveniences and discomfort of the legal process. One reason why parties go to court has been considered. But reference to test cases in itself illustrates one peculiar imbalance of curial resolution. For it may be that in civil suits one party, in that he is looking for something different, has greater reasons for going to court than the other. There may in fact be an asymmetry of relationship: the large corporation, using the courts as part of its everyday routine and conscious of the fact that it can pass court costs and losses on to consumers, has less to fear than the ordinary citizen encountering litigation for the first time, even if the latter is assisted by legal aid. Further, in such an instance, their respective goals may not be congruent: the former will seek certainty and predictability, litigation to save future litigation; but the latter will see this as an isolated incident of life, a means of justifying himself and getting as much compensation as possible.

Further, both sides will be blind to the virtues of the other's case. It is overestimation of the chance of winning plus the fact that 'to predict loss in a courtroom would normally imply doubt concerning one's own moral right'[40] that drives litigants to court.

This 'moral tinge' may be reinforced where one acts in a representative capacity as, for example, a trustee or a partner: by going to court one absolves oneself from any imputation that one has not done all that one could do. One can hide behind the objectivity of the judge's robes. It is also true that in a fit of blind rage parties act so irrationally as to rule out any possibility of their conflict being resolved other than by judicial *diktat*, and that, once having committed themselves to curial resolution, barring an agreement, they must abide by the decisions made by the judge.

A complete understanding of the motives for seeking court resolution of conflict is impossible without the realisation that the parties' advisers (the legal profession) have interests additional to, or in conflict with, those of their clients. This in part flows from the fact that lawyers uphold the general social interest and wish to ascertain and mould the law. But one must not discount the social prestige accorded a lawyer who can predict the outcome of litigation. In Aubert's words 'verification demands lawsuits'. So, for two diverse motives, lawyers may seek litigation when their client's benefit might well lie in a out-of-court settlement.

Mediation

The difference between adjudication and mediation is that a court's decision imposes a solution on the parties, whereas a mediator provides the means for differing parties to reach a solution of their own. This may be a matter of compromise, as it often is in industrial affairs, or of one party climbing down and admitting he is in the wrong, a solution posited as the ideal in the implementation of race relations legislation. In more homogeneous, less mobile societies than that of contemporary Britain, mediation is a more prevalent solvent. Thus, even where the *form* is one of adjudication, the court may see its role as one of conciliation: it may strive to effect a compromise acceptable to all parties. Gluckman so describes the Lozi of Barotseland. They 'disapprove of any irremediable breaking of relationships. For them it is a supreme value that villages should remain united. . . . Throughout a court hearing . . . the judges try to prevent the breaking of relationships, and to make it possible for the parties to live together amicably in the future.' As a result, 'judgments are sermons on filial, parental and brotherly love'.[41] In such communities courts will even try to mediate between group norms and an individual who has offended against them. In the interests of group cohesion reintegration of the offender within the community is a supreme value. Llewellyn and Hoebel's classic of legal anthropology, *The Cheyenne Way*,[42] is replete with instances of such philosophy. Thus, they cite the case of a horse thief, robbed and left for dead by white soldiers, who is reintegrated into Cheyenne society by the magnanimity of a tribal chief. Instead of excision from the community, he is given a right of passage back into it.

The success of mediation may be seen to depend on a number of variables. The conditions are clearly best where both parties are interested in having the conflict resolved. The stronger their common interest, the more motivated they are to cooperate with a 'professional stranger' to secure a satisfactory compromise. Thus marriage guidance to rescue a marriage in distress is likely to be more successful where there are young children than where there are none. It is also more likely to succeed if the matrimonial troubles are diagnosed at an early stage. Thus, a magistrate's power to refer parties to a probation officer is likely to be used more, and more successfully, than a divorce court's power to adjourn a divorce petition to see if a reconciliation can be effected. The latter power was introduced only at the beginning of 1971 and there is no evidence as to its success. But a decade of experience in Australia has shown little use for a similar provision, and minimal success. By the time the parties actually reach the divorce court it is too late to resolve their conflict other than in terms of satisfactory arrangements regarding financial provision and care and upbringing of children. By this stage, also, the parties (or an intransigent one) are not motivated for having the conflict resolved, and mediation could only succeed if pressure could force cooperation. And, as the Norwegian sociologist, Torstein Eckhoff, rightly asserts: 'Mediation under such circumstances presents difficulties . . . because it demands a balancing between the regard for impartiality and the regard for the exertion of sufficient pressure.'[43] Accordingly, adjudication and administrative ruling are, as he suggests, usually more effective procedures in such circumstances.

This problem is highlighted in the law's recent attempts to curb racial discrimination by declaring certain acts to be unlawful. The workings of the two Race Relations Acts are interesting because of the interlocking of mediation with adjudication (in the later Act, 1968) and administrative enforcement. The objective of proceedings against the discriminator is neither to punish him (though he may so see it), nor to compensate the victim (though this may be incidentally satisfied). It is rather to 'secure a settlement of any difference between [the parties concerned] and, where appropriate, a satisfactory assurance against any repetition of the act considered to be unlawful'.[44] Thus, conciliation in a race relations context is 'miles apart from the type of "conciliation" which is common in industrial practice'. For, as Hepple points out, 'the Race Relations Act procedure . . . is aimed at a settlement and assurance against further discrimination. A particular result is aimed at, and not simply industrial peace.'[45] In labour disputes there is a good deal of common ground and interest: but this may be entirely lacking in a racial conflict. Hence the necessity for the mediator to side with the party and to lay down what terms are acceptable not only to the victim but also to the community ethic. The 'agreement' may thus be closer to an administrative imposition than a genuine contract. Further, the decision to take civil proceedings against the discriminator, where he refuses to come to such an agreement, rests with the Race Relations Board, the institution with overall responsibility for the conciliation.

The role of the conciliator is thus not clearly differentiated from that of administrative organ or 'prosecutor' (though the proceedings are in a civil court). One result of this hybrid of the roles is hostility to the conciliator from both discriminator and victim. To the former he is police (for, although the Board does not initiate proceedings, it is seised with investigatory powers), judge and jury: to the latter, he is one of 'them', a middle-class white whose cumbersome, slow procedures, with their inbuilt legal safeguards, are alien. Further, about one-third of complaints about discrimination in employment find their way to voluntary industrial machinery, where discrimination is almost never found and the procedures applied are loaded against the complainant. For 're-presentatives of management and union, both of whom have a vested interest in preserving the good name of the industry and both of whom may be hostile to the complainant, sit in judgment on a complaint from an individual who is almost certainly not represented by anyone with an understanding either of industry or of the procedures followed by the machinery'.[46] Both the TUC and the CBI were adamant about the value of the British tradition of voluntarism in industrial conflict. However, that success, now challenged by the Industrial Relations Act, presupposes some common values and objects, and these are lacking in a race relations context.

Nonetheless, the Race Relations Acts have had considerable success. This is due more to the use of law as ideology, a theme discussed in the first chapter, than to the particular merits of the hybrid scheme for conflict resolution. The two are, however, related. The conciliator can frequently get the parties to renounce unreasonable demands, thus bringing them closer together, by appealing to societal norms of what is right and wrong. He can further support this by pointing to the possibilities of social disapproval of 'deviants'. Mediation has its greatest chance of success where the norms are accepted and the dispute concerns their interpretation, where in Aubert's words, the dispute can be kept within the bounds of a conflict of interests. So long as the conciliator can concentrate on the interest aspects, his mediation arguments will have an effect. Once the conflict becomes ideologised into one of values the conciliator either becomes a judge or finds it necessary to send the case for judicial resolution: he can no longer get the parties to see the wisdom of a settlement; one must be imposed upon them.

Law: behaviour and attitudes 3

This chapter explores two closely related themes and, in doing so, goes some way to explain why law is obeyed and how law is enforced. It discusses firstly the legal control of conventional morality and then the problems that the law encounters in changing existing social patterns. In the first of these areas the law follows: in the latter it leads. There is a large body of opinion which holds that morality cannot be legislated. It is this caucus which usually favours laws that support the existing moral order. It conceives the law as 'a kind of dam that is constructed after moral judgments are developed'.[1] The judgments tend to be those of 'middle Britain' for, as Svend Ranulf[2] long ago reminded us, the middle classes tend to have a monopoly of moral indignation.

Clearly, the particular problems of each type of legislation are different. In the former, law is used as a means of social control; law is secondary, obtaining its legitimacy in terms of a more primary reference point, the moral order. Law is a reinforcement agency. The problems of law enforcement concern a deviant minority. In the latter, however, law is used as an educator. Some social patterns are easier to change than others. Experience has shown that such change must be timed carefully and be compatible with acceptable values. Race relations legislation can thus be legitimated in terms of such well worn principles as equality of opportunity. Such law will encounter resistance and this must be overcome. Failure to do so not only spells the doom of the particular law but can bring the whole legal machinery into disrepute. Even more difficult than institutionalisation of behaviour patterns is internalisation of beliefs. Laws which attempt to convert depend for their efficacy on their ability to change attitudes. Where law is merely codifying existing mores it will encounter general acceptance, a sense of obligation, a feeling that obedience is right and proper, and acknowledgement that criticism in the form of criminal sanctions or the more diffuse social pressure, is legitimate. This is why most law is obeyed. One reason why the Austinian account of obedience is still prevalent is that law is seen in terms of 'them' and 'us'; law is the thunderbolt from on high imposing its will. This coercive model is best suited to those laws which transform customary practices. Their success, nonetheless, depends on the ability of law-making and law enforcement agencies to convince that the behaviour legislated for is right and proper. The more such active laws depend on a sense of obligation and the less on the need for sanctions, the more successful the laws will be. Hopefully, a point is reached where the behaviour legislated for is the acceptable norm.

A key to the understanding of this process lies in history. E.S. Turner's *Roads to Ruin*[3] is replete with examples of prophecies of doom that would befall this country upon the legitimation of such innocuous practices (to our eyes, at least) of marriage with a deceased wife's sister. Divorce for women, the prevention of cruelty to children, most public health and safety legislation was resisted at the time of its passage. Most extreme is the oft-quoted remark of Herbert Spencer[4] that it would be better for a whole population to be decimated than for one person to be vaccinated against his will. Resistance to such legislation is usually broken down in time. If not, like Prohibition in the United States, its monumental failure is erased from sight by its repeal.

LEGAL ENFORCEMENT OF CONVENTIONAL MORALITY

The question whether the law, usually but not always the criminal law, should be used to enforce the positive mores of a society is, in Hart's terminology, a question of critical morality.[5] Ever since John Stuart Mill wrote in *On Liberty* that 'the only purpose for which power can be rightfully exercised over any member of a civilised community against his will, is to prevent harm to others',[6] what is 'rightful' has been subjected to vigorous and constant debate. A decade ago the controversy was rekindled by Lord Devlin's attack on the philosophy of the Wolfenden report and by Professor Hart's searching examination of the rationality of Devlin's case. Although the nominal subject of the debate, the legalisation of homosexual practices between consenting adults, is now moot, the debate has moved, as often in the past, to new pastures, in this case to dangerous drugs and pornography.

Enough has been written of the Hart-Devlin controversy to avoid repetition here. Suffice it to say that little separates the contestants, that Hart would permit the use of law to enforce 'universal values', and Devlin would tolerate a good deal of immorality before invoking the sanction of the criminal law.[7] Fuller accounts of the debate can be sought elsewhere.[8] Concern here centres on some of the practical problems of the legal enforcement of positive morality.

Pluralism and 'middle Britain'

No one denies that the law does enforce morality. No suggestion is being made that it should not prohibit murder, rape or theft or any of the other crimes that are undoubtedly also proscribed by a practically universal morality. But once away from this undisputed core, problems are encountered. For, is there in this country today one set of conventional standards of what is proper behaviour? Even a cursory glance at contemporary society will leave one in no doubt that we live in a pluralistic society with numerous, often overlapping, cultural standards and reference groups. The breakdown of organised religion, the increase in communication facilities, greater mobility, the influx of migrants from diverse parts of the globe, have turned what may have been a homogeneous society into a heterogeneous one. Contrary to prophets of doom the existence of numerous cultures has

47

led by and large to coexistence and tolerance, and not absence of minimal restraints. The occasional clashes of cultures, racial disturbances, tensions between the young and their elders, attract attention, but are the exception rather than the rule.

One example will illustrate the way the law copes with alien institutions. In *Mohammed* v. *Knott*,[9] the Divisional Court of the Queen's Bench Division had to decide whether a girl, who was about thirteen, and was living with a man twice her age to whom she was lawfully married under Nigerian law, could be said to be 'in moral danger' by continuing to cohabit with him. The minimum age for marriage in England is sixteen, though as recently as 1929 girls could marry at the age of twelve. The court looked to the law which was operative in her home environment and decided that this, rather than English standards, should govern the lawfulness of the marriage and looked to the cultural standards of Nigeria to test whether she was in moral danger. It further refused to invoke any residual public policy under which it could have refused to recognise a status if this were contrary to English standards of decency and justice. This decision is consonant with an acceptance of moral pluralism. Any other decision would have required a criterion by which to judge which morality should be enforced.

From such attempts as there have been to enforce morality, it seems that it is the morality of 'middle Britain' that is posited as the norm. Observers of the 'Oz' trial, an underground magazine aimed at the young, convicted under the obscenity laws,[10] who asked themselves why pornographic bookshops in Soho continued to flourish free from such harassment, were quick to point out that the latter pandered to the tastes of established society, whilst the former wanted to eradicate this in favour of a counter culture. 'So long as an activity is engaged in predominantly by those in the "center" social categories the likelihood of moral condemnation for the activity is miniscule.' Troy Duster, in tracing the history of narcotics legislation in the United States, has shown how until 1914 the taking of heroin was the prerogative of the upper and middle classes, and that legislation to outlaw its use followed the trend for medical journals to diagnose the fact that the 'overwhelming' majority of users came from 'unrespectable' parts of society. He comments: 'Middle America's moral hostility comes faster and easier when directed toward a young, lower-class Negro male than toward a middle-aged, middle-class white female.'[11] One wonders what would happen to the lawfulness of cigarette-smoking should it, for example, disappear from the drawing-rooms of polite society, or what would happen to dangerous drugs legislation if such drugs became acceptable to the moral centre of society, as alcohol, once condemned by 'respectable' elements, did.

It should be added that the thesis presented is reinforced by Devlin's measuring-rod for legal intervention. Although he later admitted that he had placed too much emphasis on feeling and too little on reason, he posited that the limits of tolerance had been reached where the 'reasonable man' felt indignation, intolerance and disgust.[12] Devlin's reasonable man sat in a jury box. He himself had elsewhere described this model of rational judgment as predominantly male, middle-aged, middle-class and middle-minded.[13]

The police and victimless crime

The juryman is one measuring rod of the moral centre of society. The police provide another. To understand the role of the police two features of 'morals' offences must be emphasised. Firstly, the crimes themselves, given their relative indeterminacy of aim, are loosely worded. Thus there is the notorious conspiracy to corrupt public morals, and obscenity legislation defines obscene as that likely to deprave and corrupt. The filling in of gaps is no mechanical process. Secondly, such offences are usually crimes without victims. These have been defined as offences arising in 'situations in which one person obtains from another, in a fairly direct exchange, a commodity or personal service which is socially disapproved and legally proscribed'.[14] There are thus no complainants. Since no one, subject to one type of exception noted below, reports the offences, the police must ferret out those they intend to prosecute. Selective enforcement of crime is a well-established pragmatic principle (though by no means sufficiently acceptable to be encoded).[15] How do the police decide which 'crimes', many as suggested above defined in a vague manner, to discover and prosecute? Customary morality, as perceived by the police or as interpreted to the police through societal pressures, tends to define law enforcement. Lambert, whose survey of relations between police and immigrants in Birmingham is one of the leading studies of police in England, makes this point: 'The police force . . . tends to be an agency committed to establishing moral conformity; or in some instances achieving and maintaining social stability, by tolerating to a greater or lesser extent certain legal infractions—such as prostitution or some "social" violence— if such does not threaten the sense of well-being of the dominant moral community.' In emphasising that the police enforce what they perceive to be conventional morality, one must not overlook the fact that policemen rarely live in the locality they police. 'Inevitably', as Lambert reports, 'the suburban mores and those of the heterogeneous central residential area are in conflict.'[16] The policeman is thus the outsider enforcing the morality of an alien culture.

Victimless crime has other dangers. In seeking out wrongdoers the police have to rely on their own devices to obtain information and evidence. To catch a participant they may resort to becoming an *agent provocateur*. Not long ago this caused a minor scandal when a judge dismissed a case where a police inspector had negotiated a deal with a member of a criminal gang under which he and his gang were caught in the act, but only the accomplices were prosecuted.[17] The danger exists that a policeman face-to-face with a known addict will be tempted to act illegally to secure a conviction by, for example, planting drugs on his person. Skolnick, writing of standards applied by police in arresting for 'reasonable cause', describes the dangers graphically: 'He [the police officer] finds it necessary to construct an *ex post facto* description of the preceding events so that these conform to legal arrest requirements, whether in fact the events actually did so or not at the time of the arrest.'[18] The policeman has everything to gain and nothing to lose: at the worst he loses a conviction. But his concern with 'small fry' may be to create an informant, rather than secure a conviction. If an illegal substance is found the burden tends to switch to the defendant to show that the search was illegal. Further, 'the low status and marginality of typical offenders make it unlikely that the police version will be challenged'.[19] Nor is it likely that the addict will complain against the police officer for the very reason that he is an addict.

Privacy

There is an increasing danger of the police gaining a new information system. The growth of the state bureaucratic machinery plus the data bank makes it possible for increased information to be circulated about a person's activities. Skolnick and Woodworth, in studying the sources of complaint in cases of statutory rape, make this point tellingly: 'It does not matter very much if criminal law forbids various erotic activities, so long as it is impossible to see through walls. When such vision becomes possible, however, the totalitarian potential is enormous because . . . the surveillance potential of those performing police functions will be extraordinary.'[20] It may be that our technology is not so advanced as that of the United States, nor our concern with the value of privacy so sensitive, but the danger described by Skolnick and Woodworth is nonetheless a very real one. Their study of one West Coast town showed that the greatest single source of information in statutory rape cases was the family support division of the prosecutor's office: the adolescent girl applying for maternity assistance was sent as a matter of routine to the police who urged her in the strongest terms to present a complaint. The gradual centralisation of record systems will make prosecutions in such cases easier. One result of this is that crimes like statutory rape are punished mainly among the poorer sections of the community, since their crimes surface to visibility on applications for welfare benefits.

51

The crime tariff

One leading student of the criminal process, Herbert Packer, has argued that attempts to enforce conventional morality through law are in fact promotions of crime tariffs. Laws proscribing dangerous drugs, or pornography, or abortion create a protective economic tariff for the sale of such goods and services, since the demand for them is relatively inelastic.

> Of course, no one designed criminal enactments such as these to operate as a tariff. The object is not to enhance the profits of entrepreneurs in these particular lines of commerce by protecting them from competition. In fact, we rarely think of these activities as involving commerce. . . . But there is a common feature of some oddly disparate kinds of conduct covered by our criminal law that produces quite a different effect from that intended.

Prohibition in the United States was a classic model of the operation of the crime tariff. To quote Packer again:

> Traffic in liquor became the monopoly of the lawbreakers, who proceeded to earn enormous monopoly profits and, behind the protective wall of the crime tariff on liquor, to build criminal organisations that could rapidly take advantage of any other crime tariff with which we were willing to oblige them.[21]

Whatever the effects of the repeal of prohibition, one is undoubted: the price of alcoholic drinks plummeted and illegal suppliers would have been financially ruined had they not turned their attention to other lucrative areas, such as the traffic in drugs.

The consequences of the crime tariff are numerous. Three will be described here. Firstly, the effect of sanctions on both buyer and seller must be considered. A second consequence, the dangers of deviance amplification, has been discussed in an earlier chapter, was hinted at in the last paragraph, and needs only cursory reference in this context. Thirdly, the impact of the crime tariff on the reputation of the law and its institutions must be noted. It may be added that these three consequences are not unrelated.

Most, if not all, the crimes which purport to enforce a moral principle are, what is usually termed, expressive offences. That is to say that 'the act is committed because it is pleasurable in and of itself and not because it is a route to some other good'.[22] Sexual offences and drug addiction are clear examples. Taking the latter, Chambliss has tried to show that there is no evidence that punishment deters drug addicts. He adduces evidence from an organisation for the treatment of drug addicts in Los Angeles which suggests a high relapse rate of over 70 per cent of those who volunteer to undergo treatment. His assumption is that if treatment does not work, then *a fortiori* punishment would not. This is probably true but it leaves unanswered whether punishment deters and, though Chambliss concedes this, the other objects of punishment.[23] There is evidence to show that price is a more important deterrent than penal sanctions. For persons who are committed to a certain activity sanctions are relevant but not necessarily determinative in forestalling the activity.

> The illegal drug-using 'outsider' develops a shared set of responses and definitions including 'a special language or argot, certain artifacts, a commodity market and pricing system, a system of stratification, and ethical codes'. These shared responses and definitions serve to moderate the salience of prohibitory laws. . . . *The behaviour of the 'deviant' is not so exotic if we place ourselves in his total life situation, not merely if we ask how we would respond to his sanctions.*[24]

Looked at from the seller's point of view every increase in risk increases the potential gain to him. Packer argues that the harder we strain to make their sale risky, 'the higher we drive the price that makes the risk worthwhile. . . . The theory of deterrence, however useful it may be in the ordinary run of crimes, breaks down.'[25]

The crime tariff also leads to deviance amplification, or secondary deviance. To get the exorbitant price to purchase goods not available on the open market, a drug addict may be forced to commit other crimes. Further, contact with the underworld may induce the commission of other 'vices' to which the addict was not originally habituated. What starts as a powerful desire to experience something which the law proscribes (and that is rarely the motive), may develop into a whole deviant culture.

The effect of law on moral judgments is considered later in the chapter. It is there stressed that the symbolic value of law as law, the fact that most people want to obey the law and will do so has important consequences for long-term compliance tendencies. But we are concerned in this instance with a deviant minority. 'To be effective, authority must be "legitimated" through both consent and rationality—a genuine understanding of the *total* situation.'[26] The drug addict, for example, develops a set of meanings and definitions associated with his drug-taking that justifies his way of life and makes legal proscriptions irrelevant and irrational. If he needs to do so he can support his case with disillusionment that follows the knowledge that these particular laws are either unenforceable or unevenly enforced. Either way the image of the law is tarnished. And tarnished, also, in the eyes of respectable conformists.

There is a prevalent belief amongst wide sections of the community that there is too much law, particularly too much criminal law. The point is often made with reference to minor motoring offences: in classifying the motorist who infringes speeding or parking restrictions as a criminal one is debasing the coinage of crime. Real crimes, and the whole administration of the criminal law suffer from overuse of the concept of crime in areas where the concept cannot and does not fulfil its aim.

CHANGING SOCIAL PATTERNS

Most writing and research on the question of the law's capacity to affect behaviour and attitudes tends to focus on the area of race relations. Not surprisingly most of this has been done in the United States. However, with the beginnings of a British attempt to solve problems of racial conflict, interest has been awakened in Britain too. This is not to say that the problems are identical.

For example, antagonistic feelings are not as deeply embedded in this country as they are (or were) in the American South. We shall nonetheless rely very largely on American research and hypothesis. Little has been done in this country to test the impact of race relations legislation and implementation on behaviour and, more significantly, on attitudes. But if legislation in the United States is successful then, *a fortiori*, it should succeed here. Although the discussion will concentrate on the area of race relations, references will be made to, and parallels and distinctions drawn with, other life conditions upon which the law has tried to effect a change.

The first annual report of the Race Relations Board stated the role of legislation in five points:

1. 'A law is an unequivocal declaration of public policy.
2. A law gives support to those who do not wish to discriminate, but who feel compelled to do so by social pressure.
3. A law gives protection and redress to minority groups.
4. A law thus provides for the peaceful and orderly adjustment of grievances and the release of tensions.
5. A law reduces prejudice by discouraging the behaviour in which prejudice finds expression.'

We believe [they continued] that there is no more effective way for society to express its disapproval of discrimination, to protect itself from its consequences, or to mobilise opinion and voluntary action against discrimination than through the law.[27]

In a phrase, law is a symbol.

Law as symbol

The importance of law as a symbol has increased with the waning influence of earlier more traditional forces, notably organised religion and the family. The legal system stands out as a basic symbol of external control. Ball and Friedman, writing of the use of criminal sanctions in the enforcement of economic legislation,

55

put it thus: 'The symbolic value of law as law, the fact that most people want to obey the law and will do so, has important consequences for long-run compliance. . . . Social sanctions can be employed deliberately to modify modes of social action—not only overt behaviour, but also cognitive, affective and conative attitudes.'[28] Law shifts the balance of power. In a race relations context, once a law has been passed civil rights forces are given access to the power of the state. One of the conclusions drawn by Leon Mayhew, in his study of the Massachusetts Commission Against Discrimination, was that the law solidified 'the moral position of the forces advocating the implementation of equal opportunity'. Whilst 'those who continue to discriminate find themselves even more on the defensive than they were in opposing the original passage of the law. The normative force of legally established ideals is apparent in the unwillingness of respondents to challenge complaints at public hearings'.[29] The relative paucity of court actions to conciliation settlements in Britain bears out Mayhew's final observation.

The contention in the last paragraph should not be confused with the more extreme thesis of some Scandinavian jurists, notably Olivecrona and Lundstedt, that law is the primary factor in influencing moral standards.[30] If these jurists were right, it would be difficult to explain resistance to laws which changed social patterns. What they ignore in their analyses is the internal attitude towards law which makes the enactment of law possible. Where law fails completely, as Prohibition did, it fails because opinion is widely spread, strongly felt and deeply rooted in opposition. Law cannot operate in isolation, but it can provide the final push.

If the Scandinavian thesis were correct one would expect that trends in favourable attitudes by whites towards Negroes would rapidly increase upon the enactment of liberalising legislation. But

opinions on civil rights issues are best understood as moving in a uniform direction, and becoming increasingly more favourable to Negro aspirations, regardless of immediate events. This is not to say that events are irrelevant, but rather that shifts in opinion . . . are better understood as responding to a host of events . . . that act in such a way as to produce a climate of opinion generally favourable to Negro rights.[31]

The Scandinavian explanation of why law projects compulsive images is more satisfactory. Olivecrona regards the act of law-giving as a question of cause and effect in the natural world, on the psychological level.

> Everywhere there exists a set of ideas concerning the govern-ment of the country, ideas which are conceived as 'binding' and implicitly obeyed. According to them certain persons are appointed to wield supreme power. . . . From this their actual power obtains. The general attitude towards the constitution places them in key-positions, enabling them to put pressure on their fellow-citizens and generally to direct their actions in some respects. . . . The constitutional law-givers gain access to a psychological mechanism. . . . We are so familiar with this situation that it seems to be a part of the order of the universe like the rising and the setting of the sun. . . . The law-givers can play on our minds as on a musical instrument.[32]

In spite of its unreal, over-pessimistic image of man as a passive automaton, this passage gives a clear picture of law as symbol.

Law thus connotes authoritative, legitimate action. Some legal institutions are, however, more prestigious than others. This observation is particularly pointed where law is to play an educa-tional role. The average citizen perceives Parliament to be the proper and legitimate forum for the enactment of new laws. It is the attitude which permeates the judicial mind as well. Wahlke and Eulau[33] rightly attribute this to the fact that legislatures are more sensitive to public pressures and feelings than are other sources of law-making. If this hypothesis is accurate it should follow that the more cataclysmic the social change to be effected, the greater its chance of success if it is introduced in the legislative forum. This suggests that if the decision in *Brown* v *Board of Education* had been part of a Congressional enactment (in spite of a finding that no job had greater prestige in the United States than a Supreme Court justice),[34] it might have been more successful, and that Parliament was the right place to introduce our laws making racial discrimination unlawful. Without a written constitution embodying a bill of rights or resurrection of natural law dogma, it is unlikely that our courts could have developed such a doctrine. And, while administrative and executive orders are useful (note, for example, the introduction in 1969 of a non-discrimination clause in all government contracts), they lack the prestige and authority of an Act of Parliament, with its solemn procedure.

Thus far the effect of law as a symbol acting on people's minds has been analysed. The assumption has been that the individual believes that the law has the right to regulate his behaviour, that he justifies his conformity to the law by interpreting the legally forbidden action as 'wrong', and that in the course of time, with repetitions of this process, behaviour sanctioned by legitimate authority comes to be seen as morally improper without the intermediate behavioural compliance. In real life one cannot isolate a factor in this way. The part played by legitimacy and other factors, such as social consensus, are closely intertwined. But, in the clinical atmosphere of a laboratory, experiments can be conducted to assess relative weight and to differentiate personality traits and their effect on these different influences. The next section describes one such recent experiment, one which it is thought may have some impact on the race question in contemporary Britain.

Law, social consensus and moral standards

The Walker-Berkowitz experiment was conducted in England and reported in 1967. It followed an earlier investigation carried out by Walker, this time with Argyle, which seemed to establish that people were more influenced by the results of a fictitious survey of peers' opinions than by the information that a particular action was or was not a criminal offence.

These conclusions are reinforced and amplified in the later

experiment. The subjects were eighty-seven students from Oxford and Reading universities. They were given a two-part questionnaire designed to elicit 'student opinions regarding different forms of conduct'. A typical question was based on the statement; 'A man who is drunk in a public place is acting in an immoral manner even if he is not disorderly,' on which the subject was asked whether he strongly agreed or disagreed. The second part of the questionnaire had three versions; one group was asked if it wished to reconsider its answers; a second was told of the existence of a recent national student survey and its findings; a third of recently enacted statutes relevant to the questions.

The subjects informed that laws existed tended to alter their opinions as to the moral propriety of the actions in accord with the laws, and this change 'in the direction of the supposed laws (they were fictional) was significantly greater than the change (generally in the opposite direction) occurring in' those who were merely asked whether they wished to reconsider their opinions. 'The greatest shift in adjustments, however, arose in the *Peer Opinion* condition.'[35]

Resistance

The legitimacy behind law and the social consensus underlying it are usually sufficient forces to ensure the modification of life patterns projected by the law-making authority. But laws nonetheless encounter resistance. Where there is likely to be 100 per cent resistance, the law would be totally ineffective. Similarly, 'somewhere at the higher end of [a] continuum there is a threshold of such massive resistance to a new law that enforcement is impossible'.[36] It is at a low level, where law is enacted in the face of appreciable resistance, that the legal system takes on an educational role, in addition to its social control task. There is general consensus amongst the writers of how best the legal system should set about its task. A little will be said of each of the various factors. The importance of the law-making forum has already been stressed.

It is important that laws which modify mores should be shown to be compatible with major existing values. To Gunnar Myrdal the 'American dilemma' was the tension that existed in the United States between received ideas of 'fairness' and estimates of what was involved in producing equality of races at a practical level.[37] Thus the Supreme Court in *Brown* v. *Board of Education* could ground its reasoning upon the constitutional value of equality before the law. The British Race Relations Acts could be presented as embodiments of entrenched ideals of equality, justice and social welfare. The Road Safety Act of 1967, in introducing the breathalyser test, could be related to the corpus of road traffic regulations. The introduction by the Divorce Reform Act 1969 of divorce by consent may be held out as but a legislative recognition of a social fact, a catching up by 'law in the books' of living law. *Plus ca change, plus c'est la même chose.* It may be possible in this way to overcome objections by establishing in the eyes of the public the legitimacy of the particular law. It should be added that in contemporary society values themselves are full of inconsistencies and strains and compatibility is thus a matter of degree. A particularly good example of this is brought out by Marshall in *The Negro and Organized Labor*. He shows how the union élites were able to eradicate discriminatory practices after the passage of Fair-Employment Practice Laws, how they were able to use these laws as 'excuses to make equalitarian changes . . . not considered politically feasible before the laws were passed'.[38] What was at stake was a clash of 'liberal' values. The enactment of a law tilted the balance from freedom to equality.

Secondly, resistance may be overcome by setting up a model of compliance which is visible and even an object of admiration by potential objectors to the implementation of a similar law. Thus, the law-maker in England might point to the success of similar laws or institutions in Scotland or Europe or the United States. He might, as A.P. Herbert was able to do when piloting his extension of the grounds of divorce (in 1937) point to Scottish practice, in this case dating back to the days of John Knox *and* to no dire consequence of social disintegration. Proponents of race relations legislation can point to its success in the United States and to the consequences (race riots, the growth of Black Power) to which American procrastination and resistance have led.

A third condition of success is that deliberate and conscious use be made of the element of time. There are two schools of thought. One argues that the incremental approach is appropriate, that old patterns cannot be broken and new ones instituted over-night. The opposite view is taken by those who press for rapid change to minimise the capacity for resistance to the mooted new pattern. The American Supreme Court emphasised the first approach when it ordered schools to desegregate 'with all delibe-rate speed'. The provisions of the Race Relations Act 1968, allowing for staggered implementation of the employment pro-visions to increasingly smaller firms, adopt the same philosophy. There is no definitive solution to this problem. But success of the second approach depends to a very large degree on rapid and complete conversion of enforcement agencies to the new pattern. Olivecrona's ideal of a state organisation 'trained automatically to execute the laws . . . irrespective of their own opinion of their advisability'[39] is utopian. As a secondbest alternative one can hope for little resistance to new law by enforcement agencies. The adoption of the second approach also calls for an imaginative demonstration of the value of the new social pattern by, for example, rewarding those who conform to it. The effect of positive sanctions, cash incentives or tax rebates, may be more valuable than the traditional negative sanction. The carrot may work better than the stick. This is particularly so where there is pre-dominant opposition to the new pattern, but a state of latent readiness to accept change, due perhaps to feelings of conscience and guilt. One commentator has suggested that 'the only successful approach' to the race problem 'is to identify the relative stubborn-ness of resistance to be encountered, and then choose legal weapons that are of a correspondingly high degree of potency'.[40] Sanctions of the type being advocated here have not been tried to any great extent, though the philosophy is hardly novel. Incentives to take industry to declining regions are one instance.

The paying of higher salaries to primary school teachers in unprivileged areas, as recommended in the Plowden report, is another.

A further prescription for success is to ensure a practical method for the enforcement of the law and the vindication of the rights of those, if any, whom the law was designed to protect. This proposition may be illustrated by reference to law designed to give equality of opportunity to all persons. It is generally agreed by most American commentators that reliance on a case-to-case approach, on the initiative of the individual plaintiff, is a hopelessly inadequate technique if the goal is to eradicate discrimination as a practice. This was recognised as early as 1952 by Morroe Berger in his classic *Equality by Statute*. Law, he argued, could be more effective in producing changes if its administration were directed not to settling individual cases but to systematic discovery and elimination of patterns of discrimination.[41] This theme has been recently taken up by Mayhew. Writing of employment complaints brought to the Massachusetts Commission Against Discrimination he noted that these

> failed to give the Commission jurisdiction over the most discriminatory firms, the occupations closed to Negroes, or the various structural conditions that tend to lead to the exclusion of Negroes. The Commission emphasized justice for the individual complainant, but the complaints of individuals reflect the established patterns of everyday life. Individuals bring complaints against the very firms that offer the most opportunity to members of their ethnic group and they complain about the types of jobs in which they have already been employed. . . . *The Commission treated antidiscrimination law as a system of private law, designed to adjust disagreements that arise within an established social order.*[42]

This last comment is particularly stinging, for it shows how lawmakers fail to perceive the difference between problems of conflict resolution, and modification of social patterns. Yet, in spite of these warnings, the British system ('a new field of public law without criminal sanctions but with civil sanctions initiated by a public body'),[43] adopts basically the American private law model.

Schwartz, writing in the aftermath of the racial violence that shook America in 1967, pinpointed the failure in the process of redress as an underlying cause of black frustration.[44] Critics of the British system have focused on the passive 'letter-box' approach of the Race Relations Board as an Achilles heel of the legislation. In addition, the British system is so structured that victims rarely receive adequate compensation, and the inevitability of the law's delays all too frequently converts the issue into a moot one. No panacea can cure all these ills, but the success of the whole policy may depend on admitting group actions and encouraging spontaneous searching-out activity by the Board. In doing this, however, the danger is, if danger it be, that it will sacrifice its position as impartial conciliator.[45]

The four factors described here go a considerable way towards countering resistance to active legislation. Earlier we described the symbolic effect of law as legitimate authority and influence of one's peers upon the same process. Two final points must be made. Firstly, law is not only a symbol, but also has the effect of inducing resignation. And, secondly, law is negative and minimal; it cannot stand alone.

Law as an accomplished fact

'When an opinion is held by a slight majority or when opinion is not solidly structured, an accomplished fact tends to shift opinion in the direction of acceptability.' These qualified, cautious remarks come from Hadley Cantril's pioneer study on *Gauging Public Opinion*.[46] He attributed a 10 per cent rise in opinion favourable to conscription and allied actions to the passage of legislation. The point comes out forcefully in Hyman and Sheatsley's studies of attitudes toward desegregation in the American South. They hypothesise that 'as official action works to bring what is already regarded as a lost cause, public acceptance of integration increases because opinions are readjusted to the inevitable reality'.[47] Public sentiment is seen to accommodate itself to a new situation. Part of the modern human predicament is its feeling of powerlessness, lack of participation in government, exposure to the will and whims of central control. Accordingly, there exists a widespread feeling, documented among others by Mildred A. Schwartz, that legislation and important court rulings may be wrong but are unfortunately part of the law of the land, and it is absurd to think that they can be resisted with any success over any period of time. Sanctions play a significant role in inducing this condition of anaesthetisation.

Law—but not in isolation

The second point is too obvious to need much amplification. It has been recognised in every Race Relations Board annual report. Thus, the second referred to the need for legislation to be used 'in conjunction with other policies the government can deploy in every area, both central and local, to diminish tensions and decrease prejudice. Positive action in housing, the content of education in schools'[48] were two areas singled out as examples of non-legislative means towards an integrated society. And the fourth report noted that:

> the Act lays down the minimum requirements. . . . Management and the trade unions, the government and local authorities, estate agents and insurance companies . . . are in a position to be far more effective . . . than anything the Board can do. . . . The most important consequence of the passage of the Act is to stimulate these and other bodies to fulfil their social responsibilities.[49]

Law may coerce and indirectly thereby change social patterns, but ultimate success depends on reason, and reason upon education.

The strength of the customary practices

Much of the discussion has centred on the viability of using law to fashion an integrated society. Some account of law's impact in changing attitudes has suggested itself, and this will be considered more fully in the next section. But we must pause here to ask whether there are not some areas of life peculiarly immune to modification through the instrumentality of legislation. The evidence is that civil rights legislation both in the USA and Great Britain has by and large worked. But there is also evidence suggesting considerable lack of success in two areas of life: conditions of work and family relations. Since both areas are undergoing legal revolution in this country at this time, some consideration of this research may cast doubt on the efficacy of active legislation in these areas. But the caveat must be entered that the research comes from countries with different cultural backgrounds from our own.

Three examples from family relations and law may be briefly cited. Lipstein has shown that when Turkey adopted Western codes of legislation in a conscious attempt to modernise its society the new laws introduced had considerable impact on the commercial life of the country; businessmen adapted their practices in line with Western law; but those aspects of social action involving expressive, as opposed to instrumental, activities, and basic beliefs and institutions, such as family life and marriage customs, were very little changed despite the introduction of new laws.[50]

Dror discusses the problem of changing marriage habits of oriental immigrants into Israel. The Marriage Age Law of 1950 is a telling illustration. This set the minimum age for marriage at seventeen and 'tried to impose a rule of behaviour strictly opposed to the customs and habits of some of the sections of the Jewish population of Israel which came from Arab and oriental countries, where marriage was generally contracted at a lower age. . . . [The] act has had only limited effect on social action. Those communities which formerly permitted marriage of females at an early age continue to do so.'[51] The main impact of the Act was to create a situation where marriages were contracted without formal registration.

Thirdly, there is Górecki's socio-legal study of divorce in Poland. The Polish law, like the English, is based on irreparable breakdown but, unlike the English, a 'guilty' spouse cannot get a divorce against an 'innocent' spouse. Górecki admitted 'there was no way of testing the impact of (this provision) on human behaviour', but samples of law students, judges and barristers (a rather biased sample, one would have thought), believed that it had no preventative impact. This was the opinion of 71 per cent of law students and 85 per cent of judges and barristers ('they argued that those who are inclined to violate marital duties act spontaneously, and do not consider their procedural position in an eventual divorce trial').[52] While it is difficult to transplant such evidence from a Communist-Catholic-rural society to an English context, it is some indication that the policy underlying the English Divorce Reform Act is the right one and that the Act will not accelerate moral disintegration.

But the most important studies on the displacement of entrenched customary practices are those of Aubert and his associates.[53] The significance of these studies of the impact of the Norwegian Law of Housemaids of 1948 is their searching examination of the aetiology of failure. A sample of Oslo housewives and housemaids showed that little more than one-tenth of the relationships exhibited conformity to the law, and that barely half observed the ten-hour working day rule, regarded by legislature as the most important provision in the Act. Aubert observed that 'in spite of the law and the general economic and social development, the working conditions of many housemaids have preserved many important traits from the old *Gemeinschaft*-pattern'.[54] He found that the parties were strongly orientated toward the peculiarities of the particular relationship, and that the universalistic legal standards were insufficiently institutionalised and internalised in actual housewife-housemaid interaction. Why?

In part the problem was the insufficiency of the law's information channels. Aubert found that those rules which were fairly well known were those where the law corresponded to existing occupational culture. And, by correlating perception of norms and acquaintance with the law, he was able to show that perceptions of norms derive more from customs than from laws. Further, 'there exists a nearly significant relationship among housewives between information and the index of violations, in the expected direction', though 'information on the part of the housemaids has little or no bearing upon their actual working conditions'.[55] Ignorance of the law may not be an excuse, but it is a severe obstacle to active legislation. This conclusion is supported by Dolbeare and Hammond's work on the ineffectiveness in the Mid-West of the United States of the decisions banning school prayers. They write of 'officials and other leaders (they remark elsewhere that 'the Court is in effect almost exclusively an object of élite attention') having tacitly committed themselves to ignoring the Court's mandate as long as possible, apparently develop[ing] perceptual screens which enable them to avoid knowledge threatening or conflicting with the accommodation they have made'.[56] One lesson to be learnt is that legislation must be explained at a multiplicity of levels. At the moment it is phrased in language that lawyers can understand, but with scant regard for the subjects of the legislation.

The other reasons suggested by Aubert can be left to Aubert's own analysis. Housewives and maids are

> groups which traditionally have had little connexion with laws and public authorities. The recipients of the legal message consist of women who are not organised. . . . The law concerns an area traditionally protected against public inspection and control, the home. The place of work is isolated and the nature of the work relationship is intrinsically difficult to regulate. It is an area on the border-line between the worker and the (slightly inferior) member of the family. Paternalistic, or maternalistic, relations are traditionally very strong. . . . Many housemaids are very young, inexperienced and unfamiliar with urban living conditions. They look upon their job as temporary. The turn-over is very high.[57]

Further, actions for infringement of the law depend on the

initiative of the maid and, bearing in mind the shortage, they find it easier to leave than to complain.

'Norwegian housemaids' may be a special case, but there is some evidence which would enable us to broaden its implications to a more general hypothesis. Two studies will be cited. There is, firstly, George Break's investigation of the effect of high and steeply progressive British income taxes upon the incentives of solicitors and accountants. While admitting that the net effect, whether it was of disincentive or incentive, was not large enough to be of great economic or sociological significance, he nonetheless showed that they did not reduce working hours with a rise in taxation.[58]

Secondly, there are findings both in a famous Yale study and in Jerome Skolnick's *Justice Without Trial* that 'norms located within police organization are more powerful than Court decisions in shaping police behaviour, and that actually the process of interaction between the two accounts ultimately for how police behave'.[59] Thus, in making an illegal search the policeman knows that superiors within the police organisation will be in sympathy with him provided his search was 'administratively' reasonable.

LAW AND ATTITUDES

In introducing Berger's *Equality by Statute* MacIver wrote that 'no law should require men to change their attitudes. . . . In a democracy we do not punish a man because he is opposed to income taxes . . . or to vaccination . . . but the laws of a democracy insist that he obey the laws that make provisions for these things.' But, as Berger himself recognises, 'by altering the situation in which attitudes and opinions are formed, law can indirectly reach the more private areas of life it cannot touch directly in a democratic society'.[60] No one would deny that attitudes and behaviour are not perfectly correlated, but there is considerable evidence that a change in behaviour leads to a change in attitudes. Thus Hyman and Sheatsley found that where there was some measure of school integration in the American South, 'official action has preceded public sentiment, and public sentiment has then attempted to accommodate itself to the new situation'.[61] Muir found that the ban on school prayers had an overall positive effect on the attitudes and behaviour of officials in one school system, though he noted evidence of a backlash.[62]

Most recently, Colombotos has studied the effects of Medicare legislation upon the medical profession of New York. He found that despite bitter opposition to the introduction of Medicare before it became law in 1965 there was no evidence of a boycott (which had been threatened). Practically all doctors complied after it became 'the law of the land'. But not only had they observed the required behaviour, their attitudes had changed as well. Before Medicare was passed, 38 per cent of private practitioners in New York State were in favour of compulsory health insurance through Social Security to cover hospitalisation for those over sixty-five. Ten months after the law was passed, before it went into effect, the proportion in favour had jumped to 70 per cent; six months after the programme went into effect those in favour had risen to 81 per cent. The actual percentage increase is greater for the first interval than the second, but to argue that, as a result, the Medicare law itself had a stronger impact than experience of the doctors with the programme implemented by the law is to ignore the operation of a 'ceiling effect'. But it is undoubtedly true that 'the law had large effect on physicians' attitudes toward Medicare even before it was implemented'.[63] Laws may, in other words, influence attitudes without first changing behaviour. This accords with the thesis presented earlier of law as a symbol of legitimacy. The mere existence of the law itself may affect attitudes, not least attitudes of prejudice. Thus, Colombotos found that doctors' attitudes to other questions, which could have been expected to change had the doctors' shift in attitudes towards Medicare been part of a general, long-term liberal trend in thinking, rather than due to the passage of a law, had remained relatively stable.

Law: interests and values 4

A number of functions of law in contemporary Britain have been surveyed. We have seen how law controls deviance and enables conflicts to be resolved, how it acts as a codifier of positive morality and an active agency of social change. We must now turn, finally, to the goal which underlies and pervades all other functions. This was put by Roscoe Pound, the doyen of American sociological jurisprudence, in the following way:

> ... law [is] a social institution to satisfy social wants—the claims and demands and expectations involved in the existence of civilized society—by giving effect to as much as we may with the least sacrifice, so far as such wants may be satisfied or such claims given effect by an ordering of human conduct through politically organised society.[1]

This chapter investigates the ways in which law acts as a harmoniser of competing interests, and explains the relationship between such interests and the values of society.

Roscoe Pound (1870–1964)

Pound is one of the seminal legal thinkers of the twentieth century. Jurisprudence's debt to him is inestimable.[2] His practical programme set the legal world thinking after decades of uncritical obeisance to the shades of John Austin. His analysis of the varied and competing interests in society is painstaking and detailed. It is a thorough attempt to take the pulse of American society, to discover its requirements and to adjust them. His articulation of values, what he called jural postulates, was a brave attempt at measurement. But his success in both is questionable. Nonetheless, a belief that he posed the right questions induces us to use his structure as a model of the relationship between interests and values, and to see in its terms legal developments in contemporary England.

INTERESTS

Pound classified and expounded three types of interest: individual, public and social. There has been some debate as to the necessity of a separate classification of public interests, that is those interests 'asserted in the title of political life', such as the interests of the state as a juristic person in the maintenance of its personality and substance; and a deal of criticism over the omission of group interests, the interests of companies, trade unions, churches, ethnic minorities and the like. Critics have maintained that public interests are social interests seen in another light, and Pound would have maintained that group interests were but individual interests writ large. This will be debated no further, save as to say that the first of these disputes concerns no more than a matter of arrangement; but the second is very much a matter of substance. Pound was a real child of 1900 both in his selection and omission. Discussion will centre on individual and social interests.

Pound believed that interests existed independently of the law, that they pressed for 'recognition and security', and that the law satisfied as many as it could. Thus, the interests catalogued by Pound were those that had satisfied the litmus test of legal acceptability. But his argument had something of the *post hoc propter hoc* about it. He discovered what the interests which existed independently of the law were by looking to those which the law had recognised. In other words, he studied legal phenomena as social facts. The danger of this approach is obvious: it is all too easy to sanctify the existing order rather than to reveal those interests which are pressing for recognition. Identification of the two presupposes a social structure which enables the legislative and judicial arenas to be used as fora for the legitimation of claims, without let or hindrance. In an ideal society this may happen. It did not happen in Pound's America, nor does it in England today. A belief that it does would ignore the fact of a two-party system, the far from diverse immediate background of members of parliament, and the limited role of the private member in initiating legislation. It would pass over, too, the costs of financing legal action, which, in spite of legal aid, are a prohibitive obstacle to the airing of claims. Nor does it really take account of the juridical method, the limits of judicial creativity.

But, if one should not look to existing case law and statutory provisions, or, indeed to litigated claims that have successively failed or Bills that have failed to reach the statute book (which, to give Pound his due, he did include), how is one to determine which interests are pressing for recognition?

Pound was aware of the problem. He, indeed, had originally investigated social instincts as a possible source of nascent interests. The difficulty was that social psychologists were not agreed about them (nor are they now), and that, as Dewey pointed out,[3] they were inadequate to explain conduct without the influences of custom and habit. Pound eschewed empirical investigation: not that empirical investigation of interests is easy. Far from it. The difficulties of testing attitudes to existing law and desiderata have been discussed. So much depends on the phrasing of the question. For example, ask a group of workers whether they believe that the law ought to recognise the right to work, and the answer will reflect affirmative unanimity. But ask whether the 'closed shop' should be outlawed and this consensus will be destroyed. Further, there is the danger that, in an age of mass communication and mass persuasion, the actual desires of the public may be manipulated by organised professional persuaders, both open and hidden. Nor can the layman appreciate the implications of pressing for recognition of his interests. This point was developed in our discussion of the Nebraska project on parental authority.

The problem should not be insurmountable. It should be possible to collate from different sources, social surveys, protests, letters to the local and national press, complaints received by the legal profession, the social services, citizens' advice bureaux, a general picture of the pulse of society which would either support, or show discrepancies with, the pattern of interests which emerges from the material wrought by legislature and judiciary. This, needless to say, has only been done in small specialised areas. Royal Commissions and other public enquiries, Crowther on consumer credit[4] or Francis on rent control[5] or Roskill on the location of London's third airport[6] tend to document evidence of this kind.

The Roskill Report is a concise demonstration of the relationship between interests and values, for an emphasis on one set of values, the preservation of wildlife would have led to the recognition of the interests of Essex villagers not to have an airport imposed upon them, whilst the stressing of another, the preservation of rural life and Norman churches would have led to the recognition of similar interests of Buckinghamshire commuters. The utility of the report is that it amassed evidence and exposed policy considerations to enable a government to come to either conclusion.

We can thus rely on the results of research and public enquiry to correct the single perspective that an investigation of interests from legal sources would leave. The danger of focusing exclusively on legal phenomena, as Pound did, must be resisted. The danger in so doing is, as Patterson pointed out, that the actual may become rationalised.[7] Our survey, though using Pound's classification, will try to correct his emphasis, wherever this is possible.

Individual interests

Pound subdivided individual interests into interests of personality, interests of domestic relations and interests of substance. Each of these in their turn is subdivided. Individual interests of personality are broken down into the protection of physical integrity, freedom of will, honour and reputation, privacy, belief and expression. Domestic interests are subdivided into those of parents, children,

73

husbands and wives, with a cross-division of claims by the members of the family against each other and against third parties. Interests in substance are concerned with livelihood, with property, freedom to carry on enterprises and make contracts, the ability to rely upon promises, protection of contractual relations from interference and freedom of association.

In reality, of course, all individual interests are social interests. Individual interests are not asserted in the name of a given individual. Sawer presses this point: 'It is not the business of a developed legal system to attend to the interests of a particular individual as such, and every individual claim needs to be capable of expression as the interest, present or potential, of a class, preferably a class which potentially can include at some time every member of the society.'[8] A good example of this came out recently in *Stringer* v *Minister of Housing and Local Government*. The plaintiff was appealing against a decision not to allow him to build houses on a site some four miles from the Jodrell Bank radio telescope. His appeal was dismissed. Cooke J. held that the likelihood of interference with the work of the Jodrell Bank telescope was a 'material consideration' (the terms of the relevant statute), for while such material considerations must be of a planning nature, they were not limited to matters relating to amenity and covered any consideration, in regard to public or private interests, relating to the use and development of land. The judge refused to restrict himself to balancing two individual interests and admitted to feeling 'considerable hesitation in holding that the operation of the telescope was not a public, as opposed to a private, interest'.[9]

The case also illustrates problems of a claim pressing for recognition. The plaintiff's contention that there ought to be a right to compensation when planning permission is refused for reasons relating to the authority's refusal to grant planning permission for such reasons was rejected. 'Planning legislation is in effect an extensive system of expropriation without compensation.'[10] But, while a genuine and widely held expectation, it is not an easy one to legitimate. Take the instant case. Who should pay the compensation? Would it be right to expect Jodrell Bank to buy out every potential developer within range of the telescope? Or, if we see efficient running of the telescope as a social interest, should society as a whole compensate the individual whose land is thus blighted?

It may be added that social and economic considerations underlying such a decision put it beyond the competence of a judge, who is limited by the restrictions of the trial process. Lord Diplock put this well when he said that

> the material relevant to the assessment of the reformative effect on trainees of release under supervision or of any relaxation of control while still under detention is not of a kind which can be satisfactorily elicited by the adversary procedure and rules of evidence adopted in English courts of law or of which judges (and juries) are suited by their training and experience to assess the probative value.[11]

Yet judges have often assessed medical and actuarial evidence. American judges may be presented with a brief documenting just the sort of extra-legal information to which Lord Diplock refers (the so-called 'Brandeis brief'). This, in addition to the ability to consult extrinsic materials, such as reports of commissions, which English judges cannot do, and a broader type of legal education, means that the American judge is less hamstrung. Yet, even so, the legislature is the more appropriate forum in the United States, no less than in England.

Pound also oversimplified when he asserted that the balancing of conflicting claims assumed their existence on the same plane or level. Thus, individual claims were to be balanced against individual claims: social against social.[12] This ignores the fact that the public interest is often the criterion which determines that interest which it is the right of the individual to have protected. So, a shopkeeper has no right to an injunction to stop another shop opening next door and selling the same commodity, because in a free enterprise economy, competition is regarded as in the public interest. Another example comes out in the case of *Bull* v *Pitney-*

Bowes. An employee had been required to enter the firm's pension scheme, one rule of which provided for cancellation of all pension rights if the committee decided that a retired worker was engaging in any activity 'in competition with or detrimental to the interests of' the employer. Bull had worked for twenty-five years but forfeited his pension under this rule. The rule itself was held to be invalid, the decision so to hold it being based on 'a principle of public policy'. And, the judge added: 'I emphasise the word 'public'.'[13]

Interests of personality

No system of law could exist which did not protect the physical integrity of the individual. Laws making murder, assault and intimidation punishable offences are found universally. But only with the development of psychology have individuals been able to assert an interest in the protection of their nervous system. Even today liability for nervous shock is narrower than for physical injury. But with the shift in definition of negligence from the type of interest injured to the kind of conduct engendering liability, the days of this gap appear to be numbered. Laws can only respond to pressure. Until recently exposure of the human person to pollution of air and water by industrial waste and urban congestion had not impinged on consciousness. There were thus few demands, and those lacking urgency, for the recognition of interests protecting life and limb from pesticides, exhaust fumes, the dumping of toxic waste or other forms of pollution. In different ways the Buchanan Report in 1963, John Barr's *Derelict Britain*, other surveys and 'natural' disasters have given rise to claims and demands.

These have led recently to the passing of the Deposit of Poisonous Waste Act 1972, which was rushed through Parliament in response to the finding of poisonous chemical waste on various Midlands refuse tips to which children had access. The Act imposes both civil and criminal liability on those who deposit poisonous, noxious or polluting waste on land so as to give rise to an environmental hazard. But the Act is not directed to the more general mischief of pollution: pollution by motor exhaust is, for example, totally ignored. The decision to recognise protection from this as a new interest must depend on the acceptance of new values. So long as the value of mobility is prized above the preservation of basic human amenities, the decision to ban motor traffic from city centres will not be taken. When the increase in traffic is such that mobility is anyway destroyed, emphasis may be placed on the new value.

Reputation is another individual interest long-protected. But, as Sawer points out, the law of defamation developed to protect a different interest from the one it now serves. The English law of libel 'was devised in the Elizabethan Star Chamber in order to protect the grandees from the printing press; it has been broadened to protect a generalised interest in personal reputation'.[14] But, important though the upholding of the individual's interest in the protection of his name and reputation may be, a careful balancing of this against the equally important interest in free speech and public's interest that truth should out, must be undertaken. Thus justification is a complete defence: a combination of the latter two interests prevails completely over the interest in security of reputation. Furthermore, the law gives the critic, acting in good faith, generous scope. The interests and tension involved are well-illustrated by the case of *Fraser* v *Evans*. The Court of Appeal upheld the decision of *The Sunday Times* to publish extracts from a report made by a consultant in public relations employed by the Greek government, which had come into its hands surreptitiously, although the article would be defamatory of the consultant. He had sought an injunction to stop publication. Lord Denning, refusing one, said that the court would not restrain publication of an article, 'even though it is defamatory, when the defendant says that he intends to justify it or to make fair comment on a matter of public interest'. Commenting on previous justifications of such a doctrine, he continued, 'a better reason is the importance in the public interest that truth should out'. The Court refused to stifle free speech. 'There are some things which are of such public concern that . . . the press and, indeed, everyone is entitled to make known the truth and to make fair comment on it.'[15] If the article turned out to be libellous, then the plaintiff should seek damages after publication.

Defamation is but one of the ways in which reputation is protected. There are others: the torts of malicious prosecution and false imprisonment, for example. One striking deficiency in the protection of this interest by these torts is the inability to obtain legal aid to legitimate a claim to reputation. The reason behind the omission is the undesirability of encouraging actions of this sort. This is not convincing. One of the points in Pound's blueprint for a better society was a study of means of making law effective in action. An interest not effective in action is tantamount to no interest. When we talk, therefore, of a legally protected interest in reputation we must see this as unevenly and imperfectly realised.

Of all interests of personality pressing for recognition the right to privacy is paramount. It is part of our political culture. The desire for such a right may be comparatively modern. Most American states protect this need. The United Nations Covenant on Civil and Political Rights and the European Convention on Human Rights both recognise its existence. English law does not. There have been abortive attempts in Parliament to introduce such a right.

In default the judges have tried valiantly to circumvent the omission. Thus, where a wedding photographer sold negatives to the *Daily Express,* the bridegroom was held to have had his copyright infringed,[16] and where a famous golfer's name was used, without his permission, to advertise chocolate, the courts held him to have been defamed by innuendo.[17] Most recently, the Duchess of Argyll was granted an injunction against the Duke, her former husband, to stop his publishing in a Sunday newspaper intimate details of their married life.[18] But such innovation must necessarily be interstitial.

The need for protection has increased with the computerisation and collectivisation of society. 'The impassive, unremitting memory of the computer will prevent society from ever forgetting. . . . Although theology teaches that sin may be forgiven without necessarily being forgotten, sociology remains unforgiving for as long as it remembers.'[19] The data bank is bureaucracy's greatest ally. The danger is that one's present and future are governed by one's past. Information once given is stored for future evidence. This was the danger foreseen by those who objected to the 1971 Population Census.

It is a problem now well documented and it seems likely that steps may be taken to convert a nascent interest into a legally recognised one. As with the example of pollution it is necessary to make a decision on the basis of changing values. Hiding one's past may not have been either possible or expected fifty years ago. Mobility has made it possible but the data bank has cut down this freedom once again. This has led to frustrated expectations. In *Melvin* v *Reid*[20] a California court held a film called *The Red Kimono* to constitute an actionable invasion of the privacy of a former prostitute who had been acquitted seven years earlier of a notorious murder and who had married and assumed a niche in respectable society. The film was an accurate portrayal of her former life. If these facts were to recur in an English context, the courts would find it difficult to protect the interests of the plaintiff.[21]

Interest of substance

Property is the key to modern industrial society, and as such figures prominently in the philosophy of both left and right. In capitalist and Catholic ideologies it is a natural right: in Marxist theories it is synonymous with power. Property is, of course, wider than merely that which is tangible. The history of recent developments in the law of property show two strands, which are inter-related: an increasing recognition of different property rights and a gradual emergence of a social interest with concomitant restraints on use and enjoyment of property. The first theme will be illustrated here; the second in the section on social interests.

As Friedmann has pointed out, Anglo-American jurisprudence found it easier to accept patents, copyrights, shares and claims as property than most European countries did, as they 'labour under an artificial analytical division inherited from Roman jurisprudence, and out of step with the reality of modern industrial society'.[22] Interests in property in a complex society cannot be reduced to land and tangible movables. English law has adapted to many of the needs of contemporary society but nonetheless interests press which are not requited. Intellectual property is not fully protected. There is a flourishing trade in record piracy which is hardly deterred by the nominal fine 'levied' where an infringement is detached. The search for a spy-proof business law continues.[23]

In many European countries, both East and West, employees have property rights in their inventions which at least take the form of a right to compensation. In England, where the invention relates to employment duties in any way, the rights to the patent belong to the employer. Thus, in *British Syphon* v *Homewood*,[24] an employee who was expected to advise on 'all technical matters' by a firm manufacturing soda syphons was compelled by the court to assign the patent in his method of dispensing soda water to his employer. The Secretary of the Institute of Patentees called for a reform of the law as long ago as 1965 and a private member's Bill attempted, without success, to alleviate the plight of the employee inventor in the same year. Here is a good example of an interest pressing for recognition but failing to displace the status quo which itself reflects a competing individual interest of substance. Employee inventors will often be white-collar workers in weak (or no) unions: in other words, a badly represented interest group. The Banks Committee on patent law reform failed to grapple with the problem, passing the buck to the Department of Employment with the lukewarm recommendation that it should consider the encouragement of voluntary schemes.[25] The issue has thus been shelved once again.

Another nascent interest slowly becoming regularised as a legally protected claim is the right to work. Although the Industrial

Relations Act of 1971 is not framed in terms of any such doctrine, those cases which articulate a right to work have usually arisen in the context of the closed shop, and this has been outlawed by the Act. Thus, in *Edwards* v. *SOGAT*, Lord Denning said:

> I do not think the defendant union, or any other trade union, can give itself by its rules an unfettered discretion to expel a man or to withdraw his membership. The reason lies in the man's right to work. This is now fully recognised by law. It is a right which is of especial importance when a trade union operates a 'closed shop'. . . . A trade union exists to protect the right of each one of its members to earn his living. . . . If the union should assume to make a rule which destroys that right or puts it in jeopardy—or is a gratuitous or oppressive interference with it—then the union exceeds its powers.[26]

The closed shop is now unlawful, though a category of 'approved closed-shop agreements' has been created to cater for the acting profession and other areas where it is assumed that it is in the interests of all concerned. Further, registered unions are permitted to enter into agency shop agreements. However, few advocates of the right to work have articulated the contours of this new interest. Is it only the liberty not to join a trade union, the freedom, as Grunfeld puts it, of taking a free ride on the backs of fellow workers?[27] Or is it the right, recently asserted amongst ship-building workers on Clydeside, to remain in employment?[28] Does the right to work mean that the exercise of one's talents is valued more than the employer's interest in profits? But Lord Denning was not directing his attention to this when he said that the right to work was 'fully recognised'. Yet, as workers' control on Clydeside has shown, the expectation that one will not lose one's job through no fault of one's own is the real content of an emerging interest in the right to work.

If the right to employment is one facet of this, then protection from arbitrary dismissal is another. Until the introduction of the Industrial Relations Act an employee had no redress against his employer for unfair dismissal. He could seek damages if he was dismissed in breach of contract, and the Redundancy Payments Act of 1965 provides for lump sum payments calculated in accordance with his age, seniority and final rate of remuneration if he is dismissed by reason of redundancy. But the 'reluctance of the courts to prevent the unfair dismissal of employees stands in remarkable contrast to their astuteness to order the reinstatement in his trade union of a plaintiff whom they hold to have been wrongly expelled'.[29] This has now been rectified by the 1971 Act. Another expectation has been legitimated through legislative action.

Should welfare payments continue to be regarded as government largesse or are they 'the new property'? Should they depend on discretion or be asserted as carefully formulated legal rights? Charles Reich, best known for his *The Greening of America,* has argued that:

> The concept of right is most urgently needed with respect to benefits like unemployment compensation, public assistance and old age insurance. These beliefs are based upon a recognition that misfortune and deprivation are often caused by forces far beyond the control of the individual, such as technological change, variation in demands for goods, depressions, or wars. . . . These benefits . . . represent part of the individual's rightful share in the commonwealth. Only by making such benefits into rights can the welfare state achieve its goal of providing a secure minimum basis for individual well-being and dignity in a society where each man cannot be wholly the master of his own destiny.[30]

Is this a new interest in property pressing for recognition and, if so, who has the competence to press such a claim forward? Margaret Wynn has argued for a 'fatherless families' allowance,[31] and a committee under Morris Finer QC is at present considering its introduction. Fatherless children can hardly be expected to turn to Parliament and ask it to intervene to encapsulate this claim within the legal structure. But this is being done for them by organisations committed to their welfare.

Social interests

Social interests are interests of society as a whole, 'compromises of conflicting individual interests in which we turn to some interest frequently under the name of public policy to determine the limits of reasonable adjustment'.[32] Pound subdivides them into six categories: general security (the protection of peace and order, health and safety, the security of transactions and acquisitions); protection of social institutions (domestic relations, political, economic and religious institutions); general morals; conservation of social and human resources; and general progress.

General security

In order to protect health and safety of society as a whole English law has developed a number of restraints upon the rights of property owners and manufacturers. Individual interests of substance have been adjusted to the wider social requirement of general security.

The failure of English law adequately to protect the consumer was discussed in chapter 1. But, through both criminal and civil liability, very real attempts have been made to increase the power of the consumer. For example, the doctrine of *mens rea*, which protects the individual by giving him fair opportunity to avoid liability by only imposing criminal liability were there is fault, has been rejected in a number of welfare offences that have mushroomed in the twentieth century. Friedmann refers to these offences as 'essentially standardised'.

> In the balance of values [he writes] it is generally considered more essential that violations of traffic rules or food laws should be strictly punished, in the interests of the public, rather than that the degree of individual guilt should be measured in each case. . . . We have to accept an occasional injustice to the individual as part of the price we have to pay for living in a highly mechanised and closely settled kind of society, in which

the health, safety, and well-being of each member of the community depends upon a vast number of other persons and institutions.[33]

It may be added that, though the traditional criminal process safeguards are missing, so is the odium which attaches to criminal conviction.

There has been similar growth of civil liability for the sale of impure food or other commodities without the seller's fault. In the landmark House of Lords decision of *Donoghue* v *Stevenson* the manufacturer of a bottle of ginger beer was held liable to a lady who drank it and became ill as a result of (she alleged) finding a decomposed snail in her drink. The court held that the manufacturer of a product owes a duty of care to anyone whom he may reasonably expect to come into contact with it.[34] Another way in which the law of torts has expanded social protection at the expense of the individual's freedom to use his property is in the increasing tendency to award damages to individuals for breach of statutory duties. Thus in *Read* v *Croydon Corporation*[35] a ratepayer secured damages on being poisoned by impure water supplied by his local authority.

Protection of the institution of marriage

One individual interest not so far discussed is a spouse's interest in release from the consequences of an unhappy marriage. Individualistic philosophy postulates the individual's right to happiness. Few systems, however, sanction free dissolubility. Some Catholic states, on the contrary, reject individualism completely and make the individual's claim subservient to the sanctity of the marriage tie. England adopts a middle way. Divorce cannot be obtained on demand. Firstly, except in cases of flagrant rejection of marital obligations or exceptional hardship, divorce petitions may not be presented during the first three years of marriage. Secondly, although since the introduction in 1971 of the Divorce Reform Act 1969, spouses can mutually agree to bring their marriage to a close, the social interest in buttressing marriage is supported by the provision which requires two years' separation before the courts will presume breakdown (the sole ground of divorce) from the parties' consent to divorce. Further, the court must be satisfied that adequate arrangements have been made for the care and upbringing of children. A further example of the way in which social cohesion prevails over individual demands is in the law's rejection of any such doctrine as incompatibility[36] (unless substantiated by two years' separation). Thus, what constitutes intolerable conduct is judged largely according to societal standards, though individual weaknesses are not entirely ignored. 'A flirtatious husband', said a judge recently, 'can reasonably be expected to live with a wife susceptible to the attractions of the other sex.'[37] Fourthly, since the promotion of any viable marriage is in the public interest, elaborate provisions are built into the divorce law to facilitate reconciliation. But it is also in society's interest to bury empty shells of marriages. The Gluecks showed many years ago that statistically the chances of a child growing up as a delinquent were greater if nurtured in an 'empty-shell' family than by one divorced parent.[38] Finally, perhaps the most controverted of individual claims was legitimated in 1969 when repudiation was sanctioned. One spouse may now divorce the other without that spouse's consent where they have lived apart for five years. The social interest is nominally preserved by the length of separation required and also by defences that the respondent may raise, for example, that a divorce will cause grave financial or other hardship. In the first year of operation of the provision no court acceded to such a contention.

There is thus a conscious attempt to harmonise individual demands for freedom with societal interest in marital stability. As values change there has been shift in favour of the individual. The law until 1969 probably did not reflect the expectations of many. With the possible exception of repudiation (arguably an example of law as ideology) it may now be said to approximate to pressing individual claims. So long as society emphasises marriage as an important social institution, it can go little further.

Security of political institutions

In all states a reconciliation must be made between individual liberty and free speech and state safety. The amount of leeway given to the individual will depend ultimately on the values of the society. A totalitarian state will allow no opposition. Even a relatively democratic one may outlaw certain parties. In Britain this has not been a problem in recent years. Nor has this country faced the problem of some countries which have stretched democracy to its logical conclusion. In Australia, for example, voting is compulsory, and in *Judd* v *McKeown*,[39] the High Court of Australia upheld this practice as a way of promoting protection of the political institution of democracy.

But we have felt the necessity to adjust these conflicting interests acutely where public authorities have maintained that they should have immunity from disclosure of documents in court proceedings. The problem is that if a litigant is prevented from putting forward evidence on which he relies, he may lose an action which he otherwise might have won. 'In effect', comments Wade, a leading authority on administrative law, 'he is expropriated without compensation'.[40] On the other hand, some protection must be given to state secrets. The difficult question is whether the courts can hold the scales of justice where private right and public interest come into conflict, or whether the last word must rest with the executive. In 1942, in *Duncan* v *Cammell, Laird*[41] the House of Lords declared that a ministerial claim for privilege could not be disputed. While the decision of *Duncan* may very well have been right on its facts, since it involved the plans for submarines and it was wartime, such a doctrine can cause injustice where no danger is caused to the state. It was therefore not surprising that in 1968 in *Conway* v *Rimmer*[42] the House of Lords rejected absolute executive discretion and substituted, in effect, absolute judicial discretion. The case concerned a probationer police constable who had been acquitted of stealing an electric torch, and who wished to sue for malicious prosecution. He applied for discovery of five reports about himself, which were in the police records, and which he believed would manifest evidence of malice. The Home Secretary intervened to claim that the production of confidential police reports would be injurious to the public interest. This assertion was rejected. The court later inspected the documents, declared that their production would not prejudice the public interest, and ordered them to be produced to the plaintiff.

Social interest in general morals

Some of the problems of societal enforcement of conventional morality through legal machinery have been discussed in an earlier chapter. Concern here is focused on the harmonisation of the individual's interest in freedom of expression and society's interest in forestalling corruption, depravity and prurience. In one instance this is complicated by society protecting at the same time the interests of literature, art and science.

Thus there are laws regulating gambling, prohibiting obscene publications and censuring blasphemy. But 'the law is a living thing moving with the times and not a creature of dead or moribund ways of thought'.[43] Blasphemy is rarely invoked today, because society is now strong enough to resist activities subversive of religion.

But, in the backlash against permissiveness, legal moralism has come to the fore in prosecutions against possession of dangerous drugs and publication of obscene articles. Further, the courts have resurrected the offence of conspiracy to corrupt public morals. Thus, in *Shaw* v *D.P.P.*, the accused was convicted of conspiring with prostitutes to publish a *Ladies' Directory*, which contained details of prostitutes and the services they provided. Lord Simonds remarked:

> I entertain no doubt that there remains in the courts of law a residual power to enforce the supreme and fundamental purpose of the law, to conserve not only the safety and order, but also the moral welfare of the State, and that it is their duty to guard it against attacks which may be the more insidious because they are novel and unprepared for.[44]

87

The obscene publications legislation attempts to balance in-dividual freedom of expression and societal concern, on the one hand for moral welfare, and on the other, where the two conflict, the interests of literature, art and science. An article may be obscene and yet immune from conviction if it is for the public good, as being in the furtherance of any of these pursuits. We may not know after a trial whether the article was not obscene or was, but was so protected, for jury verdicts, as in the *Lady Chatterley's Lover* trial, may be ambivalent. Nonetheless, the recognition of a societal interest in literature *etc.* raises an interest-ing problem. Although the alleged motive for such protection is 'the public good', it is clear that the vast majority of people would not wish these activities to be advanced. What we have here is an example of recognising an interest regardless of the public's actual desires because an élite believes it is good for them. Thus, we introduce a new factor into a study of the interests of a society. For, not only will legal phenomena not give a complete picture, it may, as here, give a positively distorted one.

VALUES

At a number of points in this chapter it has been shown that the weighing of different individual interests or the balancing of individual and social interests depends upon the values of the society and how these values are articulated by lawyers. In this last section some of the values inherent in Britain today, parti-cularly as exemplified by case law, will be spelled out.

Pound's attempt to formulate such a hierarchy was a failure. He first set out what he called jural postulates in 1910. He prefaced each by 'in civilized society men must be able to assume' and listed a number of principles: security of the person from inten-tional aggression; security of possession and property in things discovered and appropriated, created by labour or acquired under the existing social and economic order; good faith in the making of representations; due care not to cause unreasonable risk of injury upon others; control of things inherently dangerous. In

1942, he updated this list a little by including job security and that risk of misfortune to individuals should be borne by society as a whole.[45] Laski's comment was well merited: 'They are framed . . . for a community of small owners such as the Middle West knew in the epoch first following the Civil War.'[46] And Sawer has commented: 'The table is a mixture of the enduring and the contemporary, and there are surprising omissions.'[47] There are no references to group activities, to the family or to the rule of law. Nor was there any attempt to rank these postulates in order of priority. Another problem is that interests often cannot be secured unless they are able to depend upon values. For example, as Barry points out,[48] if one regards racial equality as an interest ('want-regarding principle'), it is difficult to see how it can be made to work until integration and non-discrimination are accepted as postulates ('ideal-regarding principles').

Dias, surveying contemporary English legal values, concluded that 'national and social safety override all other considerations and sanctity of the person is superior to sanctity of property, but beyond this the pattern is kaleidoscopic, not hierarchical'.[49] These four primary values have been selected for treatment.

National security

The primacy of national society as a yardstick is undisputed. So magnified can it become that in the recent *Dutschke* case,[50] the tribunal, set up to review the Home Secretary's decision not to renew the permit of a former German student leader, concluded that although he had not been nor was a security risk he might conceivably become one and so the Home Secretary's decision should not be questioned. In wartime this emphasis is more understandable. Thus the detention of an alien in the thick of the second world war under a regulation giving the Home Secretary power to detain where he had 'reasonable cause to believe' that a person's continued freedom was prejudicial to the safety of the realm was held by the House of Lords to mean reasonable in the eyes of the Home Secretary. This reminded Lord Atkin, who believed in the supremacy of individual liberty, of the Court of Star Chamber in the time of Charles I.[51]

Public safety

The conflict between personal liberty and public safety comes out well in Lord Denning's judgment in *Chic Fashions* v *Jones*. The question which arose was the scope of the police search and seizure powers and the extent to which interference with private interests of property could be tolerated. Lord Denning's review of earlier cases is a discussion of 'the balance between the inviolability of personal liberty and the pursuit of public weal'. He came down on this occasion on the latter: 'upon the side of him who acted reasonably in intended performance of what right-minded men would deem a duty to their fellow men; the prevention and detection of crime'.[52] The increase in certain types of crime has seemingly placed public safety over sanctity of property in the hierarchy of legal values. De Smith's comment is pointed: 'There is a risk that the courts, having formerly leaned over backwards in their solicitude for private property, may now give too much weight to the public interest in crime detection and too little to the claims of personal privacy'.[53]

Another recent case of the conflict of values inherent in judicial law-making occurred in *Home Office* v *Dorset Yacht*. Borstal boys had escaped from custody and damaged a yacht. The question arose as to whether the Home Office was liable for the damage caused. Lord Reid summed up the conflict of values when he said that 'the responsible authorities must weigh on the one hand the public interest of protecting neighbours and their property from the depredations of escaping trainees and on the other hand the public interest of promoting rehabilitation'.[54] Holding the Home Office liable the House of Lords refused to consider the 'very far reaching effects' the decision could have, for example on the system of open borstals. The case is complicated in that public safety (in the short term) and protection of private property both augured for the success of the claim. The value which took a knock was long-term safety which lay in the rehabilitation of young offenders.

Human sanctity

Emphasis on the sanctity of the human person is only to be expected in the age of existentialism. Even the natural lawyer's creed has been invaded by stress on the human being as its foundation. Thus, Pope John XXIII's *Pacem In Terris* laid down that 'Any human society, if it is to be well-ordered and productive, must lay down as a foundation . . . that every human being is a person, that is, he has rights and duties of his own. . . . These rights are therefore universal, inviolable and inalienable.'[55]

English lawyers have long valued human inviolability. The famous enunciation of individual freedom in *Sommersett's* case[56] is often quoted. More recently, repudiation of conditions akin to slavery has been articulated in restraint of trade cases. Thus, in *Eastham* v *Newcastle United Football Club*, Wilberforce J. concluded that the 'retain and transfer' rules governing the employment of professional footballers constituted an unjustifiable restraint of trade. 'The transfer system', he said, 'has been stigmatised by the plaintiff's counsel as a relic from the Middle Ages, involving the buying and selling of human beings as chattels; and, indeed, to anyone not hardened to acceptance of the practice it would seem inhuman and incongruous to the spirit of a national sport.'[57] In *Nokes* v *Doncaster Amalgamated Collieries*, the House of Lords spoke (through Lord Atkin) of the worker's 'right to choose for himself whom he would serve' and argued 'that this right of choice constituted the main difference between a servant and serf'.[58] Their lordships refused to sanction the transfer of employees' contracts from one company to another, in spite of an act of Parliament which allowed for transfers of all rights and liabilities on an amalgamation.

The inviolability of the human person is also illustrated by the courts' attitudes to compulsory blood testing. For example, in *W.* v *W.*, when a husband petitioner in a nullity suit applied for an order requiring that blood tests be taken of himself, his wife and a baby to prove that he could not be the father, the application was rejected on the ground that the relevant rule was not specific enough to extend to compulsory blood testing. Cairns, J. at first instance, regarded the acceptance of any such doctrine as the beginning of a slippery slope which might lead to exploratory surgical operations to establish a disputed diagnosis relevant to damages in a running-down case.[59]

Sanctity of property

The cases of *Sommersett*, in which a slave's right to freedom prevailed over his owner's right to his property, *Nokes* and *Eastham* all illustrate that human inviolability takes precedence over sanctity of property. But, though not seen as it once was, as some inviolable natural right, the right to private property still ranks high amongst the code of legal values. In 1765 Chief Justice Pratt enunciated a doctrine which commands approval even today: 'The great end for which men entered into society was to secure their property. That right is preserved sacred and incommunicable in all instances where it has not been abridged by some public law for the good of the whole.'[60] Of course inroads 'for the good of the whole' have been made upon the purity of this doctrine; *Chic Fashions,* quoted above, is one. But basically the doctrine stands.

So, in *Attorney-General* v *De Keyser's Royal Hotel*,[61] the House of Lords held that a prerogative power in the Crown to expropriate a hotel was subsumed in a statute which gave the power to requisition upon payment of compensation; and in *Burmah Oil* v *Lord Advocate*,[62] it was maintained that where the Sovereign, in exercising the royal prerogative in relation to war, deprived a subject of property for the benefit of the state (in this case to prevent the enemy Japanese taking over oil installations in Burma) the subject was entitled to compensation at the public expense, and that even though battle damages could be excepted from this general rule, destruction which was part of deliberate long-term strategy, and was not also so requisite for the purposes of battle operations, could not.

CONCLUSION

Whether these values as articulated by judicial actors fairly represent those of society is a question which a later chapter will explore. In this context it is the relationship between interests and values that must be noted. The discussion has shown that the interaction between interests and values takes place on two levels. Values are a primary motivating force in the recognition of interests originally, and secondly, values are the measuring rod where there is a clash between two interests.

Part Two:

Legal institutions and the public

The legal profession 5

Lawyers are a response to a social need. They develop most fully when, according to Nonet and Carlin, 'law is viewed as an embodiment of values' for 'society then requires specialised group activities for the protection of its heritage and may find them in that occupation whose interests are identified with the preservation of legal skills and values'.[1] In England, though not, for example, in Ancient Greece or throughout much of Chinese civilisation, this is what happened. The emergence of our legal profession in the thirteenth century followed the rapid development of the common law at this time. But, though originally the product of societal exigency, lawyers gather their own momentum and develop 'autonomous power over the orientations of the legal and social order'. The danger is that they forfeit respect and confidence when the order they fashion conflicts with the expectations of the majority. This is what some critics believe has happened to the English legal profession. Thus, Abel-Smith and Stevens write that: 'In England "the law" plays a less important role than in almost any other western country. . . . English lawyers have restricted their own horizons . . . [and] their interests primarily to the "law" which is concerned with the courts.'[2] And Michael Zander is sceptical of a profession which has not grown in numbers in half a century in spite of 'the vast ramifications of the modern welfare state with its innumerable complexities for the ordinary citizen'. He rightly views with pessimism the prospects for the legal profession should compensation for personal injuries be removed from lawyers and administered as part of social security legislation, or conveyancing be 'so simplified and streamlined as to reduce greatly the profits lawyers are likely to be able to make out of it'.[3]

The legal profession in England has always been a divided one: 'the division of function preceded the profession'.[4] Today, there are only two branches in the profession: solicitors, who number about 24,000, and barristers, who total about 2,900. Formerly there were also attorneys, sergeants, scriveners and conveyancers, and the ecclesiastical and admiralty courts had their own practitioners (proctors) in addition. Most writing on lawyers in this country, of which Zander's *Lawyers and the Public Interest* is the outstanding example, has focused on the problems consequent upon today's remaining division. One result is that wider questions, problems of role, relationship with the social system, perception of values, the placing of lawyers within a professional framework, have been neglected by English writers, as has such concrete empirical investigation as problems of social origin, recruitment, ethics or organisation. Since such questions have been tackled in the United States, some reference will be made to these works. It is a matter of regret that attempts to conduct surveys in this country have been stifled. Thus, the Bar Council, a voluntary association whose function is to promote the interests of barristers, refused to support a project of Abel-Smith's to examine the social background of barristers.[5]

THE ROLE OF LAWYERS

The role of lawyers in society has been little explored. So long as 'the life of the law' was logic and 'law in action' was thought to reflect 'law in the books', there was little incentive to examine what lawyers did. 'The revolt against formalism', as Morton White has characterised the beginnings of sociological and realist jurisprudence, changed this. Thus, the American Realist movement advocated that the best way to find out what law is, is to explore what lawyers do; whilst prediction of the outcome of litigation would be furthered by an appreciation of lawyers' crafts. Llewellyn, the leading Realist, examined the former in *The Cheyenne Way*, in collaboration with the anthropologist, Adamson Hoebel; and the latter, within the scope of the American appellate process, in *The Common Law Tradition*. The scepticism of Realism engendered a sociology of legal institutions in the United States. But it had little impact in this country. Only recently has dissatisfaction with the goals and achievement of the legal profession in England activated lawyers and sociologists, and indeed agencies of government, to re-examine its role in society.

The most detailed examination of lawyers' 'work tasks' has been undertaken by Johnstone and Hopson in their comparative study of English and American lawyers, *Lawyers and their Work*.[6] They list no less than nineteen activities undertaken by the legal profession of the United States.

In England, the division of the profession is based on, what Megarry has called, 'specialisation of function';[7] so one might expect a sharp differentiation between solicitors' tasks and barristers'. Yet, whilst some of the jobs listed by Johnstone and Hopson are clearly within the solicitors' province, such as setting up companies,[8] most of the activities listed are performed by both sides of the profession.

The layman's perception of the lawyer's role is a distorted one. In his eyes the primary concern of a lawyer is with litigation. This is a minor activity for the vast majority of solicitors, who specialise in conveyancing and probate. There are two main reasons for this. Convention denies them the right of audience in higher trial and appellate courts, though the bar's monopoly is gradually and imperceptibly being eroded. Secondly contentious business is unremunerative. The Prices and Incomes Board report of February 1968 cogently demonstrates this: 'Of the proportion of 55·6 per cent of income derived from conveyancing, the corresponding proportion of expense was 40·8 per cent, whereas in the case of contentious business a proportion of 28·8 per cent of total expense was incurred to earn a proportion of 18·4 per cent of total income.'[9] Nor is the work of the bar taken up exclusively with litigation. Barristers do a considerable volume of advisory work unconnected with litigation. A few barristers concentrate wholly on advisory and drafting work and never appear in court, and the chancery bar, mainly situated in Lincoln's Inn, spends a high proportion of its time on non-contentious matters, for example, the drafting of complex conveyancing instruments, company constitutions, and the making of tax settlements.

So, much of the lawyer's work is concerned with the giving of advice, with the purpose of what Llewellyn and Hoebel characterise as, 'preventive channeling and reorientation of conduct and expectations'.[10] In this sense lawyers are part of the enforcement system of law. Their work in advising clients is supportive of the norms and values of the social system in that it often channels clients' behaviour away from the illegal into legal methods of attaining their goals. A lot of unnecessary hardship could be averted if the public sought qualified advice before taking action. The reasons why they do not do so are investigated in a later chapter.

A lawyer's advice is based not only on his knowledge of legal doctrine and its impact on the factual situation at hand, but also on his grasp of social and economic questions. Lawyers are expected to advise on non-legal matters, such as investment or the possibilities of obtaining a mortgage or planning permission. This point is developed by Rueschemeyer: 'Since the law is a generalised mechanism of social control, its application covers a great variety of social situations. Different applications require a grasp of these social contexts as well as the law. From the good lawyer we may therefore expect a generalised capacity for defining situations and a great variety of "worldly knowledge".'[11]

Apart from advice and litigation, two of the most significant of lawyers' activities are negotiation and drafting. Lawyers frequently deal with other lawyers or other parties in an attempt to reach agreement between their client and another person. It is the lawyer's ability to objectify social relations which enables him to undertake this task. Drafting, the writing and revision of written instruments, including non-legal documents, requires the skills of clarity, precision and originality. Of course, many typical instruments of documentation have been standardised in such reference works as encyclopaedias of forms and precedents and, as Johnstone and Hopson point out, 'knowledge of available forms and their merits and demerits can be more important to good draftmanship than facility at original drafting'.[12]

Lawyers are also investigators of facts. Solicitors obtain the necessary data for the exchange of contracts on house purchase (for example, they prepare an abstract of title). It is they who assemble, often under a barrister's guidance, the information essential for litigation (for example, they obtain affidavits from witnesses). In the United States investigation assumes greater importance, as finance houses and insurance companies use lawyers in private practice 'to secure credit information on applicants for loans and moral risk data on applicants for insurance'.[13] In this country senior lawyers, usually judges, are delegated by government departments to undertake enquiries into, for example, ill-treatment at mental hospitals.

Research and analysis is undertaken at different levels. The average solicitor will go no further than a standard work of reference (Rayden on *Divorce* or Lindley on *Partnership*), or a comprehensive encyclopaedia (Halsbury's *Law of England*). Few will have the resources or the time to explore any further. Difficult questions will anyway be referred to a barrister, if for no other reason than as insurance against professional negligence. The Bar, on the other hand, is close to reasonably good libraries maintained by the Inns (though local bar libraries are hardly adequate). Most research of primary materials is thus by barristers.

On a completely different plane, the lawyer undertakes a number of associated roles which depend hardly at all on his being a lawyer. He gives emotional support, sympathy, understanding, compassion, reassurance to a distraught client. The lawyer as social worker or therapist has barely been explored. But, although a lawyer is not trained to meet this role expectation, it is easy to understand why he is looked to in this way. 'Crisis, uncertainty and tension are characteristic of much of [his] work. He usually can adjust to this as a regular aspect of his profession, but most clients have great difficulty doing so.'[14] The lawyer is also his client's scapegoat. He absorbs the criticism that would otherwise be directed at clients. One aspect of this was discussed in an earlier chapter: the lawyer used by a client, perhaps a trustee or director, as an excuse for an unpopular step, as a way of rationalising a decision. The lawyer is thus a 'face-saver'. Since clients do not have direct contact with barristers, the role as 'fall guy' is played by the solicitor's branch of the profession.

Role conflict and ethics

A number of 'law-jobs' have been described. Underlying these, notably the tasks of advice and litigation, is the problem of role conflict or role strain. The problem does not arise in a totalitarian system: there a lawyer's duty is plain; it is to the state. But in a society such as England the question arises as to priority where there is a conflict between the lawyer's role as an officer of the court and commitment to the interests of his client. Johnstone and Hopson put it thus:

> When should he be the client's servant and when his critic? To what extent should he identify with the client's goals and follow his expressed wishes? To what extent should he question and challenge them? . . . [He] may decide to defy the client's wishes. He may, for example, be unable to compromise his professional or moral standards by advising on a course of conduct he thinks undesirable without stating its weaknesses and that he opposes it. On the other hand, a lawyer of different make-up, wishing to avoid the risk of client resentment, may unqualifiedly recommend what he thinks the client wants to hear.[15]

The problem is accentuated because the central value of the legal profession, which one takes to be *justice*, is so elusive. If lawyers cannot agree on its content, there is necessarily value dissensus between lawyer and layman, and different sections of the public will perceive justice differently. The lawyer is faced with a problem that the doctor, for example, does not encounter. For, while 'the interests of the . . . client may be at odds with what the lawyer considers just, it is rare that the patient's interests stand against the attainment of health'.[16]

How does the lawyer react to this ambivalence of role? This question is intimately related to one touched on earlier, the extent to which the lawyer moulds or is moulded by the social system, and to the problem of lawyers' ethics.

One of the most difficult questions to decide is the extent to which lawyers are their clients' consciences. Is there an elasticity to clients' interests and values that adjusts itself to what the lawyer will tolerate? Or are the lawyers' standards tailored to the ethics of their clients? This problem has not aroused interest or speculation in England. This may be due to the homogeneity of the legal profession. It may also stem from the fact that such an obvious obstacle to impartial client representation as 'plea-bargaining' does not exist to the same extent, nor permeate the trial process as indelibly as it does that of the United States. But faced with the problem American sociologists have reached no definitive answer. Smigel's complacent study of *The Wall Street Lawyer* viewed his subject as the conscience of big business. He quoted, with approval, Parsons's remark that they acted as 'a kind of buffer between the illegitimate desires of . . . clients and the social interest'.[17] On the other hand, Handler's survey of lawyers in a middle-sized city in America suggested that their 'ethical commitment . . . was conditioned by the characteristics of their practice'.[18] He found that pressures and conditions of practice were more significant guides to lawyers' values than social background, that lawyers would adapt to their clients' role expectation.

Research has not been undertaken in England. But one facet of the problem has created attention in an adulatory way. English lawyers are accustomed to quoting Erskine's famous response to the decision to deprive him of the office of Attorney-General for defending the radical, Tom Paine:

'From the moment that any advocate can be permitted to say that he will or will not stand between the Crown and the subject arraigned in the Court where he daily sits to practise, from that moment the liberties of England are at an end.'

The 'cab-rank' principle, which underlies this, by which a barrister is bound to take any case within his range of practice, provided that the fee is agreed (between his clerk and the solicitor) and he has no prior engagement, has the important consequence that a barrister can take on a client, but not his values. A solicitor, on the other hand, is not forced to work for a client and the concomitant danger is that he may be accused of identifying with the values of those clients he does take on. But both sides of the profession are strongly controlled internally. The ideal is clearly formulated, for barristers in Boulton's *Conduct and Etiquette at the Bar*, and for solicitors in Lund's *A Guide to Professional Conduct and Etiquette*. Whether these normative statements wholly represent living law may be doubted, but sanctions for failure to observe them, including deprivation of professional status, are stringent enough to ensure that deviation is rare. Furthermore, the bar at least is a small, well-integrated profession. As in the case of members of a commune, breaking rules is difficult as activities are carried out in view of the group. Megarry, a Chancery judge, put it thus:

> There is the atmosphere of chambers, of hall and of the circuit mess. The newest recruit soon sees many instances of counsel unhesitatingly rejecting the easy half-truth or equivocation that would help him or his client, or scrupulous respect . . . for the profession secrets in his care . . . and, in short, of honourable and responsible conduct which fully matches the demands made by the long traditions of the Bar.[19]

This, plus professional opinion, ensures that 'conscious wrong-doing is . . . the last thing that would be associated with the English Bar'.[20] However, that which constitutes 'conscious wrong-doing' is characterised by the professional group, not the wider community. Thus, a distinguished law lord could urge that there is no dishonesty in arguing a bad cause, for the barrister is not asserting his opinion or judging the merits of the case, but merely putting before the court 'all that his client would have said for himself if he had possessed the requisite skill and knowledge'.[21]

The area of role conflict is thus drawn conspicuously narrower by the profession than it might be by society.

To what extent does the social system of the legal profession affect its role in the legal and political order? What impact does legal education and a divided profession have upon this relationship? This section raises these issues.

Legal education

Legal education is socially significant for three main reasons. First, the values of the profession are in part dictated by the social composition of its entrants; second, the scope of legal services is circumscribed by the content of courses of legal education and training; and third, the juridical skills of the profession are closely related to methods of legal training.

No study of the social composition of the English legal profession has been conducted. Remarks therefore tend to be speculative. It 'is widely thought of as being distinctively middle class or even upper middle class'.[22] This is particularly so of the bar. Thus, an examination of the educational background of the judiciary (recruited exclusively from the higher echelons of the bar), reveals a high percentage of public school Oxbridge graduates. But in a social system no subsystem can be insulated from all the others.

As long as British social structure is such that the traditional ruling class can still command some deference, the law, to be sure of respect, must partake of the style of that class. Until the thought of a High Court Judge pronouncing a life sentence in a Birmingham accent no longer seems incongruous, High Court Judges must speak with the tones of Oxbridge, and so must ambitious barristers, and so must solicitors who do not wish to be thought inferior to barristers.[23]

Hence a vicious circle which legal education alone is not capable of breaking.

How is one to account for the relative social homogeneity of the English legal profession, particularly of the bar, and what consequences does it have? The reasons are complex and multi-farious: the ruling class association, as depicted above by William Plowden, the image conveyed by schools and the media, often based on dated misconceptions (for example, that solicitors' articled clerks pay premiums[24] or young barristers starve), but, above all, the cost of qualification must be prohibitive to a number of potential recruits. The ambivalent nature of legal education (is it education or vocational training?) has meant that local authorities show less interest in financing the training of recruits than in assisting university education. The Inns are generous in their provision of scholarships, though their bounty is over-distributed to Oxbridge students. The articled clerk, though no longer paying for the privilege, is remunerated very poorly. But he is fortunate at least that on admission he can take a position as a salaried assistant solicitor. One of the least desirable consequences of the rejection of partnerships at the bar is that there is no one to employ the novice on a salary. Zander rightly believes that 'one of the most important contributions the Bar could make to equalising opportunities would be to permit partnerships which could employ the entrant on a salary whilst he was beginning his career.'[25] Provided he can get a seat in chambers (there are only some 250 sets in the country), the current boom in bar practice, activated by extensions in the provision of legal aid, the 'devilling', the pleas of mitigation, the work in county and magistrates' courts will see him through. But to qualify he must spend a considerable sum of money.

This means that the legal profession, particularly the Bar, tends to be drawn from that part of the population with independent means. The danger is that the services of the profession may be geared primarily to that same élite. One oft-cited answer is that the poor have no legal problems, that only the business and pro-perty communities are seised of justiciable issues. This is not so, as a later chapter demonstrates, but what is true is that legal education is oriented towards solving disputes of this type of person.

The content of courses of legal education changes but slowly. The legal profession itself tends to assume a finite quality about traditional subjects of study. The result is that the content of courses studied by law students serves the needs of prosperous private clients, particularly those who have patronised the courts over centuries. Thus, to cite an example used by Abel-Smith and Stevens:

> The emphasis given to land law . . . suits the needs of land-owning clients and . . . owner-occupiers. The strict settlement . . . loom[s] much larger than the few references to town and country planning. Discussion of the lease . . . is . . . allowed to exclude entirely dilemmas of housing policy. . . . little is taught about land planning, virtually nothing about the long-term use of land, new towns, publicly provided housing, commercial land finance and the like.[26]

And this example could be multiplied from almost any other area of law. This narrowness of perspective was recognised in the Ormrod report on legal education which reported in 1971. It warned that lawyers must adapt to the changing structure of society or lose work to other professions, but it saw the extension of private practice (as opposed to neighbourhood lawyer services), into areas such as welfare and housing as 'likely to be slow'.[27] The problem is not a novel one: lawyers have lost work before, to accountants, civil servants and social workers, among others. Nor, so long as the current boom continues, are they likely to fear the 'nascent' profession of neighbourhood law firms. Indeed, the danger is that the legal profession does not even perceive neighbourhood lawyers as competition. There is a certain irony in the fact that, after initial hostility, legal organisations expressed approval of, and pledged support for, the establishment of salaried lawyers in underprivileged areas, on the basis that they would stimulate and nourish private practice. This they may indeed do, though indirectly, by helping to reshape the content and context of legal education.

Only recently has there been any real examination of the rationale of legal education. Its pragmatic growth, ambivalence of aim, the splits between university and professional training schools, academic training and apprenticeship, the bar and the solicitors' branch, hinder such an examination. Of course, if legal education is to produce legal practitioners, then the mapping out of its contours should be within the prerogative of the profession. But if its aim is to produce law-trained persons then something more is required beyond the acquisition of requisite technical skills. It is now universally accepted that law is a means to an end, that the lawyer is a social engineer who employs his skills to regulate the conflicts and tensions of society. But so long as he only learns his 'law' from reported cases he studies pathology (like a horticulturalist studying solely cut flowers, was how Judge Jerome Frank,[28] a leading American 'skeptic', put it); and even more significantly adjusts his focus to social conflicts of earlier ages.

It may be that the failure to teach law in a social context, and the glossing over of underlying social policies bear the main responsibility for the failure of lawyers to develop legal services to meet changing needs. If this is so, and one must not discount other factors such as the natural conservatism of the profession, then there are hopeful signs of a increased awareness of the value of socially oriented law teaching in many of our universities and polytechnics.

Juridical skills inculcated into law recruits also affect the social order they mould. It was Max Weber,[29] one of the fathers of legal sociology, who noted the relationship between type of legal education and responsiveness of the legal order to social change. He contrasted the common law system of apprenticeship with the more conceptual and formalistic study of the law which prevailed (and still does), in continental countries under Roman law influence. Apprenticeship produced a pragmatic, inductive approach to legal problems and enabled the common law to accommodate to social change whilst retaining continuity with the past. The history of almost any branch of English law demonstrates the accuracy of this. The law of torts has seen transitions from agricultural to industrial and industrial to technological societies with little statutory intervention. But Weber drew the contrast with civilian systems too widely. If continental traditions of legal education induced *rigor legis*, as he suggested they did, then it is difficult to account for the fact that juridical creativity has enabled the French *Code Civil* to do service to a very different society from the one for which it was fashioned. However, it must be conceded that a legal system so constrained that it is unable to keep pace with social transformation may be unable to resist extra-legal means of social change to which dissidents resort.

It affects the legal order in a number of other ways. If law students study judicial decisions, usually of appellate courts, then recruits perceive the law as the result of litigation rather than as a programme for living together; they overlook fact-finding; they ignore the fact that much important law is made by legislators and administrators and, indeed, by custom, for the law in action is rarely examined in the course of a law degree. One of the results of this narrowness of horizons is that much law is relegated by lawyers to the class of being 'not really law'. Thus welfare law is so depicted, originating as it does in statutes and ministry regulations, directives and officials' discretion. There is little case law and less appellate case law because disputes are taken before tribunals and legal aid is unobtainable in these fora. The circle is thus a vicious one. Law students will not study welfare law so long as it remains outside the boundaries of appellate case law and it will not achieve this status (hardly an enviable one), until legal aid is extended to tribunals. Another consequence of legal education is that, as little foreign law is taught, a rather insular arrogance towards foreign institutions is endemic in the legal profession. Thus, codification was long frowned upon, and administrative law and a Ministry of Justice were anathema to the 'democratic' English lawyer. The attitude towards codification springs directly from an emphasis in legal education on the study of case law.

Precedent is seen as the tailor's cloth, the statute merely as a stitch in time.

A divided profession

The divided English legal profession is currently an issue of controversy, and not for the first time. Indeed, in 1887 a Bill to fuse the profession was submitted in Parliament. It is an issue on which, as Johnstone and Hopson point out, most commentators are partisan. Though the arguments of both sides are couched in terms of social good, it is not difficult to detect self-interest not far below the surface. Successful barristers rarely advocate fusion, though 'younger and financially marginal elements' figure prominently in that lobby, as do solicitors who have most to gain from a single profession.[30]

The case for fusion rests largely upon cost and efficiency. The hiring of two lawyers where one could do the work (a premise always assumed but never satisfactorily proved) means duplication of effort or shrugging-off of responsibility, but whichever results cannot produce the best value for the client's money. The solicitor, further, is likely to be in greater control of the facts, to have greater knowledge of his client's desires and the witnesses' statements. This mastery is accentuated by the late briefing that a barrister often gets; but since he collects the fee marked on his brief even if the case is settled before he does any work on it, and this is by no means a rare occurrence, it is not surprising that many briefs are delivered at the eleventh hour.

Most interesting of other arguments in favour of fusion is the proposition that it would give a wider choice of judiciary. 'By maintaining the Bar's monopoly over judicial appointments', argues Zander, 'one is artificially depriving the country of the benefit of selecting its judges from a wider talent pool than is now available and therefore of raising the level of these appointments.'[31] Exclusive eligibility to judicial office also acts as a symbol of the superiority of an élite. But the criticism goes not so much to a divided profession as to a particular monopolistic practice which could be removed without fusion. One must distinguish here between trial and appellate courts. The argument against appointing solicitors to the bench of trial courts without giving them the right of audience before those courts is a strong one: extensive experience in advocacy must prove invaluable to a trial judge. But the argument against appointing solicitors (or, indeed, academic lawyers) to an appeal court has doubtful validity. Ironically, the first hesitant step towards dismantling the Bar's castle, taken in the Courts Act 1971, has reversed this process. Under a Practice Direction issued pursuant to this Act by the Lord Chancellor, a solicitor's right of audience before the new Crown Court (before which all trials on indictment are held), is limited to appeal and committal for sentence proceedings from magistrates' courts in which he, or a member of his firm, appeared for the defendant (in civil proceedings he may have represented either party), but he is eligible for appointment as a circuit judge after five years as a recorder. He thus gets advocacy rights in appeal cases and the possibility of elevation to the bench for trial actions. Of course, to give solicitors full right of audience and competence for judicial office without fusing would be to give solicitors the whole cake.

The case against fusion is built upon the benefits that a separate bar bestows upon the public. Megarry, in his *Lawyer and Litigant In England,* gives a spirited defence of the status quo. 'The main advantage', he argues, 'of the English system of a divided profession lies in the obvious benefits that flow from all specialisation: each becomes an expert in his own field.'[32] A separate bar means a client gets an expert in advocacy as well as a specialist in a relevant field of law. He also gets the knowledge that there will be a degree of parity between his counsel and his opponent's. This equalisation argument is a cogent one. For, though it assumes an adequate system of legal aid and a solicitors' profession versed in the wares of particular counsel, it overcomes a problem much commented on in American literature. Some account of the American dilemma will demonstrate the boon of a separated bar at the disposal of all solicitors.

The American legal profession is not divided into solicitors and barristers, but it is certainly divided. It too has specialists, as we would have, were we to fuse. But its dividing line is socio-economic. Our bar may be an élite: top American firms are almost a caste. A cursory reading of Smigel's *The Wall Street Lawyer* and Carlin's *Lawyers On Their Own*[33] will demonstrate the chasm dividing the apogee and nadir of the American legal profession. On the one hand, there is the upper middle class graduate of an Ivy League law school, such as Harvard or Yale, who gravitates towards partnership in a large Wall Street firm: on the other, the ambitious, upwardly mobile working or lower middle-class boy, often from an immigrant ethnic minority group who studies his law at night school, works for another lawyer as an apprentice and office boy whilst building up his own practice on the side, and finally becomes a 'solo' or individual practitioner. The process of stratification has a number of consequences.

The wealthy and powerful have access to the best lawyers: those who are not so affluent must be satisfied with what is left. This syphoning off of the best law graduates perpetuates an imbalance in the distribution of lawyers, and in its turn engenders developments in certain areas of law to the exclusion of others. Ladinsky articulates this problem thus:

> Partly because legal talent from quality law schools has flowed heavily into the large firms for many years, there has been an extensive elaboration of legal procedures to handle the problems of corporate enterprises as opposed to those who care for the problems of private citizens. The result has been a high development of corporation protection often at the expense of individual citizens. In addition, areas of law unrelated to the operation of corporate enterprises have not had the same level of creativity devoted to them.[34]

A further consequence is the identification of lawyers with clients. Our élite is open to all, but the American élite runs the risk of total identification with the aims of its clientèle, big business and government agencies. In doing so it sacrifices autonomy. Nonet and Carlin encapsulate the distinction succinctly:

> One organisational device [to secure a viable autonomy] is to create within the profession an élite specially charged with the protection of legal ideals. While this segment insulates itself from outside pressures, others in the profession are left free to respond to and accommodate the variety of demands that are made on the legal order. The British system has achieved this differentiation by developing a small and specialised class of barristers.[35]

They also point out that the greater the stratification 'the more difficult it becomes to incorporate in the legal order the demands that are brought to' the lower levels of the profession. And Carlin in *Lawyer's Ethics* commented that this increased the willingness of low-ranking lawyers 'to influence official decision-makers though such illegitimate means as bribery or the prospect of political favour'.[36] No suggestion is being made that any of this would happen if the English legal profession were fused: the American situation is in part a product of the educational system, the political structure and comparatively poor provision of legal services for the underprivileged. What is being argued is that isolation of the Bar plus open access to it go some way towards preventing the evils of the American legal profession.

Specialisation and equalisation are the two most frequently used arguments against fusion, but there are many others. The importance of the atmosphere and setting in which a barrister works is often stressed: the sheltered calm of chambers, isolation from the distractions of being 'a man of affairs', no letters to write or telephones to answer. To this Zander replies: The seclusion of the cloister may be more congenial than the hum of the world to some professional men; but the main question is whether the cloister's relative peace produces significantly better work. Lawyers all over the world seem to manage to produce work of good calibre without the degree of isolation peculiar to the English barrister'.[37] Further, Megarry points out, the Bar's efficiency in research is assisted by proximity to law libraries and by having 'its finger on the pulse of judicial opinion'.[38] Neither of these points is persuasive: a unified profession would have advocacy specialists and they would doubtless congregate near law libraries and spend their time in and around courts, thus absorbing the titbits of information not otherwise available. The argument that isolation from client affairs promotes objectivity assumes that a solicitor's involvement with his client is such that his powers of analysis are blurred by emotion; this is completely contrary to any lawyer's training. Nor can too much faith be placed in the argument that the witness being unknown to the counsel cannot be coached and that, therefore, is more likely to tell the truth.

These are some of the main arguments put by advocates of no change. Weak as many of the propositions are, there is unlikely to be fusion. Interest groups favouring the status quo are well represented in Parliament. Further, the system works. This surprises Johnstone and Hopson who, from their American background, would have expected it to break down from evasion and non-compliance. They are surprised by the fact that solicitors 'with their almost total control over the work flow of barristers . . . have not financially subjugated [them] or become their status superiors'.[39] The answer to this is that each needs the other: the English legal profession is structured upon an intellectual division of labour. Indeed, the provision of better legal services through specialisation must remain the ultimate rationale of a divided legal profession.

But, though fusion is unlikely, the current debate has at least stimulated some reform. Thus, the implementation of the Ormrod report will ultimately mean common educational requirements, and this in turn will improve the facilities for transfer from one branch of the profession to the other. There may be continued dropping of restrictive practices: the Bar has already relinquished its two-thirds rule (under which a junior appearing with a QC automatically received two-thirds of the fee asked by his senior) and the special fee demanded for appearing off circuit. Further, the Bar Council has recently endorsed the Kerr report which advocated the dropping of all restrictive practices which would obstruct the Bar undertaking legal work within the Common

Market.[40] The solicitors, however, show no desire to forfeit their conveyancing prerogative. But they may themselves get improved rights of audience before superior courts: the Courts Act 1971 provides just a hint of this. Piecemeal reform may just be enough to silence the critics temporarily, but the debate will reactivate periodically so long as a divided legal profession survives.

A PROFESSION?

Throughout this book the assumption has been that the legal profession is a profession. One must now examine what such a classification connotes, and whether the characteristics of lawyers merit such a designation.

One sociological model of a profession, constructed by Goode,[41] postulates it as a service occupation which sets out to solve the problems of society by using specialised, technical competence, and in so doing promote a value central to society's consciousness. There are those also who picture the profession as at the opposite end of a spectrum from business. Talcott Parsons, however, disagrees believing that the difference is a matter not of motives but of institutional patterns; 'the essential goals in the two cases' are, he maintains, 'substantially the same [viz.] objective achievement and recognition: the difference lies in the different paths to the similar goals'.[42] But a professional man's paths are circumscribed by standards internalised during education and training. His calling is characterised by a high standard of ethics. In return, it is assumed, society grants him privileges and benefits (a high income, prestige), and safeguards his profession's autonomy against lay control and interference.

Although much of this could be a description of the English legal profession there are difficulties in fitting features of the legal profession into the model set out. A good examination of these problems is Rueschemeyer's study of doctors and lawyers in the United States. [43] Part of the difficulty, as he points out, results from the fluidity and elusiveness of a lawyer's technical competence. For he is expected to possess more than legal knowledge. Since, however, this is not based on systematised learning 'the customer may be in a position to judge ... for himself', and society accordingly does not 'imbue [it] with the same moral significance as strictly legal activities'. Another of the keys to a lawyer's competence is his possession of interpersonal skills, the ability to negotiate, to act as intermediary. Much of his work is thus taken up with non-legal activities in which 'the gap in competence between professional and laymen may be considerably reduced'. There is some truth in this, but a lot of a lawyer's work tasks are intimately concerned with the purely legal, more so in this country than in the United States. Even so, out of the realms of the purely legal, the lawyer's training still enables him to create a gap between himself and the layman. But it is not so much his specialised knowledge that erects the barrier as his rationality, matter-of-factness and failure to be impressed by other than commonsense solutions. Riesman's hypothesis that 'the ceremonial and mystification of the legal profession are ... veils or protections underneath which this rational, all too rational, work of the lawyer gets done'[44] is near the mark. The development in sophisticated legal systems of an elaborate law of procedure reinforces this image.

The problems inherent in measuring the legal profession against the value limb of the model are greater. Even if all are agreed that the central value to be promoted by the legal profession is justice, it is unlikely that there will be anything like consensus on the contours of the concept. The ideal of treating like alike remains constant, but what constitutes likeness is a shifting criterion.[45] Further, that something is lawful raises a presumption that it is just, but the notion of an unjust law is not uncommon. The problem is aggravated because different conceptions of justice are associated with subgroups, socio-economic strata and cultural or ethnic enclaves. The legal profession cannot insulate itself from the interplay of value systems. Law is not a lifeless entity with logical momentum. The development of legal norms hinges on the value orientation of the legal profession. The danger is always that a legal profession will become captive to a class or group and promote its interests exclusively, hence sacrificing autonomy and self-control and subjecting itself to the pressure of a powerful clientèle. This danger may be accentuated by the costs system, which can act to deprive a large slice of the population of the services of lawyers. A concomitant effect of this may be that the lawyer is shielded against the full impact of value dissensus.

The problem is a real one. The English legal profession has not obviated it, though the provision of legal aid and advice has softened its blow considerably. The societal consensus on justice is greater in England than in the United States. The best lawyers are not the exclusive preserve of large corporations as has happened there. Yet, much as rich and poor are treated alike, one cannot get away from the difficulty that this assumes they have the same problems and require the same legal expertise and skills. The technical competence of the average lawyer barely touches many of the areas of life on which the underprivileged have legal problems. The interpersonal skills cultivated by the legal profession are highly class specific; for example, 'skill in negotiating with executives is quite different from competence in handling minor officials in local administration'.[46] There are signs that this is changing as legal education and research improve, but change is likely to be slow. Until it is accomplished it will be difficult to escape the conclusion that it is the values of a limited class which the legal profession promotes.

Judges   6

With the exception of lay justices of the peace (and many of these are as well), judges are members of the legal profession. Thus, much of the comment and discussion in the previous chapter, is equally applicable to this. Similarly, some of this chapter, particularly the account of judicial techniques, describes an intellectual process adopted by all lawyers. Indeed, the close identification of Bench and Bar reinforces this intimate relationship, particularly when the contrast with civilian systems in Europe is brought out.[1] We recruit our judiciary from our ablest practitioners at the Bar, whereas they have a career-structured government legal service. The continental system means that promotion depends on ability at judging rather than at advocacy, which is a good thing, but it leads to the danger that a safe man may secure promotion for that very reason: it is also thought to result in more appeals to higher courts.

The English system of selection also differs from that in operation in much of the United States, where judges are elected (under the Missouri plan[2] adopted widely, direct election has been attenuated by executive nomination). Nonetheless, the English system can boast that legal ability, distinguished practice and the judgment of peers are hallmarks of selection, not political platforms.

This chapter is about the judiciary of superior courts and county courts. Unless otherwise stated, remarks are not directed to lay justices who administer minor criminal jurisdiction (they hear 98 per cent of criminal prosecutions), nor to chairmen of tribunals who hear many of the disputes arising out of the administration of the welfare state. Sections at the end of the chapter survey problems concerned with them. As far as empirical research is concerned, more has been directed to lay justices and the working of tribunals than to superior courts of record or county courts. In the case of magistrates' courts this is probably because of the political nature of appointment as well as discrepancies in sentencing felt by the vocal, middle-class defendant, the motorist. Tribunals have probably been subjected to sociological research because of their integral role in the development of the social services.

No research, apart from a few none-too-specific surveys, has been undertaken on the judiciary. The reasons for this conspicuous failure (judges must be the only decision-makers of importance not subjected to the enquiries of social scientists) are: first, the long-prevailing myth, still perpetuated by some, allegedly to maintain public confidence in the judicial process, that decision-making has the inevitability of a slot-machine; second, the hesitant growth of a sociology of law in this country; and third, a conservative judiciary which fears diminution of its status through exposure of its mysteries, and obstructs it in the name of public policy; it further can use resurrected powers to commit for contempt of court those who criticise the functioning of the legal process. This power has lapsed[3] somewhat since the judiciary, along with other institutions of the establishment, came under public scrutiny in the 1960s, but by then the damage to legal sociology had been done.

The result is that data is sparse and comment necessarily speculative.

The judicial role

The legal values underlying the British system of government necessitate a social ordering by rules and judges to adjudicate on these rules. The role of the judge is thus intimately related to the institution of adjudication. An appreciation of the standards expected of a judge entails in its turn an examination of these legal values. This calls for a rational justification of adjudication according to established rules (established both by other institutions such as legislatures and administrative agencies and also, under a system of judicial precedent, by judges) as the optimum process of decision-making. No definitive list can be drawn, but some reasons why this model is promoted may be suggested.

The system supports the orientation of human conduct in the directions approved by society. The knowledge that judges and other officials, including the police, apply rules enables members of society to channel behaviour in accordance with these norms. Law in official action must approximate closely to law in the books. Of course, the majority of individuals do not know the law, beyond the outlines of criminal prohibitions. This legal value thus assumes that lawyers are consulted.

Secondly, the system enables and increases the likelihood of private settlement of disputes. It does this by enabling lawyers to predict with reasonable degree of success the outcome of a court hearing. Counsel's opinion thus has a quasi-judicial function, something that is often stressed when a divided legal profession is defended. The desire to settle out of court is reinforced by the costs system. Under 5 per cent of writs issued come to trial, and the majority of potential court actions do not even reach the writ stage. Of course if facts were always certain, rules as mechanical as used to be pretended, and damages totally conventionalised, few, if any, cases would ever reach a judge. If, on the other hand, every dispute were to require trial by a judge, the judicial system would break down.

A small number of cases thus reaches trial. The institution of adjudication is viable because of a shared consensus between Bar and Bench as to the arguments that will be used to justify judicial decisions. Without this agreement the adversary system, under which lawyers representing each side adduce arguments to persuade the judge that they have the better legal case, would collapse. For any case worth submitting to a judge there are arguments both ways. There are always a variety of competing considerations, and the judge, unlike, for example a legislator, is expected to give a reasoned decision. The process of argument will not, Wisdom notes, constitute a chain of demonstrative reasoning.

> It is a presenting and representing of those features of the case which severally co-operate in favour of the conclusion, in favour of saying what the reasoner wishes said. . . . The reasons are like the legs of a chair not the links of a chain . . . it is a matter of the cumulative effect of several independent premises, not of the repeated transformation of one or two.[4]

This argumentation takes place within the framework of judicial precedent.

Precedent is the practice of following past decisions. It is a natural enough convention, a time-saving convenience, which exists in all walks of life and in the judicial process of all modern legal systems. But cultivated by the English it is a fetish. Happily for legal and social development the days of its irrational reverence are numbered. At the height of its worship,[5] all courts in the judicial hierarchy were obliged to follow higher courts, and the House of Lords, the highest in the land, laboured under self-imposed fetters which bound it to its own previous decisions. It was a religion which involved such mental acrobatics as convincing oneself that a long line of wrong decisions had metamorphosed itself into correct legal principle (the doctrine of *communis error facit ius*). *Stare decisis*, the name given to the common law form of precedent, is no longer as rigid as it was, and some of its worst excesses have been removed. The House of Lords is no longer bound by its decisions and, though it shows great reluctance to depart from a previous decision, will do so where an existing rule 'has been rendered obsolete by changes in physical and social conditions and has become an incumbrance impeding the proper development of the law'.[6] The introduction of the 'leap-frog' appeal, empowering a litigant to appeal straight from a first instance judge to the House of Lords, where under the system of precedent prevailing, the Court of Appeal would prove a cul-de-sac, has also relaxed the burden of *stare decisis* somewhat. Yet the civil Court of Appeal still remains bound by its own decisions, in spite of efforts by Lord Denning to loosen its chains. Indeed, the Court recently received a sound reprimand from the House of Lords for transgressing the restraints of judicial orthodoxy by refusing to follow a House of Lords' decision.[7]

In the present context precedent has an important role to play. We have already referred to adjudication according to established rules enabling human behaviour to be properly channelled, and heightening the chances of disputes being settled out of court, thus relieving the courts of an intolerable burden. Neither would happen without a system of precedent. Nor would we get legal justice, the assurance that litigants at any particular time will be treated by the courts equally. But these arguments must not be stretched too far. Thus Weiler argues that 'the reasons why we want to protect private expectations about the legal quality of their conduct do not extend so far as to safeguard the right of anyone to rely on the stability of the extreme boundaries of the letter of the previously-stated law'.[8] The burden is not so much a strict doctrine of *stare decisis*, but a technique of overruling which has it that the new principle being enunciated has always been the law, rather as America was there before Columbus discovered it. If cases were to be overruled prospectively, as happens in the United States and as Lord Simon has suggested might be introduced here, this justification of *stare decisis* would evaporate.[9] Further, as far as the value of legal justice is concerned, this assumes that the rule itself is a reasonable one. For legal rules which conflict with community mores impel litigation and ultimately produce instability in the law.

Despite, or perhaps because of, precedent, judges are able to adapt the law to meet changing circumstances within the perimeter allowed by the rules. Legislative activity is directed towards the general, the typical, core problems. By their very nature many disputes concern open, marginal questions. A judge's attention is often focused on a specific issue, and is always directed towards the human implications of law-making. And, although judges are working within the framework of precedent, judgments are sufficiently discursive and open-ended to allow for considerable flexibility. Further, in appellate courts there is usually more than one judgment and accordingly variations on a theme, different reasons and illustrations. Legislation's abstract blueprint is more limited and produces rigidity rather as the choice of a mosaic worker is more restricted than that of a painter who can mix his paints on a palette to achieve infinite variation. The tendency for the appellate courts to give one judgment is, as has recently been pointed out by the House of Lords, unfortunate.[10]

No one doubts today that judges do make law. If they do so less in this country than in the United States,[11] it is because of the greater activity of the British Parliament as compared with Federal and State legislatures in the United States. In spite of opinion to the contrary, judicial law-making can quite properly be regarded as adjudication in conformity with established rules. It is an unfortunate legacy of positivism that a clearly defined boundary exists between law and policy. The role of the judge, in terms of this ideology, is seen as a narrow one: to find the facts[12] and apply the law. We are just emerging from some of the worst consequences of this philosophy: a slavish reliance on precedent, a literalist interpretation of statutes, and image of the judge as objective, impartial and totally independent of the pressures of society, which in its own turn led to the 'pedestal' theory of the judiciary, the placing of judges apart from all mankind, outside the range of scrutiny or criticism. But rules require interpretation, elaboration, qualification: they are purposive instruments, means to ends. The ends do not remain static and it is part of the judicial role to adapt them to changed social conditions. It is a limited creative role: the judge does not have *carte blanche*, but must innovate within the interstices of established rules, fashioning them in accordance with the principles and policies at the basis of those rules.

Judges then are law-makers. What advantage do they have, and what drawbacks has their activity, over parliamentary legislation?

Judges are not elected and, therefore, not answerable to an electorate. They hold office *quamdiu se bene gesserint*, and are thus not subject to the same pressures as elected members of Parliament. No English judge has ever been removed. Nor are they subject to the pressures of lobby groups or interest organisations as Parliament is, though as litigation is developed as a means of legitimising claims this difference may become more apparent than real. It is easy for Parliament to ride roughshod over minority interests, and it is with respect to these that courts can anticipate the earliest pressure of group actions. If the United States proves the example, the key to this development lies in the growth of neighbourhood law services and the strengthening of the declaratory action.

Judges are, of course, lawyers, recruited from the élite of the Bar, whereas members of Parliament come from diverse backgrounds (though 93 of the 630 members elected in 1970 are barristers). The relationship of social origin to values is discussed later in this chapter. In this context one must note that the information fed to judges is of a narrow legal character. In an adversary system he relies upon what information counsel present. He does not even have, save in very exceptional circumstances, power to call any witnesses. He may hear expert witnesses but what he does with their information is up to him.

Judges often adopt a rather bigoted attitude to expert evidence.[13] In comparison with his American brethren he labours under two other handicaps. Firstly, the practice of presenting what is known in the United States as a 'Brandeis brief' has not been recognised in England. Secondly, he may not use such extrinsic material to legislation as reports of committees or parliamentary debates.

The 'Brandeis brief' takes its name from a brief presented successfully to the United States Supreme Court in 1908 in *Muller* v *State of Oregon* by Louis Brandeis, later to become one of the greatest justices of that court, in which the danger of women working long hours in laundries was substantiated by reference to over ninety reports of committees: bureaux of statistics, commissioners of hygiene, inspectors of factories from Europe as well as the United States.[14] The institution has never taken root in this country, though there is the isolated example of a judge buttressing his legal arguments with statistical data. The more typical English stance is the one taken Pennycuick J. in the Chancery division in *Re Craven's Insurance*.[15] A brief testifying to the effect on employment in Keighley of winding up an insurance company was held not to be information upon which a judge could act: the question was not justiciable.

The exclusion of extrinsic material (*travaux préparatoires*) is more controversial. The Law Commission recently recommended that this should be admissible, at least in so far as reports of law reform committees, such as the Law Commission itself, were concerned.[16] Attempts were made in 1970 to introduce clauses to this effect into two Bills, but both clauses were rejected. It was a liberal, progressive proposal which had the support of the judiciary. The judges undoubtedly saw the convenience of the suggestion for not only would it save time, but it would also enable the judges to develop the law in partnership with Parliament, as they would get guidance on the social background of the law, the mischief the Act intended to cure and the scope of the remedy provided.

A judge is expected to develop the law in the directions required by social needs, but in comparison with Parliament he is severely hamstrung in his attempts to ascertain these. Parliament is nourished by departmental investigations, sometimes even full-scale Royal Commission enquiries, in which expert knowledge of various kinds is brought to bear. Parliament can also give a proposal a formal first reading and then await reaction from informed opinion and interest groups. Judges must pronounce there and then, though consultations with other judges may take place while judgment is reserved. Once judgment is given, the judge is *functus officio*, though depending on the vagaries of litigation, he may get another chance to consider the problem, should his solution be challenged by a litigant disgruntled at the first decision. The judge may then be torn between a desire to conform to community standards and a wish to respect the established law. The result may be instability, with some judges going some way and some the other. Advising a client then becomes perilous, for so much depends on who hears the case.

However, once Parliament has passed legislation it is difficult for it to undo its work. Pressures on parliamentary time are such that mistakes are characterised as experiments, and the fullness of time panaceas for the evil they perpetrate. Of course, legislation is a symbol of legitimacy so that resistance to parliamentary dictate will anyway be eroded by the efflux of time. But judges get the opportunity to reconsider the doctrines they fashion. This is because the judicial decision-making process is *ad hoc* and incremental. Shapiro thus characterises it: 'In the face of uncertainty about consequences the best decisional tactic is to take minor steps which will elicit new information and allow one to pull back without excessive loss if the new information indicates unexpected trouble.'[17]

The development of the tort of negligence in this country is ample testimony to this model of decision-making. Courts have been able to proceed thus because they are confronted with real human problems: legislatures, by contrast, perceive the problem in issue in an abstract, generalised fashion.

Finally, one insuperable problem to judicial law-making may be noted. Judges are confined to litigation and circumscribed by the techniques available to them. They do not have available enforcement or licensing machinery or positive rewards. They are limited to damages and specific orders, injunctions, specific performance, certiorari, declaratory judgments and so on. Without this institutional machinery the steps they can undertake are limited. Thus the judges could be convinced of the iniquity of the doctrine of common employment or the unfairness of the common law position on contributory negligence and be able to alleviate the position by careful pruning and adaptation (using, for example, the standard law reform ploy of fictions), but they could neither abolish the former nor introduce a better scheme for the latter: both steps had to be undertaken by the legislature. Similarly, the judges may feel that the state should compensate victims of crimes of violence or perjury, but such schemes require administrative machinery to be operable, and judges do not have this.

Origins and recruitment

The dropping of the myth that judges do not create law has led to a questioning of the directions in which judges are fashioning the law, and in its turn to speculation about their background and attitudes. In the United States, and some other countries such as Japan, this has led to the development of a new social science, judicial behaviouralism.[18] In this country its impact has been relatively slight. Without wishing to belittle the achievements of the behaviouralists, in some way this is an advantage. For they (Schubert, Lawlor, Nagel, Danelski are leading exponents) have indulged in excesses of hypothesis and prediction. In correlating independent variables such as political affiliation, ethnic background, religion or previous appointments with what they take to be dependent conclusions, they gloss over the problem of causation. Because a judge is a Catholic Democrat of Irish ancestry who represented trade unions while at the Bar, and because his decisions are consistently in favour of unions in labour disputes, it does not follow that his decisions are such because of his background. What the behaviouralists fail to consider adequately is the institutional setting in which judges act. They ignore such crucial factors as judges' common training and environment, the 'taught tradition', and other institutional factors such as *stare decisis*.

Dorothy James, using Nagel's version of the role theory, has shown the importance of this in a recent article on two of Roosevelt's Supreme Court appointments (Jackson and Douglas) who stood at opposite sides of the spectrum of thought on the Supreme Court of their day. In so far as those attributes of role were concerned which are considered essential, she found that the Court fashioned the Justice's conception of his role, rather than his previous experience and opinions. She concluded:

Most analysis of the Supreme Court focuses on the differences between Justices. Role theory indicates how broad is the area of similarity in their behaviour, because of the structural factors of the role. It also indicates those areas where personal factors may influence decisions. Yet even where personal factors come into play, there arfer equent constraints placed by the institutional setting.[19]

One lesson is that attempting to redress the political balance by appointing, for example, socialists, to the Bench will not change legal values much. Sawer, commenting on the overt, political appointment (something England has not succumbed to except from about 1832 to 1906 when claims of party held sway) of Evatt and McTiernan in Australia in 1930, noted that each 'went on to distinguished judicial careers in which the general social evaluations resulting from their Labour background (they had each been Labour MP's) were evident in some marginal cases, but no more evident than the different social assumptions of colleagues in the same cases'.[20] Nor must it be forgotten, when the different social assumptions of the English judiciary are stressed, that appointment to a judicial post is a right of passage into the establishment (if the judge is not already an initiate): that part of his role consists in symbolising national consciousness and upholding the social system.

This is one of the reasons why judges are frequently chosen to head enquiries, though their judicial qualities (impartiality, assessment of evidence, sifting of relevance, rationality) are more important reasons. It is also part of the explanation why 'judges on the whole free of positive political attitudes, think on the same wave-length as the governors, it is hard for them to conceive of bad faith or mis-management by our masters'.[21] Certain executive-minded decisions, the Soblen affair in 1963 being an outstanding example,[22] may be seen in this light.

Although it is fashionable to comment on the narrow social background of the judiciary, there is very little concrete evidence presented. What there is supports this hypothesis. One recent sociological study shows that between 1820 and 1968 47.4 per cent of the High Court Judiciary came from the upper middle class.[23] *The Economist* noted in 1956 that 76 per cent of judges had been to public schools (one-fifth of these to Winchester) and that 76 per cent had attended Oxbridge (two-thirds of these went to Oxford). It noted also that 'in their recreations and pursuits they seem to belong to the "county" rather than to the intelligentsia'.[24] Henry Cecil's random survey of 117 out of 235 Supreme Court judiciary, county court judges and stipendiary magistrates as at July 1970, shows a slight move away from public schools (though it is negligible) and an increase in those attending university. He reports no great change in judges' sparetime activities, though music has now caught up with shooting.[25] Goldstein-Jackson's findings, based on every one of the 359 judges named in the 1968 *Law List* (covering the complete professional judiciary) showed that 292 of the 359 went to public school (over 85 per cent went to Oxbridge). He also found, hardly surprisingly, that the ages of the judges went up as one climbed the judicial hierarchy. The average age of Lords of Appeal in Ordinary was sixty-nine (it still is). Further, 'as one progresses up the judicial hierarchy, one finds more members attending public schools and either Oxford or Cambridge'.[26] There are variations in the different surveys, but the general picture is a clear one.

Significantly, there are occasions when this background comes to the fore. They are isolated examples, but nonetheless unwelcome for that. Some are just risible. Oft-quoted, but eminently repeatable, is the remark of prosecuting counsel to the jury in the *Lady Chatterley's Lover* trial in 1961: 'Is it a book that you would even wish your wife or your servants to read?'[27] He later became a judge. More insidious are chance remarks that may give a key to the judge's reasoning. Two adoption cases in recent years illustrate this point. In the famous blood-tie adoption case *(Re C (MA)*,[28] the fact that the natural father, who together with his wife wanted custody of his natural child, was a wealthy businessman seemed to weigh unduly with the court; whilst in *Re B*, Davies LJ, in very properly deciding what was best for the child, noted in the adopters' favour that they had put the child's name down for Eton.[29]

Even if there were not this uniformity about a judge's background and education, the method of recruitment of the judiciary ensures a sameness about those appointed. He will almost certainly be a Queen's Counsel (Junior Treasury Counsel, junior barristers retained to argue for the government, are normally promoted to the Bench without taking silk). Abel-Smith and Stevens have estimated that this reduces the field for recruitment to about 25 active Chancery and 145 common-law silks.[30] Thus, he will have been at the Bar many years. He will have had a busy practice and little time for social contacts outside his narrow circle of legal acquaintances, or for widening his intellectual horizons. The case for giving new judges (and existing judges, periodically) a sabbatical year or term during which they could widen their experience by participating in seminars and discussions with lawyers (including foreign lawyers) and social scientists, and visiting penal institutions and slums is thus a strong one.[31] Perhaps because their salaries do not give them the degree of wealth they once did, judges are not as unworldly as they once were. The point is recognised by Henry Cecil in his Hamlyn Lectures:

> When a judge never went by public transport, was never called 'ducks' by the conductress and only moved about in moneyed circles, it may be that he had less understanding of popular ideas or popular ways. [But now] nearly all of them travel by public transport, many help with the washing-up and most of them have learned from personal experience how the man on the Clapham omnibus lives. Most, if not all of them, have radio and television and have heard of the Beatles even if they do not all listen to them.[32]

Yet one still wonders whether the Bench can really understand and communicate with the working classes: whether it can, for example, understand the problems of poverty, or the different tensions, expectations or social values to be found in classes of society other than their own. The ethical norms of different strata of society by no means coincide. A good example of the problem is recounted by Alfred Hinds in his *Contempt of Court*.[33] He tells of a judge's inability to comprehend how anyone could buy goods in a public house. What to Hinds was a normal working-class incident of life, was perceived by a judge as akin to a criminal activity. Yet, whilst working-class judges (from what has already been said a contradiction in terms) might understand this better, if working-class magistrates may be taken as a model they would be no more tolerant of it. This differential perception of social norms can be a real problem when a judge expects a witness to have the standards of common sense and composure that he, or someone with his education or status, would have. It was the leading American realist, Jerome Frank, who pointed to the uncertainty inherent in the trial process because (*inter alia*) no one could predict how a judge would react to a witness. His solution was to psychoanalyse judges.[34] More useful would be their education so as to enable them to get a better understanding of those who appear before them and to become more socially tolerant.

Another reform would aim to achieve a broader base for the selection of judges. One of the strongest arguments in favour of appointing solicitors as judges is their wider social, educational and political background and their contact with a wider spectrum of society. But the caveat has already been entered that judges recruited from a different background would anyway take on the characteristics of the body they were joining.

Judge and Jury

A quantitatively small (less than 2 per cent) but qualitatively important number of criminal trials and a few civil actions, almost all concerned with reputation, are tried by a judge together with a jury of twelve men and women. What distinctive contribution does the jury make to the trial process, and what is the relationship with the judge?

We know very little about the workings of the jury. It is an institution deeply rooted in history. It gives no reasons for its findings because it replaced the inscrutable ordeal. Jurors were at the outset of the institution illiterate. The jury deliberates in secret and jurors are reminded of their solemn obligation not to reveal what has taken place in the jury room. Bugging a jury room would undoubtedly constitute contempt of court.

We do not even know how many criminal trials are heard by juries; 27,395 persons were 'found guilty' in 1970 at Assizes and Quarter Sessions (their jurisdiction has since been transferred to the Crown courts), but we do not know how many of them pleaded guilty. It is typical of the lack of sophistication of socio-legal methods in this country, that *Criminal Statistics*, an official Home Office publication, does not distinguish pleas of guilty from findings of guilt. However, research carried out in 1965 showed that the national average of acquittals was 39 per cent.[35] This would suggest very roughly that about 15,000 persons are convicted by a jury in a year. Until 1972 this meant twelve men and women (a greater proportion of the former) who owned property of a negligible rateable value had formed the opinion on the evidence presented to them that the accused was guilty beyond reasonable doubt.

The Criminal Justice Act 1972, accepting belatedly a recommendation of the Morris report of 1965[36], has now replaced the property qualification by evidence of inclusion on the electoral role. In social terms this should mean a broader-based jury: more women, more younger jurors (until now it was generally a middle-aged institution), a few older ones as the upper age limit has been extended to sixty-five (it is seventy for magistrates and seventy-five for superior court judges), and more working-class members. These changes in themselves will strengthen the intellectual underpinnings of the jury, though the exclusion of many professions, but not, for example, teachers or accountants, will preserve the essential middle-mindedness of the typical jury.

What are the social consequences of the composition of the jury? Bredemeier describe it as a mechanism by which the court's output of justice may be balanced with community sentiment. 'Although nominally only a "trier of facts" when facts are in dispute, the jury probably tries a good many things besides facts behind its closed doors. Without overt changes in the legal doctrines, then, justice—according to the community's views—may nonetheless be served.'[37] Hitherto, the input of values will have been those of 'middle Britain'. Note, for example the reluctance of juries to convict for 'motor' manslaughter and drunken driving: in each case their resistance was a catalyst to reform. The male character of juries may have been seen in a reluctance to convict for sexual offences. Weber commented on the same trend in German juries. Research in the United States has shown that social status and contribution to jury deliberation are related. Strodtbeck, James and Hawkins found that: 'Men, in contrast with women, and persons of higher-status, in contrast with lower-status, occupations have higher participation, influence, satisfaction and perceived competence for the jury task.' They were of course using mock deliberations, but their juries were recruited from voting registers and reflected similar categories exempted from service. We can thus expect the behaviour noted to compare closely with jury deliberations in England in the future. In this light the fact that the choice of foreman was $3\frac{1}{2}$ times more likely to be made from professional or managerial occupations than labouring, the acts of foremen accounted for one-quarter of jury acts, and that high participation indicates a greater ability to influence others, all suggest that the removal of property qualifications may not have as great an impact as may be thought. It is also interesting that all groups, except labourers, preferred to have a member of their family tried before a jury of professional or managerial members: labourers would opt for trial by skilled workers. Yet 'face-to-face experience caused lower-status persons to be evaluated more highly'.[38]

Weber described trial by jury as 'irrational Khadi Justice'. To him it was a force weakening legal rationalism. 'It appeals to the sentiments of the layman', he noted, 'who feels annoyed whenever he meets with formalism in a concrete case, and it satisfies the emotional demands of those underprivileged classes which clamour for substantive justice.'[39] There are occasions, examples have been given where popular justice, jury equity, has prevailed over the letter of the law. But the common view that there is considerable discrepancy between jury verdicts and those to which a judge would have come, sitting alone, has been shown to be unfounded by Kalven and Zeisel in *The American Jury*.[40] They show, in a monumental study, that the incidence of agreement is as high as 75.4 per cent in criminal cases and 78 per cent in civil actions. More significantly the judges classified only 30 per cent of cases of disagreement as arbitrary decision-making 'without merit'. Even here, comment the authors, jury lawlessness is only a quest for justice giving 'recognition to values which fall outside official rules.' To amplify one example, already referred to, one may illustrate this from the law of rape:

> The law recognises only one issue in rape cases other than the fact of intercourse: whether there was consent at the moment of intercourse. The jury. . . . does not limit itself to this one issue: it goes on to weigh the woman's conduct in the prior history of the affair. It closely, and often harshly scrutinizes the female complainant and is moved to be lenient with the defendant whenever there are suggestions of contributory negligence on her part (p. 249).

Kalven and Zeisel also found that there was often more than one reason for disagreement.

> Disparity of counsel, for the most part, will not make a difference by itself but will require materials which superior counsel can exploit. . . . Again, sentiments about the individual defendant are seldom powerful enough to cause disagreement by themselves. . . . The implication again is that for the defendant to be poor and crippled or beautiful and blonde is by itself rarely a sufficient stimulus for the jury to disagree with the judge (p. 114).

The authors asked Lord Parker, then England's Lord Chief Justice, for English statistics on coincidence of judge and jury verdicts. He pointed out, not surprisingly, that none were kept, but 'as a matter of impression' he surmised that it was rare for a jury to convict where a judge would acquit (and such cases resulted often from a judge's legalistic attitude towards, for example, corroboration of a sexual offence), and that jury acquittals, where a judge would have convicted varied between 3 and 10 per cent. He added that there were too few civil trials by jury in England for statistics to be meaningful. Lord Parker's figures suggest that English juries dissent less often than their American counterparts. Kalven and Zeisel comment: 'Whether this is due to a greater conformity of sentiment or to the greater control of the English judge over the trial process would be a most interesting topic for future investigation.' (p. 516).

Whichever of these factors plays the greater role, and there is no doubt that neither can be ignored, it is ironical that, as the social base of the jury is broadened (though not necessarily its deliberations), there are moves to relax judicial control of juries, by for example, not keeping from it the accused's record.[41] The judge-made laws of evidence are, of course, the very embodiment of judicial rationality, against untutored jury emotionalism. Can one, therefore, expect a spiralling of judge-jury dissensus? A research project conducted at L.S.E. suggests not.[41a]

Magistrates

There are two types of magistrates: legally qualified stipendiaries who sit in inner London and eleven other conurbations, and lay justices of the peace, who number some 21,000. This note is about the latter.

In origin part of governmental response to the economic difficulties attendant on the Black Death, the justices of the peace have had six centuries of changing fortune. Until nineteenth-century reforms they were local government, but as they lost their administrative functions (they retain vestiges in their licensing powers) their judicial functions increased. At the same time, the last two centuries have seen a diminution of their judicial powers: once they could impose the death penalty and now, with the introduction of suspended sentences, their powers to commit offenders to prison are severely circumscribed. The last hundred years have also seen the lay justices take on some civil jurisdiction, largely in response to the recognition that the working classes do have legal problems, albeit not the sort that would dignify a court presided over by a legally qualified judge. Thus, the working-class wife, unable to afford or perhaps even want a divorce, is able to go to her local magistrates' court for a separation order and a maintenance award, the enforcement of which latter, through the ultimate sanction of imprisonment, is also administered by local justices.

The surprising thing about lay justices is their continuing survival. Yet just when they seem to be at their lowest ebb they get a new injection of life. To Brougham, the great nineteenth-century reformer, there was 'not a worse constituted tribunal on the face of earth'.[42] They might have died in the nineteenth century when their administrative powers were sapped, but the resistance of the Bar to the appointment of solicitors as judges necessitated reliance on these unpaid factotums. In this century they have faced two Royal Commissions, opposition to their manner of appointment and the type of person appointed (a property qualification was abolished in 1906), hostility from motorists, the scrutiny of sociologists like Hood, who demonstrated disparities in sentencing,[43] yet they refuse to lie down. Or is it that society cannot afford (either in terms of manpower or expense) to let them go? Thus, a Royal Commission, reporting in 1948, noted that it would be 'impossible to find a sufficient body of persons equipped with knowledge of law and . . . with judicial temperament and knowledge of the world to provide that large body of stipendiary magistrates which would be required'.[44]

Lay justices, however, are not equipped with knowledge of the law. They do not need to be trained in law, for their clerks are legally trained, but they need training in sentencing techniques, in criminology and penology. It was the occasional, notorious case of magistrates' lawlessness, together with the more sober criticism of books like Roger Hood's *Sentencing in Magistrates' Courts*, which led to a White Paper in 1965, the implementation of which has meant that justices appointed after 1 January 1966 must undergo training.[45] Three years earlier the Lord Chief Justice had initiated one-day conferences on problems of sentencing and the social factors involved for the professional judiciary. It is vital that all those who administer justice should be aware of the social problems underlying it. It may, however, be said in the magistrates' favour that they are not as far removed from society as the professional judiciary. For a start, they will almost certainly have an interest in local affairs. Many as local councillors will have sat on committees dealing with children or education and will have knowledge and experience of the working of social services. Although the majority will come from upper-middle-class backgrounds, just as the judges do, there are a few with working-class backgrounds. Hood's *Sentencing the Motoring Offender* provides, for the first time in recent years, a profile of the social background of a sample of magistrates. This shows no evidence of any significant changes in the social-class backgrounds from which magistrates came in the years between 1946 when the Royal Commission conducted a survey, and the second half of the 1960s, when Hood's sample was taken. He notes that 'the combined proportion of salary and wage earners has not increased', though those 'with independent means have decreased at the same time as the number of those from professional backgrounds has risen'.[46] There has also been an increase in the proportion of women justices, but this trend has reinforced the middle class base of the magistracy still further. Nonetheless, with increased allowances a wider based magistracy is a possibility.

In view of this greater intimacy with society and its problems it is not surprising that many of the main advances in treatment of offenders have originated in the magistrates' courts, before being adopted on a higher level. Examples are the institution of probation, social enquiry reports before sentence and a means inquiry before imprisoning for failure to pay a fine or maintenance. But what is disturbing is the apparent dislike of magistrates' courts felt by matrimonial litigants, and that what they most dislike according to McGregor, Blom-Cooper and Gibson, was the attitude of magistrates.[47]

Tribunals

This chapter would give a misleading picture of the world of law if some attention were not focused on the retreat from judicial resolution of conflict. Dissatisfaction with courts and judges has nourished in turn the development of private legal systems of arbitration, and the growth of administrative tribunals.

Tribunals are a product of the welfare state, which has increased immensely the potential area of conflict between government and citizen. A balance between state and individual has to be struck. The natural choice as guardians would be the judiciary. Since Coke's time they have set themselves up as protectors of civil liberties. Parliament instead turned to tribunals, and since 1911, when a tribunal was established for settling disputes in the new health and unemployment insurance schemes set up by the National Insurance Act of that year, over 2,000 tribunals have been established.

In part this decision is explained by judicial attitudes, in part also by shortcomings of ordinary courts.

Part of the explanation, then, can be sought in the consciously-narrow role that a prevailing positivist philosophy of the judicial process had marked out for the judiciary. The fallacy of believing that there is a rigid demarcation line between law and values or social policy has been commented on. But judges who believed it (the majority still do) had by 1911 shown themselves incapable of resolving questions that would be justiciable under a welfare state. They had refused to fix rates under railway and canal legislation, to regulate competition (*Mogul* v *McGregor* is the classic instance), though not trade unions (*Taff Vale*), to control central government (*Arlidge*).[48] As guardians of civil liberties they cherished an individualist concept of society and, accordingly, of litigation. Today, as is shown by cases such as *Stringer* v *Ministry of Housing* and *Bull* v *Pitney-Bowes*, judges are not unaware of the social implications of a dispute between two individuals. In the early part of this century they were. So they made a mess of workmen's compensation before it was taken from them in 1946: in such disputes, and in cases between landlord and tenant, little or no cognisance was taken of wider insurance or housing policy. Thus, by the early years of collectivism, 'the judges had been removed, had removed themselves or had been restrained from entering large areas of competence in the modern state'.[49]

The formative era of tribunals was also the period when a rigid doctrine of precedent and a literalist emphasis on statutory interpretation were at their apogee. Social welfare legislation abounds with flexible standards. It was feared that, for example, once a judge had declared that $£x$ was 'a fair rent' or 'reasonable compensation', another judge, perhaps years later, would blindly follow the first judge's precedent.

But what governments may have feared most about the judiciary were not these rigid attitudes so much as their forthright independence, and their staunch support of the 'rule of law'.[50] Governments felt they could control tribunals, whereas they knew they could not control courts. Of course, courts and tribunals are not the only choices open to government; in some instances, then as now, ministerial discretion is the last word. The importance of the independence of tribunals has been stressed many times, notably in the Franks report,[51] but the evidence shows that at the outset tribunals were though of by the executive as part of the administration. Kathleen Bell, in her *Tribunals In the Social Services* illustrates this from the history of assistance services.

> In the early years (i.e. from 1934), the newly created Unemployment Assistance Board kept a close hold on the appeal tribunals, because . . . there was anxiety that they might get out of step. . . . Deliberate provision was made to diminish the risk of serious divergence and keep the tribunals close to the Board. For example, one of the members on every tribunal was appointed by the Board as its own representative. . . . Hearings were always held in the Board's offices with the clerk . . . always present.
>
> . . . As economic conditions improved, as the Board slowly became more acceptable and as its confidence increased, it was able to relax its hold over the tribunals.[52]

Yet McCorquodale has shown that, even in 1960 in the North West Region, there is evidence of consultation between the

Board and the Ministry about particular appointments to national assistance tribunals.[53] No ministry could have exercised this type of power over the judiciary.

Reasons for the use of tribunals may also be sought in the failings of the courts and judges. Thus, it was said that the issues raised under social welfare legislation were of a complexity which required the competence of specialists to handle. The judges are, of course, quite used to complexity, but what is really meant is that the judges are lacking in the experience to get a full comprehension of the dispute. Judges are not wont to have experience of working-class life: they are unlikely ever to have worked in a factory, or lived in a substandard flat.

Further, judicial hearings are expensive, and what was needed was a cheap procedure for settling diputes. To paraphrase Street,[54] there are occasions when a Mini is more useful than a Rolls-Royce. Judicial organisation is incapable of coping with the volume of litigation transacted under social security legislation.

It is possible, also, as Katherine Bell suggests, that the decision to transfer disputes from courts to tribunals may have something to do with the stigma attached to a court ruling. She gives the example of the change of direction in mental health policy in 1959, with the abolition of the judicial process of certification, and its replacement by medical recommendation subject to review tribunal which would investigate medical and non-medical aspects of detention.[55]

So tribunals were set up and have become an accepted part of the legal structure. To the average person tribunals are of greater significance than courts of law. Sir Carleton Allen, a leading public lawyer, wrote in 1959 that 'to be ignorant of our extensive and extending supplementary justice is to be unaware of half the legal issues which are affecting the rights and liberties of innumerable lieges every day'.[56]

It is pertinent, therefore, to ask in what tribunals are different from courts. Firstly, they differ in composition. Courts are staffed by a judicial élite, recruited from the cream of the Bar. Tribunals have a chairman and usually two other members. The

Franks report emphasised the importance of choosing a legally qualified chairman. The report was impressed by the need for such qualities as 'objectivity in treatment of cases and the proper sifting of facts' and believed that these 'are most often secured by having a legally qualified chairman'.[57] Of course, there is no distinction for these purposes between barrister and solicitor, or indeed academic lawyers. It is difficult to find enough lawyers to take these jobs. Since legal aid is not available for tribunal proceedings (except in the Lands Tribunal, which is anyway more like a court), lawyers are not particularly interested in, or knowledgeable about, tribunal work. The practice varies: the mental health review tribunals and the National Health Service tribunals are always legally chaired, whereas supplementary benefit appeal tribunals are often not (Street points to the desirability of such chairmen having 'acquaintance with working class life and conditions')[58] The other members of a tribunal are chosen by the relevant Minister for their expertise in the area of work of the particular tribunal. In social security tribunals the other members will come from the two sides of industry; in planning appeals there will always be an expert in valuation.[58a]

Secondly, appellants may be represented, other than by lawyers (a heading which includes non-admitted legal executives). Trade unionists are often represented by a trade union official. Appellants are unlikely to be represented by lawyers, because of the unavailability of legal aid. Bearing in mind the importance of tribunals for the average person, this is a major gap in the provision of assisted legal services. The decision to exclude tribunals from the benefits of legal aid may be grounded in deliberate policy: the belief that lawyers would destroy the informality of tribunals. Bell's comment is pertinent: an examination of mental health review tribunals has shown that patients represented are twice as likely to be discharged.[59] Doubtless, though no statistics are forthcoming, this pattern would repeat itself over the whole spectrum of tribunals.

Thirdly, tribunals are cheap. The tribunals members are poorly (if at all) remunerated. 'We do not seem to have made up our minds whether tribunal work is to be remunerated at a realistic level or treated as voluntary service.'[60] Appellants are not charged fees, nor is there any risk of large bills to pay the costs of the other side. Overhead expenses are less than 10 per cent of the benefits distributed. Proceedings are speedy and efficient, though delays in getting a tribunal hearing can be lengthy. Further, tribunal hearings are by appointment; one of the greatest criticisms of court procedure is the lack of fixed dates.

Fourthly, tribunals give greater privacy. There is greater willingness to sit in private when personal details are being aired. Anyway, tribunals are not the public spectacle that court hearings are, and few members of the public attend, and the press are rarely represented.

Fifthly, there is more informality. The tribunals do not stick closely to an adversary procedure. A good chairman is anxious to elicit from an inexperienced appellant the merits of his case. The exclusionary rules of evidence (such as hearsay) are not applied rigidly. Chairmen, rather as many magistrates do, often invite the appellant 'to tell his story'.

Sixthly, whilst both judges and tribunal chairmen are expected to articulate the reasons for their decision, judges are expected to do this as matter of course, but tribunals need only rationalise their decision-making when a request is made for them to do so.

Finally, tribunals act in the knowledge that the ordinary courts are in the background. Although there are restricted rights of appeal, the ordinary courts can review the findings of tribunals where there is an error of law on the face of the tribunal record (the fewer reasons given the more difficult it becomes to use this ground of appeal), or where the tribunal has infringed lawyers' principles of natural justice, by, for example, not hearing one side's case or showing scant regard for impartiality and objectivity. A glance at the Law Reports will demonstrate the truth of Abel-Smith and Stevens's contention that 'judicial supervision over administrative tribunals provided an important practical and psychological boost to the work of the Courts'.[61] What is surprising is that in half a century so little of the experience of tribunals should have rubbed off on lawyers and courts. Law today still connotes for the average lawyer the activities of the courts, and this in spite of the importance and volume[62] of legal work undertaken by administrative tribunals.

The police 7

To many people the police are 'the law'. Relatively few will ever consult a solicitor or see a judge in action, but the presence of the police is perceived by all. To some the police are even identified as 'the government'. Thus, according to Laurie, political demonstrators see the police as 'the State made flesh: in their single blue bodies they focus a thousand resentments against the omnipresent machinery of government'.[1]

These views may be untutored, yet in a strange way they uncover sociological truth. The police wield great power and exercise an inherent and virtually uncontrollable discretion. The decision to invoke the criminal justice system is taken more often by policemen than it is, for example, by judges. Changes in police powers or the way they exercise them can have a more profound effect on the social system than the passing of a new piece of legislation.

Yet the myth is perpetuated that the police are but ordinary citizens. This does obeisance to the English cult of the amateur, but how true is it?

Historical perspectives

The institution of a professional police is alien to English culture. Until Peel's reforms of 1829, the country was policed by constables who held unpaid part-time appointments. But it was the duty of everyone to maintain the King's peace, and it was open to any citizen to arrest an offender. The community itself was thus responsible for the level of social control. There is no reason to believe that in the stability of the Middle Ages this system did not work well, but it broke down under the weight of the Industrial Revolution.

The alternative, a professional police, was regarded as anathema by the English public. At the time of Pitt's abortive attempt to introduce police into England in 1785 the very word had a sinister ring. Its emotive power darkened men's minds to any advantage its introduction might bring. It was believed that 'once admit a police force into England, and the long-cherished liberties of Englishmen would be swept away in a regime of terror and oppression'. When Peel did succeed in establishing the Metropolitan Police, it was widely believed that his 'bloody gang' was but the machinery to put the Duke of Wellington on the throne.[2]

The myth that the police were but private citizens thus helped to soften the blow, whilst at the same time preserving essential continuity with a long-established English institution. But the police today owe more to Peel's reforms than to the ancient office of constable.

Police and government

The constitutional status of the police today is anomalous, in part reflecting this history. There is no national police force. The individual retains powers of arrest and has limited powers to initiate prosecutions, which are useful balances to the growth of police bureaucracy. At the same time the individual has duties, such as that to come to the assistance of a police officer when called upon to do so. In legal theory the policeman is not a Crown servant, in spite of declaring on appointment that he will well and truly serve the Queen, for he is not paid directly out of central government funds. Further, if he commits a tort by, for example, falsely detaining someone, the Crown is not liable in damages, but nor is local government. Vicarious liability, however, attaches to his chief constable, who is entitled to be indemnified out of local police funds.[3] Nevertheless, central government through the Home Secretary exercises very real control over the activities of police forces.

One must distinguish the Metropolitan Police force from local police organisations. The 'Met', which has a manpower of over 21,000 and is thus nearly a quarter of the country's police, is directly under the control of the Home Secretary. He is answerable in Parliament for its activities, but not for those of police forces outside the metropolitan area. Home Secretaries tend to take a restrictive view of their obligation to answer parliamentary questions about law enforcement in the metropolis. The handling of the Challenor case by Henry Brooke in 1963–64 is ample testimony to this.[4]

The Home Secretary appoints the Commissioner who commands the Metropolitan Police and can give directions to him as to deployment of the Force. In practice the Commissioner exercises great independence, but in theory '[a] government which wished to would be able to arrest the opposition's M.P.s by means of the Metropolitan Force. In addition, they would have under their control the main Special Branch, which is the nearest equivalent we have in this country to a "political police".'[5] The precise legal relationship between the Home Secretary and the Commissioner has not been determined. It was aired for the first time in 1968 in *R* v *Commissioner of Police for the Metropolis ex parte Blackburn*, when Lord Denning MR stated: 'I hold it to be the duty of the Commissioner of Police of the Metropolis. . . . to enforce the law of the land. . . . But . . . he is not the servant of anyone, save of the law itself. No Minister of the Crown can tell him that he must, or must not, prosecute this man or that one. . . . The responsibility for law enforcement lies on him. He is answerable to the law and to the law alone.'[6]

The 'Met' provides a number of specialised services for local police forces, of which the most important is the Criminal Record Office. Otherwise police services operate on a local basis. The Royal Commission on the Police (1962)[7] rejected the setting-up of a national police force, but recommended rationalisation of provincial police forces and closer Home Office involvement in their running so as to promote coordination and efficiency. These recommendations were implemented in the Police Act. As a result amalgamations have taken place, and there are now forty-nine local police authorities. The composition of each of these is two-thirds local councillors and one-third lay magistrates. Local responsibility for, and participation in, local police activities is thus preserved. But 'the powers of the Home Office now dwarf those of local police authorities'.[8]

The police authority, which is charged with the duty of securing the maintenance of an adequate and efficient police force, appoints the Chief Constable, his deputy and assistants, subject to the concurrence of the Home Secretary. It is responsible for determining the size and establishment of the force and for providing and maintaining buildings and equipment. But the Home Secretary's regulations govern discipline, pay, pensions, training, duties, uniform and equipment. He has powers of inspection, and may call upon chief constables to provide him with reports on the policing of their area. There is a central inspectorate of police. The Home Office meets 50 per cent of the net expenditure of local forces and can withhold this grant if dissatisfied with the efficiency of a local police force. The Home Secretary can conduct independent *ad hoc* inquiries into the conduct of a force. All in all, and in spite of local fragmentation, there is government control of police. The Royal Commission recognised this reality and recommended that the Home Secretary should be made fully responsible in Parliament for the conduct of the police. The Police Act did not implement the proposal, with the result, as the Royal Commission put it, of 'the worst of both worlds, in that control is in fact exercised by anonymous Home Office officials whose conduct cannot be examined or questioned'.[9]

Police bureaucratisation

The power which central government exercises over the police is neutralised by internal bureaucratisation of the police. The police force is organised, trained and controlled in such a way that commitment to occupational community takes precedence over other social commitments. There are dangers in this, as this chapter demonstrates: an individual policeman may look to organisational norms rather than to legal ones. But the principal benefits are the unimportance of social origins in recruitment, and the reliability of the police to enforce unpopular legislation. Those who advocate more recruitment of coloured policemen, as a means of improving relations between police and immigrants, fail to perceive this process.[10] It also enables the police to define their role in terms of political neutrality. They are there to protect the public no matter from what source danger comes.

The role of the police

There is no better introduction to the role of the police than the instructions framed by Rowan and Mayne, Peel's first commissioners, to guide the first recruits in 1829.

> The primary object of an efficient police is the prevention of crime; the next that of detection and punishment of offenders if crime is committed. . . . It should be understood at the outset that the object to be attained is the prevention of crime. To this great end every effort of the public is directed. The security of person and property, the preservation of public tranquillity, and all other objects of a police establishment will thus be better effected than by the detection and punishment of the offender after he has succeeded in committing the crime. . . . Every member of the Force must remember that his duty is to protect and help members of the public no less than to apprehend guilty persons. Consequently, while prompt to prevent crime and to arrest criminals, he must look upon himself as a servant and guardian of the general public and treat all law-abiding citizens, irrespective of their social position, with unfailing patience and courtesy.[11]

This passage is still used today to teach police recruits their role. It pinpoints two work tasks as the norm: prevention of crime and its detection. One of the main criticisms levelled at the work performance of the police is their concentration on law enforcement to the undue exclusion of more primary prophylactic measures, such as establishing a viable relationship with the communities they police. The blame for this fixing of priorities can be attributed to three main factors.

Firstly, the image that the police project to potential recruits. Advertising campaigns, career booklets and the like present the police as a career of adventure, rarely one of social service. This may of course be attributable to the social and educational background of the potential recruit. In the past a large proportion of recruits were graduates of the armed services, and the image may have been fashioned to appeal to them. The standards of height and weight set by the police reinforce the image presented. That 'tact, emotional stability, balanced social attitudes, and intelligence are infinitely more vital to the successful performance of the police role . . . than pounds of flesh'[12] is a truism, but one which is only slowly penetrating the police bureaucratic machine.

Secondly, law enforcement is the role for which education and training equip the policeman. The sixteen weeks' crash course which initiates recruits into the rites of police work is universally condemned as sterile. The students are expected to consume titbits of assorted information, large chunks of criminal statutes and principles, inventories of occasions when arrest without warrant is permissible, details of Home Office instructions, and sundry courses of action to be adopted on finding anything 'from the Koh-i-noor diamond to an anarchist's bomb'.[13]

But in all this indoctrination there is precious little attempt to instil the principles of criminology or penology or the psychology of behaviour; no attention is devoted to the development of interpersonal skills; problems of social administration, of immigrants or drug addicts are peripheral to the learning by rote of procedures that a policeman could pick up in a fortnight of station and beat experience. The system is geared to producing manpower as quickly as possible; the training to ensure that a policeman does not commit an act which might cost the police authority more than he earns in a lifetime. According to Maureen Cain, 'policemen themselves maintain that 80 per cent of the information is no further use to them'.[14] In fairness, one may add, the police staff college at Bramshill provides the broader education advocated here, but only for a select few.

The drawback to this narrow legalistic education is that it does not assist policemen to understand the communities they police. To geographical isolation, for they do not live among their charges, is thus added social isolation. Instead of comprehension of other cultures, the young, the underprivileged, the immigrant, the police fall back on stereotyped expectations. To understand the effect of this one must explore the policeman's working personality. Skolnick, in his *Justice Without Trial*, postulates that a policeman's role can be understood in terms of two variables, danger and authority. Police, he suggests, enjoy the possibility of danger: most would opt for detective work rather than station duty. Police mythology thus cultivates 'symbolic assailants' (a youth dressed in a black leather jacket and motorcycle boots is a good example). The police learn to be suspicious of these objects of danger; this forestalls meaningful interaction and in its turn breeds social isolation.[15] Lambert, in his study of police and race relations in Birmingham, develops this:

> Stereotyped expectations of an adverse nature are possible so long as there is a limited context in which the contact can occur. The social system which promotes widespread prejudice, because it involves policemen as citizens in a set of attitudes which cannot but affect their attitudes as policemen, also promotes barriers to effective policing.
>
> Stereotype is of very great importance for normal police duties: policing is largely an ever changing series of contacts demanding an individually directed response. A policeman must be able to sum up a person very quickly and determine a suitable manner with which to treat him. . . .
>
> In this stereotype of the coloured immigrant the social context provides an unfavourable starting-point. . . . This stereotype when tested by experience is reinforced rather than modified for the policeman, who, in the main, will have contact with

only those sectors of the population in only those situations where his suspicions are confirmed. He is unlikely to have the kind of contact which might break the ignorance barrier to a complete idea of the immigrant community.[16]

A third reason why law enforcement is the favoured role situation is that it constitutes the measuring-rod of police efficiency. The public must be able to judge the success of the police organisation by some criterion: that constructed as an index of efficiency is the clear-up rate of offences known to the police. It is, to say the least, an artificial and suspect method of judging the competence of the police. It ignores the predominant role played by the citizen in solving crime, both in indicating offenders to the police, and asking for offences to be taken into consideration. The statistics are misleading. For example, they show a remarkably high clear-up rate for shoplifting offences (89 per cent in 1970), but these are usually only reported where the offender is caught redhanded, so that there is little for the police to do. The clear-up rate for theft from parked cars is very low (24 per cent in 1970), but this offence is perceived by the police as more akin to nuisance than to crime and they devote little effort to apprehending the culprits. To get a more realistic understanding of police efficiency through clear-up rates one needs to consider offences which the police regard seriously. A good example would be robbery. The clear-up rate here is shown to be 42 per cent in 1970 and the percentage of reported cases cleared up has declined (it averaged nearly 48 per cent in the years between 1955 and 1959). But it may be more significant that 6,273 robberies were made known to the police in 1970, whereas the earlier period averaged 1,315: in other words, the police are solving more robberies, but the numbers of reported robberies are rising faster than the numbers which they solve.

This is the institutional setting in which the policeman works. 'The worker', Skolnick points out, 'always tries to perform according to his most concrete and specific understanding of the control system.'[17] A policeman is left in no doubt what his control system expects of him. To give an example, he spends the first two years on probation pounding a beat for eight hours a day. During this period he is a fairly free agent. To prove that he has been spending his time usefully, he must produce tangible results. C.H. Rolph recounts that to substantiate his candidacy for promotion to sergeant he was advised to 'embark on a sort of prosecuting blitz'.[18] But inherent in this method of measuring efficiency is a graver danger.

The danger is, in Packer's words, that the police may prefer the "crime control model" of the criminal process to the "due process model", that factual guilt may prevail over legal guilt.[19] Skolnick puts the problem thus:

> The police in damocratic society are required to maintain order and to do so under the rule of law. As functionaries charged with maintaining order, they are part of the bureaucracy. The ideology of democratic bureaucracy emphasizes initiative rather than disciplined adherence to rules and regulations. By contrast, the rule of law emphasizes the rights of individual citizens and constraints upon the initiative of legal officials. This tension between the operational consequences of ideas of order, efficiency and initiative, on the one hand, and legality on the other, constitutes the principal problem of police as a democratic legal organisation.

He finds that 'the police [in the United States] are increasingly articulating a conception of professionalism based on a narrow view of managerial efficiency' and urges 'a significant alteration in the ideology of police, so that 'professionalism' rests on the values of a democratic legal order rather than on technical proficiency'.[20] And Banton comments that 'the efficiency of the police may therefore be less important than their responsiveness to the community they are required to serve'.[21] The dangers may not be as great in England as they are in the United States: there is less serious crime and the police lack the reputation for venality and lawlessness that attaches to their American counterparts. The English police may even, as Lambert suggests, enjoy 'some prestige and a great tradition of community service'.[22] Nonetheless, the problem is a real one. Zander has recently shown how access to a solicitor in the police station, guaranteed by Administrative Directions accompanying the Judges' Rules, is frequently refused by the police.[20] With threatened abolition of these Rules[24] there is no room for complacency.

The dangers of police bargaining with suspected offenders also cannot be ignored. If the goal is an optimum level of solved crimes then the incentive for the police to persuade an offender that he would like other offences to be taken into consideration is great, for an offence taken into consideration counts as a cleared-up offence. The practice, therefore, is to confront a thief or house-breaker with a list of similar offences known to the police and to ask him if he wishes to admit to having committed such offences. The consideration for such confession is (according to prisoners) that a good word will be put in for them when the judge, at the sentencing stage, asks the police whether anything is known. If he has committed these other offences he cannot lose (his sentences are at worst likely to be concurrent): if he has not, he is unlikely to suffer unduly. But fiction is undoubtedly a production standard tolerated by the police in the industry of crime-solving.

But the most unfortunate consequence of the 'crime control model' and the emphasis on clear-up rates is that success can camouflage the sort of ruthless illegality that isolated scandals like the Challenor case or Sheffield 'rhino whip' affair of 1963 reveal. Of the Challenor affair Mary Grigg writes:

> Faced with the job of breaking up the West End rackets, answerable to public opinion, prodded by the press and harangued by the Home Office, the men responsible for the success of the Metropolitan Police could hardly be expected to see anything questionable about an officer who was only too keen to carry out his duties. Looking at his record of arrests they might not have thought of inquiring into his methods.[25]

The Challenor record of framing, illegal arrests, assaults in police stations only came to light because Challenor happened to pick on an articulate newspaper cartoonist. Similarly, the most frightening aspect of the Sheffield incident was the disclosure in the subsequent Inquiry, of wholesale concealment and even fabrication of evidence by several police officers. 'The other grave revelation', comments Whitaker, 'was that, although. . . . many officers must have known the truth, not one member of [the] force had the integrity to come forward and speak out. The trouble is that the wrong loyalties are, at times, uppermost and strongest in the police today: comrades and service come first, with justice and the public a poor second.'[26] The Sheffield police were over-bureaucratised. But the blame should not be attributed wholly to the police; the public must share the opprobrium. Two-faced it expects the police to eradicate crime, but it allows them only 'sporting' methods. So long as the public measures police achievement in terms of crimes cleared-up, it must expect the police to put a premium on achieving an optimum level regardless of the rule of law.

Law enforcement may be the favoured role situation and the factors just outlined conduce to such a choice, but the majority of a policeman's time is nonetheless as a 'peace officer' rather than a 'law officer'. This is illustrated by Banton's experiences in Edinburgh and in four American cities. He saw that far more time was spent 'keeping the peace' by supervising the beat and responding to requests for assistance than was taken up in enforcing the law in the sense of arresting offenders. Police officers can act in this way because of public response. Relations with the police are better than they were in the last century or fifty years ago. There are less prosecutions for assault on the police, though this may indicate a reluctance to prosecute rather than a diminution of such attacks.[27] The public's willingness to cooperate is also assisted by the breakdown of closely knit communities and a sense of belonging to a wider society. But there is no room for complacency about relations between police and public. The Social Survey undertaken by the Central Office of Information for the Royal Commission in 1960 disclosed that 42.4 per cent of the public thought that some policemen took bribes, 34.7 per cent that the police used unfair methods to get information, 32 per cent that they might distort evidence in court, and 17.8 per cent that on occasions they used too much force.[28] The police cannot do without public approval and cooperation.

The establishment of a viable relationship with a community will have three consequences. First, it will help to prevent crime. Too often the police, realising this, concentrate their public relations activities on crime prevention, by arranging, for example, exhibitions which advise the public on how not to be burgled or have a car broken into. What is needed are true community relations. Bordua and Tifft[29] suggest that there is a strong case for a greater need on the part of police departments to evaluate on a continuing basis all of their operations by means of feedback interviewing of citizens. Areas of most crime are also areas where non-criminal police work is most demanding. Secondly, when a crime has been committed the police rely on the public to help them solve it. Better public relations will create a climate where the public is willing to give active assistance. Thirdly, as W.F. Whyte noted in *Street Corner Society*, when a policeman takes 'a strictly legalistic view of his duties [he] cuts himself off from the personal relations necessary to enable him to serve as mediator of disputes in his area'. But against this must be balanced the fact that 'the policeman who develops close ties with local people is unable to act against them with the vigour prescribed by the law'.[30]

The first steps taken by Robert Mark, the Commissioner of the Metropolitan Police who took up his appointment in April 1972, in integrating the CID within the force as a whole augur well for the future of police-public relations.[31]

Police and discretionary justice

Like all officials the police have and exercise discretion. The problem with the police is the low visibility of their activities so that control by a higher authority is not easy. Of course, absence of discretionary powers would produce rigidity in relationships with the public. Discretion in allowing for less formal relations is thus to be treasured. But at the same time it can lead to an arbitrary interference with individual liberty. More rigid enforcement would undoubtedly uncover more crime, but in the long run it might lead to a reduced willingness to notify the police. Hood and Sparks report that when police in California decided to prosecute all crimes of violence, whether or not the victim wished to proceed with the case, the number of reported cases dropped 11 per cent in a year.[32]

Discretion is exercised in a number of ways. Thus, the police may ignore a trivial offence to get at a 'big fish'.[33] The informer system works on this basis. In return for information leading to the conviction of a drug pedlar the police may be willing to drop a charge (or reduce it) against a possessor of dangerous drugs. Police also ignore crime for other reasons. La Fave identifies the following categories:[34] (i) ambiguous or anachronistic laws; (ii) where the offender belongs to a minority group[35] among whom the conduct in question is thought to be common or where the victim is unwilling to press charges; (iii) where the prosecution would achieve nothing, as, for example, in the case of prosecuting a drunken husband for assaulting his wife, where the burden of a prison sentence would be borne by the wife and children, and where the police would suffer opprobrium when the wife forgave the husband and sided with him against them. Further, the police must allocate their limited resources: crime clear-up rates, as has been intimated, reflect police perception of different offences. There may even be local variations of practice. In 1963 the Chief Constable of Southend announced to the astonishment of many that he did not intend to prosecute shoplifters at the public's expense unless there were very good reasons for doing so. The police may also downgrade an offence. In a study of robberies in London, McClintock and Gibson showed that the police classified a considerable proportion of aggravated robberies as less serious types of robbery (95.5% of cases were classified legally as aggravated robberies: the police only classified 70.4% as such).[36]

Another technique employed by the police is the use of cautions. Empirical research into the way in which police use this power is mainly American, but there is one recent English study. The *Criminal Statistics* are not very helpful. They tell us that in 1968, for example, the police cautioned 34,926 offenders for indictable offenders for indictable offences, a further 28,655 for non-indictable and 243,709 for motoring offences. But they do not reveal instances of informal warnings or cautions to prosecutions administered by government departments and local authorities. Steer, in his study of the exercise of police discretion,[37] did not use the information contained in the *Criminal Statistics*, but relied on information made available to him for five medium-sized borough police forces. From an examination of the official reports of some 300 cases, Steer puts into four categories the principal reasons given for cautioning adult offenders instead of taking them to court. They are: (i) the complainant declined to prosecute (cases such as domestic quarrels, petty thefts and pilfering by employees); (ii) where the victim was a voluntary participant (particularly sexual offences, such as unlawful sexual intercourse with a girl under the age of sixteen); (iii) where evidence is insufficient to prosecute;[38] (iv) where the offender's circumstances aroused sympathy (old age, illness, mental instability) and police concern that his plight should be brought to the attention of welfare agencies. Steer also found that the lower social classes were more likely to be cautioned than the upper classes.

Cautions are used more frequently with juvenile offenders. In the first year of criminal liability more children are dealt with by caution than by being found guilty by a court. The proportion of cautions to prosecutions declines with advancing age of juvenile offenders. Research on decision-making factors is exclusively American. Piliavin and Briar[39] found that the response of the youth to the police officer was crucial. If he confesses and appears penitent he will be classed as 'a victim of circumstance' and dealt with informally. If, on the other hand, he reacts with hostility and is uncooperative he is more likely to be classified as not respecting the law and to be prosecuted. They also found that possession of a record meant the offender was usually charged. Goldman[40] found that a lower proportion of middle-class children were prosecuted, and a group of 90 police officers admitted taking family background into account. Terry,[41] on the other hand, found that socio-economic status and race were not related to the use of police discretion when previous record was taken into account. To Skolnick,[42] the fact that 'Westville' police arrested Negroes more frequently than whites for failing to pay traffic fines was due not to racial bias but possession of characteristics (being unemployed, for example) which suggested a high risk of inability to pay.

One of the main benefits of police discretion is the ability to experiment with new techniques or methods of treatment. The highly praised Juvenile Liaison Scheme is the result of such experimentation. Beginning in Liverpool in 1949 it has spread to a number of other forces. Under the Liverpool plan, volunteer police officers supervise cautioned juveniles in liaison with their parents, school or youth club authorities and the probation service. The idea is to keep offenders or potential offenders (for they do not have to have committed any offence) out of court, just as in an earlier age a 'cuff-on-the-ear' was used as a friendly warning. Mack reports that 90 per cent of graduates of this scheme are not known to have offended in the next three years.[43]

Should police discretion be controlled? The difficulty is heightening the visibility of police decisions without impairing the administration of justice. One cannot control what one cannot see. Of all administrative agencies the decision-making power of the police is regulated least. But how could police activities be controlled? Davis, in his *Discretionary Justice*, makes this suggestion:

> The problems of the police. . . . can and should be guided by detailed and meaningful rules—rules that will be realistic and enforced, not the kind of rules now in police manuals that all officers know they have to violate. Enforcement policies resting upon social values usually should be determined not primarily by individual patrolmen but by top officers of the departments, as well as by other officers of the local government. And the

community should be informed and allowed to participate, except when confidentiality is necessary.[44]

This must be worth consideration in this country. The other possible reform would be to take the prosecuting process away from the police and put it in the hands of an independent authority. This is the Scottish system, and is one commended by Justice,[45] an all-party organisation of lawyers, but it has not met with any enthusiasm in this country.

Complaints against the police

It is important that complaints about the police should be heard in a manner satisfactory to the public. Most complaints are probably unfounded. In 1971 there were 12,271 complaints made, of which 8.7 per cent were substantiated. The number of complaints is going up annually, but the percentage found to have substance is declining (in 1969 there were 11,814 complaints; 10.28 per cent were substantiated).[46] All complaints are informally investigated, but not by an outside body. The police themselves (in serious matters often a chief constable of another force) undertake investigations, a procedure not calculated to enhance public confidence. The alternatives are a special inquiry, as happened in the Challenor case, more recently in relation to the Leeds police and allegatins of bribery amongst Metropolitan Police detectives, and a judicial tribunal of inquiry. The Parliamentary Commissioner for Administration has no power to investigate complaints against the police. It is said that independent investigations would affect the morale of the police, but it could do this only if complaints were substantiated in large numbers of cases: in which case the police would deservedly lack morale. Mack's new procedure is an improvement (he is establishing a new branch to investigate complaints) but the police will still sit in judgment on themselves.

The dangers of police discretion are arbitrariness and illegality. A strong police bureaucracy eliminates the worst of this but it also enables residual abuse to remain below surface. No agency which exercises the power the police do can resist much longer the mounting pressures for independent investigation of complaints against it.

Indeed, this has now been accepted by Robert Carr, the Home Secretary. His response to Philip Whitehead's attempt in February 1973 to amend the Police Act so that unsatisfied complainants would be able to appeal to an independent review tribunal was to promise the introduction by way of experiment of independent superintendence of the complaints machinery along the lines of the Parliamentary Commissioner for the Administration. This reform cannot come too soon.

Law, lawyers and the public 8

This chapter is about the consumer of law; what he thinks of law and lawyers; how he acquires his knowledge; what contact he has with legal institutions; how his sentiments are fed into and affect the working of the legal order; whether his expectations of the legal process are legitimated or thwarted. None of these questions has been thoroughly researched. Indeed, differential access to, and perception of, law have only been noticed comparatively recently. The reason for this failure may be attributed to the entrenchment of the myth of equality before the law, and the belief that, since any form of stratification was alien to the legal process, those sections of the population which did not use legal services had no legal problems. It may also be due to apathy of the legal profession: Abel-Smith and Stevens's comment that law was 'the last citadel in a capitalist economy, where the concept of consumer sovereignty had failed to penetrate'[1] rings very true.

Lawyers and differential access

It is remarkable that no one has researched how many people in England go to solicitors and for what kinds of problems. A project is being undertaken in the Institute of Judicial Administration in Birmingham which should answer these questions. In the meanwhile we must rely on information received by quota sampling undertaken by Mass Observation Limited in 1968, and written up by Zander.[2] There is also considerable American research, to which reference will be made.

Mass Observation questioned 2,004 respondents, who were

representative of age, class and area, on whether they had had any dealings with a solicitor in the twelve months preceding the interview. Of the 19 per cent who said that they had had contact with a solicitor, it is not certain from the replies how many were speaking of their own, as opposed to a spouse's or family member's contact, 81 per cent had had no dealings.

The research demonstrated the importance of variables of age, class and geographical location. More respondents in the 25 to 44 age group consulted solicitors than younger or older respondents. Since reasons given for consulting solicitors showed a high preponderance of property problems (45 per cent), this is explained by more house-buying amongst this age group. The proportion of each social class to have seen a solicitor increases significantly with the rising level of the social class. The proportion of the AB[3] group is 2.5 as high as the DE group (30 per cent to 12 per cent): in the C1 group 26 per cent had visited a solicitor and in the C2 group 17 per cent had. The figures bear out the widely held belief that solicitors are used by a much larger proportion of the middle class than working class.

The reasons given for coming into contact with a solicitor show a preponderance of property problems: 45 per cent of the sample gave this as their reason; claims and business accounted each for 8 per cent. Apart from property the numbers involved in the other categories are too small to be statistically significant. Class was a significant variable. Property accounted for 55 per cent of the problems of AB respondent taken to solicitors but only 37 per cent of the reasons why DE respondents consulted solicitors. Business problems account for a much higher proportion of consultations in the higher social class groups (18 per cent and 10 per cent for AB and C1 groups respectively, as compared with 5 per cent and 0 per cent for the C2 and DE groups). Matrimonial difficulties seem more common among the working class (8 per cent and 9 per cent of C2 and DE groups compared with 0 per cent and 5 per cent of AB and C1 categories). This may be explained by the fact that the lower classes can identify matrimonial difficulties as a legal problem. The legal aid statistics showing that

in 1969–70 84 per cent of certificates issues were for divorce or
family cases before magistrates bear this out.[4] The survey, however, failed to elicit the relationship between consultation with
lawyers and the availability and knowledge of the legal aid
scheme.

The results of Mass Observation's survey are substantiated by
work done in the United States. American research must be
treated carefully as legal aid services are not as well-developed as
they are in this country, and because of the stratification of the
American legal profession. The latter means, for example, that
even where poorer classes obtain legal representation it may be
of a poorer quality. There are a number of American studies.

Five of these have been tabulated by Carlin and Howard.[5]
They show that the use of lawyers is considerably less prevalent
among lower than upper classes in the United States. About two-
thirds of lower-class families have *never* employed a lawyer,
compared to about one-third of upper-class families. Carlin's
study of New York City practitioners, *Lawyers' Ethics*, substan-
tiates this differential access. The earlier studies had asked laymen
whether they consulted lawyers: in Carlin's study lawyers were
the respondents. Less than 5 per cent of them reported that the
median income of their clients was under 5,000 dollars (such people
accounted for half the population), whilst 70 per cent of lawyers
reported it to be over 10,000 dollars, the income of less than 10
per cent of the population.[6]

Mayhew and Reiss[7] have shown, however, that while resources
(income, and to a lesser extent other resources such as education,
confidence, and social connections) make a difference (there is for
example, a positive association between income and legal representation among Conard's[8] sample of persons injured in motor
accidents), 'nevertheless this fails to account for the extent of use
of legal services even among those with the least resources'. Their
survey of Detroit residents showed that seven out of ten had seen
a lawyer at least once, and one in four in the last five years. But
only 39 per cent had ever sought advice on a matter other than
property. They concluded:

The association between income and legal contacts is in part an organisational effect. The legal profession is organised to service business and property interests. The social organisation of business and property is highly legalised. Out of this convergence emerges a pattern of citizen contact with attorneys that is heavily oriented to property. . . It is an interesting commentary on the legal frame of reference to note that [Reich] has argued that such interests as rights to welfare benefits . . . will only be adequately protected when lawyers come to see them as property right.

Studies, both English and American, show that legal contract is predominantly an activity of the middle and upper classes. Why do the working classes not consult solicitors?

(a) *Recognition of problem as legal*. Firstly, the potential client has to recognise the character of his problem as one susceptible to legal solution. Too often a layman will fail to appreciate that a legal remedy exists. He may, for example, overestimate the problem of evidence: common misconceptions are that contracts have to be in writing, or the need for independent witnesses. Zander's survey of 402 tenants in eight 'poor' streets in Islington showed that 43 per cent had never heard of the rent acts. Of those who had, 36 per cent said they did not know 'what they do for you'.[9] The *Report of the Committee on the Rent Acts* (1971) also draws attention to ignorance of tenants of their rights under the Rent Act.[10]

Further, too few people become aware of the legal potentialities of a problem until some disaster occurs: there is little recognition of the preventitive skills of a lawyer. This is one of the reasons for the relative success of legal aid, and the abysmal failure of legal advice.

(b) *Awareness of legal aid*. Equally disturbing is the unawareness of the availability of legal aid and advice. One survey in 1969 reported that of people who had been in road accidents only 67 per cent of those interviewed had received advice from a solicitor as to the possibility of making a claim for damages, and that 46 per cent of respondents professed no knowledge at all of the Legal Aid and Advice scheme.[11] But then, compared with other social services, no real attempt has been made to publicise the working of the scheme. Yet when posters were put up in some Post Offices for one month there was an immediate 34 per cent increase in the volume of advice given. This fell away in the following six months to reach the same level as before.

(c) *Legal competence.* Awareness of a legal problem and knowledge of legal aid services available does not mean that a potential litigant will seek a lawyer's help. He is not sought out. He must take the initiative and be willing to take action. It is here that his perception of the legal process becomes important. If he does not accept the appropriateness, efficacy and fairness of legal solutions to his problems he may not contact a lawyer. It is a problem of what Carlin, Howard and Messinger call legal competence: 'the ability to further and protect one's interests through active assertion of legal rights . . . the competent subject will take initiative . . . will see law as a resource for developing, furthering and protecting his interests.'[12] But a combination of helplessness, apathy and fatalism, together with previous experience of legal encounters, reduce the chances of many working class citizens seeking advice from a solicitor. He may instead seek advice elsewhere. Or he may resort to self-help or violence. One of the most important areas of research is into the socialisation process that leads to a consciousness of right, and a channelling of claims into legitimate avenues of redress.[13]

The law for many is a hostile maze. The poor are accustomed to being on its receiving end, the target for threatening letters from creditors or landlords, the whipping-boys of social security administrators. It is not easy with this background or experience to appreciate that the legal system can also operate to secure rights. Further, his claim may well be against his employer, landlord, welfare department or supplier with all of whom he will have ongoing relationships and all of whom are in positions of power vis-à-vis himself. His reluctance to challenge these people is understandable. Research is lacking in England, but Carlin has shown that the more often people had come into contact with courts the less likely they were to take action to recover damages for injuries sustained in car accidents.[14] This was markedly so with low socio-economic groups (42 per cent who had been in court two or more times, compared with 15 per cent of high status groups, took no action to recover for their injuries).

The problem is well illustrated by the failure of people who have made initial contact with advisory agencies, such as citizens' advice bureaux or poor man's lawyer centres, to follow up references to solicitors. The Cobden Trust has recently investigated what happened to applicants who were referred by two citizens' advice bureaux and by the Mary Ward Centre's legal advisers to outside solicitors. In spite of the introduction and the knowledge that the client had that the solicitor was willing to tackle legal aid cases (knowledge which was occasionally frustrated), up to 25 per cent of the cases failed to contact solicitors to whom they had been referred.[15]

(d) *Access to a lawyer*. The individual who recognises a legal problem and wishes to take legal advice must nevertheless have access to a lawyer. Lower-class individuals are less likely to have this access. They are unlikely to be acquainted with a lawyer because of their different social milieu. Citizens' advice bureaux have lists of solicitors but even with such an introduction there are social and psychological barriers cutting the working-class individual off from the solicitor's office. The legal profession projects to many a deterrent image. There is the fear of looking foolish in the surroundings of a professional man's office; there is a wide chasm in symbols of communication, dress, language and behaviour. The clinical austerity of the average solicitor's office gives no indication of its intention to serve the ordinary man's needs. But all this supposes that he will be able to find a solicitor's office at all.

Solicitor's offices are clustered in the commercial hub of cities and towns and in middle-class suburbs. In 1968 69 per cent of London solicitors were located in six of the 118 postal districts, thirteen postal districts had no firm of solicitors, eighteen had one, including Poplar with a population of 68,000, and nineteen had two, including Bethnal Green which had a population of 46,000.[16] Young and Wilmott's study of family life in East London[17] shows that the mobility of these working-class communities can be overestimated. The prospect of venturing into unfamiliar territory to locate a solicitor must be daunting to many working-class individuals.

He will also be lucky if he finds one open in the evening or at weekends. If he does not he will have to take time off work. Many will feel uncomfortable about having to ask for time off to see a solicitor or go to court. He will also have to weigh up loss of wages against the possible advantage of a solicitor's advice. With so many barriers he may well take the line of least resistance and do without a solicitor's consultation.

(e) *The services provided.* The lower socio-economic groups do not usually have a family solicitor. Their contact with a solicitor is likely to be of an isolated rather than a recurring character. Much legal work is more time-consuming than feeproductive. Nonetheless, a solicitor will be reluctant to turn away a regular client. He may feel no such compunction with a casual caller. Of the sample of solicitors interviewed by the Consumer Council some said that they would advise in a consumer case only if the person concerned were an established client.[18] A solicitor may cloak his unwillingness to act by pronouncing that the claim of the prospective client is unfounded in law. But, as Carlin and Howard point out, 'lawyers who reject clients on this basis may be unwilling (given the small fee) to put in the time and effort to find a legal solution'.[19]

This tendency is accentuated by the way a lawyer's skills are developed. By education, training and practice his energies are channelled into solving problems of higher income groups. Very often he lacks the knowledge to perform the services that lower socio-economic groups require. Thus, because consumer and welfare problems do not generally receive legal advice, most solicitors do not develop any expertise in handling them. Nor is a solicitor usually sufficiently conversant with the day-to-day problems of the underprivileged to coordinate legal advice and welfare succour. Further, subsidised legal assistance has to date emphasised litigation: it has engineered divorces and personal injuries claims of the less well-off with relative success. But the prudent citizen with resources to employ a solicitor privately uses him also for advice, preventative channelling, reorientation of expectations and negotiation, and in all these areas the state scheme has woefully failed.

Hopefully, the passing of the Legal Advice and Assistance Act 1972 will correct this emphasis. This Act introduces a '£25 scheme', first proposed by the Law Society in 1968, whereby solicitors can give £25 worth of advice and assistance without first obtaining a legal aid certificate. Of course, £25 buys less of a solicitor's time in 1972 than it did in 1968, and the scheme will wane in importance with the passage of time, unless the limit is kept flexible. The Act also provides for the establishment of special centres, staffed by solicitors employed by the Law Society to do work under the legal aid scheme in poorer areas. But these will not be established until the effects of the £25 scheme are seen. The success of the improved advice and assistance scheme depends on its becoming widely known.

Another problem is that solicitors cannot advertise. They have no means of publicising the services they provide. Of course, a solicitor who wishes to secure a business clientèle will join the local rotary or golf club or Conservative Association. But what organisation is open to the solicitor who wishes to make known his desire to serve the underprivileged or small consumer, or who wishes to specialise in other problems common to prospective '£25 scheme' clients? He can make himself known to local citizens' advice bureaux and he can rely upon personal recommendation, but that is all.

(*f*) *Cost*. A final barrier to the seeking of legal advice is an economic one. Even those people who know about the state scheme will not necessarily know whether they come within it or what the terms of the service are. Further, ignorance of legal costs is widespread. This breeds suspicion and usually exaggerated estimates of a lawyers' fees. But so long as the public are not told what lawyers charge, one can expect them to fear the worst.

The present legal aid and advice scheme helps in theory about a third of the population (the proportion may increase slightly with the 1972 Act). But it would be fantasy to pretend that the remaining two-thirds have the financial resources to assert legal competence. Too few are helped by the state scheme. For the purposes of litigation, it extends to those whose 'disposable' income, as assessed by the Supplementary Benefits Commission after making deductions for rent, loan interest, taxes, maintenance of dependants etc., does not exceed £700 a year, and whose 'disposable' capital does not exceed £500. To qualify for *free* legal aid a person's 'disposable' income must not exceed £250 a year, nor his 'disposable' capital £125. In between upper and lower limits an applicant is called upon to contribute up to one third of the amount by which his 'disposable' income exceeds £250 or his capital £125.

For advice not (or not yet) involving litigation the limits have been more stringent. But the 1972 Act provides that a person is eligible for advice and assistance if his 'disposable' income does not exceed £20 a week or his 'disposable' capital £125. The state scheme is thus hideously complex and productive of occasional but glaring injustice.

A legally aided litigant not only has the advantage of state assistance but, unlike unsubsidised litigants, he is always made aware in advance of what the action is expected to cost. Further, there is a limit to the amount he will have to pay towards his opponent's costs if he loses the case. Nor is he expected to provide his contribution in a lump sum: it can be spread over twelve monthly instalments, and he can be exempted from paying any or all of these should his income fall owing to unemployment or sickness or other such circumstances. With these advantages the rigid limits set by the state scheme are all the more anomalous and intolerable. The consequence is that the real sufferers are not the very poorest, provided they recognise the problem and take the initiative, but those with sufficient resources to put themselves outside the state scheme, but not wealthy enough to chance the vagaries of litigation; and they are a very large slice of the population.

Two other consequences of the costs system must be noted. Firstly, the cost of litigation has increased the predictability of consequences that will flow from the acts of private parties. The price device had led to, what Friedman calls, 'reciprocal immunities'. These 'help define and stabilize many common, continuing relationships. For example, the formal legal relationships of a landlord and his tenant are spelled out in their lease. Minor infractions of duty on either side may amount to breaches of the lease, but *both* parties are protected. . . by the costliness, in money and disruption, of claiming one's 'rights'.' But, as he points out, the fairness of this is more apparent than real where the relationship is onesided in power or authority, as the landlord-tenant relationship often is. 'The call for subsidy of tenant's rights is a call for means to break through the wall of immunities.'[20] The criminal law is thus invoked to protect the poor tenant from harassment and eviction.

Secondly, costs operate as a conservative force, limiting access to courts of recognised causes of action. Legal aid may be refused in cases where there is some justification for the application, but only a limited chance of success. The criterion applied is what a 'reasonably prudent man of moderate means' would do. But other options open to men of moderate means are often closed to poorer sections of the population because they lack those moderate means. Thus a man of moderate means might repair his accommodation himself, given the problems of suing his landlord, but a poorer person might lack the means to do this. 'The English legal system operates on the principle that the test of the amount of care and expense that should be lavished on a dispute is the size of the claim involved, in absolute, rather than (which would be socially correct) in relative terms.'[21] Test cases are thus rarely financed by the state. The success of the scheme is quantified in terms of percentages of successful actions (the success rate is consistently high—it was 79 per cent with 7 per cent settled in 1969–70), rather than in terms of novel claims legitimated. It is thus left to pressure groups, tenants' or consumers' associations or groups such as the Child Poverty Action Group, (CPAG), to finance the determination of what, in absolute terms, are trivial claims despite their qualitative importance for large numbers. The question, which affects some 400,000 people, whether it is wrong in law for the Supplementary Benefits Commission to reduce automatically long-term additions when discretionary allowances are granted has been taken to the High Court by the CPAG.[22] The particular case is about 15p a week: a reasonably prudent man of moderate means would cut his losses and pursue the claim no further, so legal aid is not forthcoming. But it is important that claims like this should be litigated: until they are social welfare benefits remain discretionary bounty, not rights of citizenship.

(g) *The Alternatives*. There are thus social, psychological and economic barriers to the seeking of legal advice from a lawyer. The individual nevertheless has several other sources of advice and assistance to which he can turn. There are the types of organisation described in the previous paragraph. The CPAG has a Citizen's Rights office which advices on homelessness.[23] There are trade unions, if the individual belongs to one, but many of the most inarticulate do not. They will usually only advise on matters related to employment, personal injuries, redundancy payments, wrongful dismissal and the like. Some unions pass the matter straight to solicitors, but some of the bigger unions do the legal work themselves, though they do not employ qualified lawyers.

Another source of advice and help are the 500 or so citizens' advice bureaux. The staff are mainly voluntary and not legally qualified, though most have an honorary legal adviser, some of whom hold evening legal advice sessions. In some bureaux private solicitors do work of this kind without charge. They also make referrals to local solicitors. Some local law societies have started liaison schemes with Citizens' advice bureaux. For example the Holborn Law Society has appointed a liaison officer who allocates cases to willing solicitor members of that society. Prospective clients have an initial interview with the CAB, which prepares a note for the liaison officer. Such schemes are of immense value. As *Justice For All* puts it: 'They can solve what may be the greatest difficulty of all—of effecting a personal introduction of the ignorant and bewildered to a solicitor who has experience of handling their particular problem, who practises in the appropriate court, to whom they can talk, and who talks to them, congenially, and with understanding.'[24] The introduction of Part II of the Legal Advice and Assistance Act 1972 will extend and enlarge on the scope of the liaison service.

Poor man's lawyer centres were set up before the legal aid and advice scheme. It was assumed that they would atrophy with the development of the latter but this has not happened; in itself that is implicit criticism of the workings of the legal aid system. The centres are located in community halls in poor areas, staffed by lawyers doing charity work one evening a week, and generally give limited advice to the very poor. Their continuing success may be attributed to the unmet need they provide, their location, opening hours and casual surgery style. They provide a service 'more attuned to the ways and expectations of their clients than a private solicitor can normally provide'.[44] In *Justice For All* it is estimated that London's three main settlements, Mary Ward, Toynbee Hall and Cambridge House give 'at least as much free legal advice to the poor as all London solicitors in private practice together give under the 1949 Act'.[25] It remains to be seen what impact the 1972 Act will have.

If he lives in North Kensington, or new in a number of other localities, he may also turn to his local legal centre. This was set up in 1970 on the model of the American neighbourhood law firm.[26] It is a charitable foundation and, under the terms of its trust, may dispose advice only to local residents. It is staffed by a solicitor, an articled clerk, secretarial assistance and a good deal of voluntary help. It runs on a shoestring. The West London Law Society provides a rota of solicitors, at least one of whom is available at the centre every weekday evening. The centre works in co-operation with community organisations such as the Notting Hill Social Council, Notting Hill Community Workshop, the Family Service Unit and others. This, a move towards seeing the totality of an individual's problem, is in line with Seebohm's proposals on local authority services,[27] now implemented in the Local Authority Social Services Act 1970, and is to be welcomed.

The centre is a strong contrast to the imposing offices of many solicitors. It is situated in an old butcher's shop in the middle of a bustling shopping centre. Its hours are flexible: its clients get a friendly reception. People can drop in casually without the need for an appointment. The majority of problems[28] brought to it to date concern housing: rent tribunal cases (there is no legal aid for tribunals), notices to quit, evictions, disputes between landlords and tenants; but minor criminal cases, consumer disputes, juvenile court cases and matrimonial difficulties feature prominently in the files of the centre.

The Law Society's initial opposition on the grounds that it would take work away from solicitors was soon retracted when American experience was repeated and it was found that the centre generated business for solicitors in private practice. As Peter Kandler, the centre's solicitor, put it: 'I have obtained three injunctions for tenants against landlords. Because the tenants came to me, their landlords had to get solicitors to defend the cases.'[29] The Law Society's own plan, now implemented in the 1972 Act, but not yet in operation, is based on a similar idea.

The blueprint for the North Kensington centre is the Society of Labour Lawyers' report, *Justice For All*. This advocates a widespread extension of the local legal centre after initial experimentation. The report envisages a new public service financed by the State, which would directly employ the lawyer running the centres. Such centres would not bounder the control of the Law

Society, as the centres to be set up under the 1972 Act will be, but under a Management Committee, an *ad hoc* body consisting of representatives of the centre, Bar Council, Law Society, citizens' advice bureaux and other local organisations. The need for independence from government control is stressed: for many cases undertaken by the centres will be directed against government agencies.

The centres would be set up in underprivileged areas. They would advertise, concern themselves with the education of the public about legal services in general and maintain contact with social groups in the locality. A principal advantage of such a centre would be the acquisition of specialised knowledge of legal problems of lower income groups. The Labour Lawyers hypothesise that

> their experience and expertise would provide a counter weight to the profession's over-emphasis on the problems of the middle classes. . . . No one can predict what the consequences for English law would be of a real concentration of legal talent and resources upon the hitherto under-represented interests of the tenant, the consumer, and the citizen, in his relationship with the public bureaucracy. But the effect would undoubtedly be beneficial.[30]

It is difficult to dissent from this view.

Among other benefits of local legal centres the following may be mentioned. They are likely to increase local consciousness of the role of lawyers and in doing so destroy or at least counter the fear and hostility in which the profession is held. If American experience is repeated they will attract law graduates of the highest calibre, and many who would not have gone into private practice because they find it socially remote. In time this may have an impact on private practice, as those with experience of local legal centres move into it. Smigel, in his *Wall Street Lawyer*, has shown how neighbourhood law standards have penetrated the elite of New York firms.[31] Finally, the centres will take off the hands of private practitioners work which is more time-consuming than profit-productive. A local legal centre will gain from processing in bulk where the private practitioner dealt only with the isolated incident—if he dealt with it at all.[32]

County courts and small claims

One conspicuous failure of lawyers and legal institutions to penetrate working class consciousness is its mismanagement of consumer's small claims.

In medieval England a multidimensional system of justice operated. The medieval common law, operating in royal institution, consisted of rules made by the upper classes for themselves. The lower classes had a system of informal local courts which applied a different set of rules. Indeed, royal courts were even known to refuse remedies because the action pertained to some other jurisdiction.

The last hundred years have seen something like a return to such a system. Thus a network of administrative tribunals has grown up to regulate in informal manner social welfare benefits. Increasing civil jurisdiction has been bestowed upon magistrates' courts to enable them to dispense speedy justice to fatherless families. More working-class marriages end[33] in the magistrates' court than in the divorce courts. Similarly, the business community, exasperated by the delay and formality of High Court litigation, instituted its own private legal system in the form of adjudication by arbitrators.

The county courts are part of this same trend. Localised and operating within a narrower jurisdiction, they were set up to serve a different segment of society from that which frequented the High Court. Yet the major demand for them came from the middle classes who required machinery to enforce their business debts.[34] They have now been in operation for over a century and a quarter, and the demand for them still comes from the same source. During this time their jurisdiction has increased many times over and they can now, for example, hear contract and tort actions where the amount in dispute is up to £750, and more if the parties agree. But the evidence is that small claims by the lower socio-economic groups have been edged out by the costs system. Not that small claims are not heard by county courts: 73.6 per cent of claims are for under £30 and 85 per cent for under £100.[35] But the majority of these are debt claims by credit grantors. A random sample of 2 per cent of summonses recorded for six county courts undertaken in 1967 by the Consumer Council showed that 89.2 per cent of these summonses were taken out by a firm or a utility board, and only 9 per cent by individuals. The sample also shows a remarkable preponderance of mail order houses among the trader plaintiffs.[36] This might be thought to demonstrate that individuals have few grievances, but that this is not so is substantiated by evidence that 5,000 individuals a year contacted the defunct Consumer's Council, citizens' advice bureaux handle over 120,000 consumer cases a year, and local authority consumer advisory services receive large numbers of complaints.

Few of these people get to court: many do not even defend or counterclaim actions brought by retailers and other firms. The individual suffers a number of disadvantages, social, psychological and economic. It may be his only experience of litigation, whereas for the seller it is normal business routine. It is uneconomic to litigate a single small claim, but the seller may process them in hundreds. An example is furnished by the Law Society's estimate that the costs of bringing an action in the county court to recover £100 damages for a faulty house heating system, assuming a one-day hearing and an expert witness on each side would be £250 if the plaintiff lost, and £15, plus other expenses and possible loss of wages, if he won.[37] Legal aid is not usually granted for small claims unless there are exceptional circumstances.

Two solutions have recently been suggested. The Consumer Council, in *Justice Out of Reach*, advocated the setting up of a small claims court with jurisdiction for claims up to £100 in contract and tort. It would be run as an adjunct to the existing country court structure by the county court registrar. The hearing would take place in his office, not in court. It would be informal with no rules of procedure or evidence and no legal representation would be allowed. The cost to the parties would be limited to a small filing fee. The Registrar's job would be to find out as many relevant facts as possible and 'to apply his own judgment to assessing the parties' stories'. If possible he would try to effect an amicable settlement. American experience points to such courts becoming an agency for debt collection. To obviate that problem the Consumer Council envisages that companies, partnerships, associations and assignees of debts would not be allowed to sue.[38]

Ison's blueprint is more radical. He doubts the public policy of utilising court machinery for the enforcement, often, as he points out, regardless of legitimacy, of retail debt claims, and advocates their abolition. He recognises a residual category of small claims that must remain: these include disputes over a seller's right to repossession and claims by a cash buyer for fraud or defective goods. For these he urges a new procedure. Adjustments to the county court system, as recommended by the Consumer Council, are rejected as grossly inadequate. 'If justice is ever to be done in small claims', he argues, 'the approach must be far more iconoclastic. . . almost every principle that a common lawyer has cherished must be abandoned. The adversary system, the rules of evidence, the dignity of the courtroom, the concept of the trial: all must go.' He envisages the *modus operandi* of the judge as approximating more closely to a police detective or weights and measures inspector than a High Court judge. To insulate the system completely from adversary influence, no representation would be allowed, and judges would be selected from non-practising lawyers and social workers. He sees the judge as mobile, the court as the initiative-taker. Litigants would, for example, be helped to formulate their claim and frame defences. As Ison says, implicit in this model is 'a recognition that different categories of litigants have different capacities to function within the legal system'.[39] But the English lawyer's inveterate belief in the equality of the legal process does not permit him to appreciate this.

Ison's proposals can have little chance when the milder case of the Consumer Council, despite the support of *Justice*, the all-party group of lawyers, is rejected out of hand by the government. Its principal objection is the absence of legal representation. Not surprisingly, a Small Claims Courts Bill, introduced in February 1971, made no progress.

In the meanwhile an interesting experiment is being conducted in Manchester by the local Law Society in conjunction with the city's citizens' advice bureaux[40]. Under this claims under £150 may be settled by the institution of arbitration if both parties agree to accept the findings of an arbitrator appointed by the president of the local law society. The maximum fee is £5, though a technical expert may cost another £6.50. Unlike the two schemes outlined above there is no element of compulsion, and it remains to be seen whether large firms will accept its jurisdiction. It, together with both other proposals, deserves support, for only through inventiveness, experimentation and research are our legal institutions going to be aligned with community needs.

Public sentiment and judicial process

The task of ascertaining the ideals prevailing in a society is a difficult undertaking for a judge. Yet if his judgments are unrelated to a community sentiment he runs the risk of making the judiciary seem irrelevant in society's eyes. He has to decide scores of questions such as whether a litigant has acted as 'a reasonable man' or is of 'good moral character', yet is deprived of institutional machinery to gauge the community ethic. Even if he were able to carry out a Gallup Poll, it is doubtful whether its conclusions would help him. He does, however, get indications of social needs and attitudes from a number of sources, two of which, the jury and custom and morality, have been touched upon earlier and are discussed in more detail in this section. Of course, much of a judge's work, an increasing part of it, is taken up with statutory construction, and the legislator has more sophisticated techniques at his disposal to measure interests and ideals prevailing in society. Judges in England, however, are not allowed to consult *travaux préparatoires*, the very documentary evidence which would give insight in the policies underlying the legislation.

It must be stressed, firstly, that courts do not act on their own initiative. They depend on the action of the public in bringing conflict to their attention for judicial resolution. Nor would the system retain viability if every dispute required adjudication. Limitation of resources necessitates rationing, which is reinforced by the costs system and public opinion. People go to courts for justice. If they do not get this feedback, they will no longer go. Similarly, if taking suits to court did not meet with general community approval, the initiator of such action might earn public opprobrium.[41] This process is paralleled for lawyers. They also do not act on their own initiative: the profession would break down if every trouble were taken to them. People go for help, solace and a pill of common sense sugar-coated with a lawyer's rationality. Again, if they did not get this they would not go. Nor would they use lawyers if public opinion denigrated the taking of legal advice. Macaulay's study of Wisconsin manufacturers bears this out.[42]

Countervailing power—the jury

The importance of the jury is as a principal countervailing force built into the criminal legal process. It acts as both safety value and symbol. Juries may refuse to convict where they disapprove of a rule of law or the punishment for its infraction (a good example was reluctance to convict mothers who had killed babies whilst suffering the effects of childbirth, until the crime of infanticide was introduced in 1929); or mistrust police evidence;[43] or perceive a difference in ability between counsel;[44] or where the defendant has some personal characteristic which attracts sympathy.[45]

As well as keeping lawyers in check, the power to create law is delegated to them in limited circumstances. It appears, for example, that in an offence such as conspiracy to corrupt public morals, the jury must decide whether certain conduct amounts to such a conspiracy. This means, as Lord Reid pointed out, that it is impossible to tell 'what is criminal except by guessing what view a jury will take, and juries' views may vary and may change with the passing of time'.[46] The jury thus acts as a popular institution curbing the bureaucracy of the law. But that shrewd political observer, Alexis de Tocqueville, saw it in another light: as a medium through which the judiciary could teach legal ideals. In his *Democracy in America* he noted that: the jury may be regarded as a gratuitous public school, ever open, in which every juror learns his rights, enters into daily communication with the most learned and enlightened members of the upper classes, and becomes practically acquainted with the laws'.[47]

These two views of the jury are not incompatible. De Tocqueville's student need not be a passive recipient of knowledge, nor need communication be a oneway process. But the jury acts as a brake on judicial power in an imperceptible way. The fact that laymen are there (the effect of the public gallery also cannot be ignored) is more significant than the occasional act of jury 'justice', just as the presence of the police is socially more important than the limited number of arrests they can effect. Both are important symbols of power.

Law, Morality and Custom

Morality and custom are two primary inputs of community sentiment fed into the judicial process. The method of their impact makes valuable comparison.

The problem which confronts the judge, having found the facts, is a twofold one: he must extract from the precedents the *ratio decidendi*, the underlying principle, and must determine the line along which the principle is to develop.

English judges have for long favoured the analogical direction; emphasising consistency with logic above all else. But there are increasing signs of a shift in direction towards social welfare, the mores of the day, public policy. Current trends in the law of negligence are indicative of this new emphasis on societal conceptions of public policy, though it must be admitted that such an emphasis is more apparant in this area of law than many others.

Thus, in deciding that the Home Office ought to pay for damage done by escaping borstal boys[48] or in holding that a local authority owed a duty of care to ensure that the inspection of the foundations of a house was properly carried out,[49] judges were deciding questions of policy. They were taking constructive polls and articulating in lawyer-like fashion considerations which would weigh with an intelligent layman in deciding whether liability should exist or not. Such articulation cannot be value-free, but these decisions do show an attempt to align the law with the expectations of society.

Public opinion is thus a catalyst of judicial law-making. It acts more directly, of course, within legislative process. The status of custom is less certain. For a start it operates on a number of different levels and each must be distinguished. Secondly, whether it can be said to impel law in a similar way or is law *ex proprio vigore* is a long-standing jurisprudential conundrum. There are three types of custom. There is *local* custom. The courts originally accepted this subject to certain conditions of antiquity, continuity, precision, and consistency with other customs in the same area. They continue to accept it provided it does not infringe a fundamental principle of common law or statute and provided it is reasonable by contemporary standards. The courts thus exercise a wide discretion to exclude local custom. *Mercantile* usage is of greater significance, for, although the last occasion on which a mercantile custom was accepted by the courts was in 1898 (when debentures payable to bearer were held to be negotiable instruments by such custom), there are more means whereby the commercial community get its practices accepted by the legal process. The medium of standard-form contracts was discussed in chapter 1. It is also recognised that the courts will imply terms in a contract from trade usage or even by showing that it is reasonably necessary to the commercial efficacy of the contract to assume that it was entered into on the basis of some established usage of the trade. There is thirdly a residual category of *general* custom. To quote Bovill CJ, 'what has been commonly received and acquiesced in as the law raises a strong presumption of what the law is, and at least throws upon those who question it the burden of proving that it is not what it has been so understood to be'.[50] As discussed earlier the *Volksgeist* is strongest in expressive relationships, such as the family, and not surprisingly many social customs accepted as living law are in this area: for example, that a wife takes her husband's name.

Thus habit of a locality, a group, or the generality, coupled with growth of a sense of obligation that it constitutes a model of behaviour, is a law-making force. There are those who hold that it is not law until clothed with legislative or judicial sanction. But, although legislature and judiciary have wide powers to reject custom, it would be sociologically unreal to pretend that what is felt and acted upon as law was not so until approved by a law-making agency. Nor must it be forgotten that community sentiment can reject or exile into oblivion laws made by a properly-constituted authority.

PUBLIC EXPECTATIONS AND LEGAL OUTPUT

Earlier sections of this chapter have described differential access to lawyers, and the way that public sentiment is fed into the judicial process. This section shows how legal output fails to legitimate public expectations of that process. This, together with the costs system and lack of access to lawyers of all but a small section of the population, plus the fact that business interests prefer commercial arbitration to litigation, eases pressures on court time. The whole legal structure would collapse if every grievance were litigated. But this does not mean that the factors to be considered can be justified as legitimate rationing processes. Nor must they necessarily be rejected in deference to consumer sovereignty. Each must be considered on its merits.

Litigation neurosis

The English are not a litigious people. We manage with a smaller judiciary proportionate to population than almost any other European country.[51] In other cultures litigation is resorted to more frequently. Amongst the Lozi of Barotseland, to take an example from another culture, there is no fear or anxiety at all about litigating.[52] Part of the English reluctance may stem from a feeling that litigation is an invasion of privacy. The washing of dirty linen in public is an unpleasant experience, particularly when the laundry characterises those who need its services as unreasonable people, incapable of managing their own affairs. This attitude which courts exude increases tension and anxiety and makes litigation disagreeable for all except a pathological minority who obtains some outlet from its process. Litigious paranoiacs are a rare breed, and are usually restrained. For most litigation is a thoroughly disturbing experience, shaking normal routine of lives of families for months, even years.

On the other hand litigation may alleviate distress. A day in court, a sublimated court room fight, acts to relieve tension that might otherwise be channelled into violence. Goitein, in his *Primitive Ordeal and the Modern Law*,[53] one of the few investigations of the psychology of litigation, suggests that the ceremonial of adversary contest, with its vestiges of the ancient ordeal, has immense emotional value for litigants. One may add that the ceremonial rites surrounding a trial for murder or rape satisfies the public craving for vengeance in a way that a less formal investigation might not.

Litigation is also a pleasant form of appeasement. Individuals experience distress after injuring others and can reduce this distress by compensation. But Macaulay and Walster's study of the legal process of assessment of fault and adjustment shows that many features of the trial process aggravate tensions and distress, rather than restoring equity. They cite the problems concerning determination of fault; a law of contributory negligence that encourages the harm-doer to derogate his victim, the delay in judgment increasing the harm-doer's motivation to put his actions in a better light; and cost which predisposes parties to bargain. They note 'the difference between society's strong support for a goal and it's minimal support for the means of achieving it'.[54]

Procedure and setting

To a layman court surroundings are strange and its procedure baffling. The court building is often austere and formidable, and few look as if they are there to serve the ordinary man. Even in the new court houses, the architectural tone is often one of austere grandeur rather than a design for a functional and attractive service industry. The ordinary man does not feel at ease. He is venturing into a strange world for probably his only experience of litigation.

Legal procedure is similarly alien. If he loses, the legal procedures which structure a trial may not even allow him to understand why this has happened to him. Legal judgments are not pitched at the level of the litigant. For him, if he can rationalise it at all, all legal procedure achieves is a longer trial, greater need for lawyers, greater cost and more of an element of chance in the whole process. He does not come for a charade, but for justice, and cannot understand why so many formal barriers need to be surmounted on the way to achieving it.

No research is forthcoming on differential perception of different reference groups. But, clearly, the trial procedure with its structure of fair play will appeal to the better educated and those whose occupational milieu accustoms them to formalised modes of conducting business.

Language

The layman would be forgiven for thinking that the 'esoteric technical patois'[55] used by lawyers was merely a means of protecting their monopoly. Even if the laymen did know the meaning of the bastard French and Latin terms used by lawyers, he would find it difficult to pronounce it properly. Law Latin was in fact abolished in 1730, but two years later an Act was passed to permit proceedings to continue 'in the same language as hath commonly been used'. This language continues to be used by lawyers for lawyers, and gives the layman the impression that he is really an interloper on the proceedings.

Legal judgments suffer from the same deficiency. As Bredemeier points out the written opinion could help the losing litigant to adjust to his loss, but it 'does not in fact function towards that end, and it is not intended to do so'.[56] It is really an explanation addressed to other lawyers, using a logic of persuasion comprehensible to them, but to no one else. It is up to the legal advisers to translate it (in an appellate court there may be three, five or more opinions, emphasising different factors of the case, and some may even be on the side of the losing litigant) for clients so that they understand and accept its legitimacy. Aubert's criticism of the language of statutes, referred to in chapter 4 is relevant.

'Stare decisis'

The gap between a litigant's conception of justice and a judge's is sharpest in their respective concepts of justice. Justice for the litigant is individualised for the court it is the treatment of this litigant like all others. The mechanism used by judges to ensure this is *stare decisis*.

The workings of this were explained in chapter 6 on the judiciary. In this context its importance is as a method whereby expectations built up on the basis of previous decisions are not frustrated. It is assumed that contracts, wills, fiscal arrangements and the like are drawn up in reliance on past precedents. The value of this is undoubted, though a system of prospective overruling whereby existing arrangements would not be disturbed, but the law changed for the future, would obviate this problem. Commitment to precedent interferes with the need felt by the public for a flexibility sufficient to adapt to changed circumstances and new claims. A litigant may fail because a similar claim failed fifty or a hundred years ago. The dangers that this will happen are less then they were, for the judges are taking a more flexible attitude towards precedent and a keener awareness of the prospects of law-making. Further, the setting up of the Law Commission in 1965 has enabled more of the grosser injustices to be weeded out by legislation than happened in earlier generations.

Legalism

Legalism may be defined as rule-following to the oblivion of social consequences. As such rigid doctrine of *stare decisis* is an apt example. Another instance which may frustrate public expectations of legal output is the rule, mitigated in one of two areas of law such as negligence, that in any dispute right is on one side. There can only be one winner. To some extent this is mitigated by the costs system (the court has discretion not to award the winner costs, though it rarely exercises it), and also by awards, in defamation, for example, of derisory sums of damages. But in essence the rule remains rigid. If you do not quite prove fault you get nothing, if you prove it you may get astronomical damages. The law sees opposite poles of a spectrum but ignores the shades in between.

The adversary system

The judicial process is not a healing process. It is a method of deciding a winner. The winner is he who presents the most convincing case. There is no attempt to understand his or the loser's psychology, to help the loser adapt to his loss, to understand why he acted as he did.

> Once rights and obligations have been authoritatively stated [Bredemeier states] individuals have only one mode of adaptation available to them: acceptance: the assumption . . . is that *learning* is the only response to a deprivation. . . . [But] the legal system does not include the machinery for insuring the amount of permissiveness, support, denial of reciprocity, and conditional reward required to make the court experience a learning exercise.[57]

He examples the baffling procedure and language and technique of legal judgment, both discussed above.

Evidence

Litigants find the traditional common law method of eliciting truth, by examination-in-chief, cross-examination and re-examination alien. They cannot understand why they cannot 'tell their stories' as they might recount their version of what has happened to a friend. Certain of the exclusionary rules are outside the comprehension of many people. Thus assertions of persons other than the witness who is testifying are inadmissible as evidence of the truth of that which is being asserted (the rule against hearsay). But the natural thing for many people is to tell what they have been told by others. A litigant may also find it difficult to understand why counsel does not ask the obvious questions: the reason, which may be unintelligible to many litigants, is that leading questions are regarded as objectionable by lawyers. The institutionalised expectations of lawyers and laymen are different, and it must be difficult for a losing litigants to adjust to this failure when he feels facts that may have helped them were not elicited by the trial process.

Delay

The law's delays are notorious. They affect the litigant in a number of ways. They produce hardship as evidence is likely to deteriorate over a passage of time. There will be loss of witnesses, memories will blur, litigants may die. The knowledge of this may force the parties into unjust settlements. This in turn tends to nurture a sense of injustice, of denial, and breeds cynical disdain for the law's processes.

What causes delay? Rosenberg distinguishes court system delay from lawyer-caused delay.[58] He is writing of the United States where lawyers bear most of the responsibility for legal delay. In this country delay is inherent in the system. A principal factor is the absence of fixed dates for the hearing of trials. Attempts made to correct this deficiency have regularly failed.[59] So litigants remain uncertain until the last moment as to when they will get their day in court. It must impress the layman, who sits in the gothic corridors of the Courts of Justice, that the courts care little for his convenience.

Delay is also caused by lawyers who use it as a threat, a bargaining counter. The longer one can prevent trial by dilatoriness, the greater the chances are of persuading the other side to settle for less than the court might award. Much litigation is personal injuries claims and the plaintiff may not be in a physical or emotional state to resist a lesser sum immediately rather than the prospect of a larger award some years hence. Rosenberg and Sovern noted that cases with large economic stakes were more likely to persist to trial than cases of small size.[60]

Litigants delayed by lawyer's bargaining and court structural devices may be forgiven for thinking that the legal process is not a functional service industry designed with them, the ultimate consumer, in mind. The procedure, the language, the legalism, the techniques employed by courts for eliciting the truth or achieving what they regard as justice reinforce this image. It is doubtful whether the average litigant's expectations of the trial process is legitimated by his experiences of it.

Perception of lawyers and courts

What does the public think of lawyers and courts? We do not know, for until recently no one bothered to find out. Not that it was thought to matter, for legal services have always been provided on a 'we know best' take it or leave it basis. The opinion of the consumer, or more important, the potential consumer, was not considered. But since both lawyers and the institutions they worked in largely served a clientèle from a similar milieu to the lawyers themselves, the level of complaint was mooted. The business community had long ago lost the patience with the law's delays, cumbersome procedure and lack of expertise in commerce and had opted for arbitration, where lawyers who were prepared to attune themselves to consumer's needs were to be found. The needs of the underprivileged remained largely unmet and unsolicited. One result was that no research was carried out to determine what the consumer or potential consumer thought of lawyers and the services provided. Recently, however, there have been two studies. Neither does more than scratch the surface, but each in its own way gives valuable insights into a perspective hitherto neglected.

Separated Spouses, an investigation by McGregor, Blom-Cooper and Gibson into the matrimonial jurisdiction of magistrates' courts, was the first study of any court in this country which attempted to discover what the users thought of it. They noted that 'convenience and feelings of litigants have hardly ever been considered in the administration of his branch of summary justice'. However, the authors rightly regarded reactions of consumers as a vital element in the social results of the exercise of this jurisdiction. To test these the authors obtained a sample of attitudes by inviting readers of the *News of the World* who had had experience of magistrates' matrimonial jurisdiction to answer a questionnaire, and subsequently by interviewing a proportion of the respondents. Such a survey must necessarily be imperfect, but it gives some clues as to how largely working class people perceived the only legal institution with which most of them would ever have contact.

The results are not edifying: 55 per cent of respondents found court officials unhelpful. 90 per cent of the husbands involved and 66 per cent of the women who obtained maintenance orders from the court thought the hearing was unfair. 75 per cent of the husbands and wives thought that the court had failed to get at the truth. When asked what they had most disliked about the magistrates' court (an admittedly loaded question), 41 per cent referred to the attitude of magistrates and 26 per cent to the fact that they were made to feel like criminals. 18% instanced the 'lack of care by the court', 10 per cent (all wives) slowness in taking action when money was not paid, and 11 per cent the attitude of court officials. Others cited the attitude of their own solicitors or counsel, the lack of privacy in the court and the procedure for collecting or paying money.[61] None of this shows that any of these putative defects in the system actually exists, but it does show that magistrates' courts do not obtain the confidence of the majority of the matrimonial consumers.

A second survey, undertaken by Zander, concerns attitudes felt by convicted criminals to their legal advisers. Whilst no one would regard their perception as a definitive statement of the quality of legal services their perspective is a proper one. Zander surveyed whether legal advice was received by convicted prisoners on the question of an appeal. In at least 9 per cent of cases, and possibly in as many as 26 per cent, no advice was given by lawyers to legally-aided prisoners, despite the statutory obligation imposed on them by s.74 (7) of the Criminal Justice Act, 1967. Many appealed despite any lack of advice, thus risking a direction that time spent awaiting an appeal should not count towards sentence, where the appeal court regarded the application as hopeless. A high proportion of prisoners felt let down by their lawyers; 54 per cent of them were not seen by their lawyers after the verdict. They were critical of their absence during the trial, their lack of trouble to consult them, the fact that their counsel was instructed so late that he could not meet them save hurriedly before the trial. According to the prisoners, too many lawyers gave the impression of not being interested in the case. A number felt they were being bullied into pleading guilty. Further, legal aid work had a bad reputation amongst the prisoners: it was generally thought to be inferior to private work.[62]

Again, except where they have failed in their statutory duty, these comments are not to be taken as criticism of lawyers. There may be perfectly adequate answers to all these complaints, though an element of truth seems probable at the very least. But it does show that lawyers are failing to convey to their clients a satisfactory picture of their work performance. The time has come for lawyers to defend themselves for they stand accused of failing to consider or even care about the needs or feelings of their consumers—the public.

References and further reading

Titles referred to in the notes to individual chapters are not repeated in the further reading sections which follow, except where further reference details are provided. Publication details given in the first section of General Sources are not repeated in the chapter references.

The following abbreviations are used:

L.R. for Law Review, H.C. for House of Commons, and U.P. for University Press.

References to law cases follow conventional usage, giving the date, usually in square brackets, followed by:

A.C. for Appeal Cases

All E.R. for All England Reports

Ch. for Chancery Division Reports

Q.B. (or K.B.) for Queen's (or King's) Bench Division Reports

P for Probate, Divorce and Admiralty Division Reports (now Family Division)

U.S. for United States Reports (Supreme Court)

W.L.R. for Weekly Law Reports.

GENERAL SOURCES

Aubert, V. *Sociology of Law*, Penguin Books, 1969.

Chambliss, W.J. *Crime and the Legal Process*, McGraw-Hill, 1969.

Friedman, L.M. and Macaulay, S. *Law and the Behavioral Sciences,* Bobbs Merrill, 1969.

Schwartz, R.D. and Skolnick, J.H. *Society and the Legal Order*, Basic Books, 1970.

Simon, R. J. *The Sociology of Law*, Chandler, 1968.
These are readers with a certain amount of commentary. Most of the material is American. A number of the articles and extracts from several of the books referred to in the text of this book are to be found in these volumes.
Abel-Smith, B. and Stevens, R. *Lawyers and the Courts*, Heinemann, 1967.
Abel-Smith, B. and Stevens, R. *In Search of Justice*, Allen Lane, The Penguin Press, 1968.
Fuller, L.L. *Anatomy of the Law,* Praeger, 1968, Penguin, 1972.
Jackson, R.M. *The Machinery of Justice in England*, Cambridge University Press, 1972.
Jackson, R.M. *Enforcing the Law*, Penguin Books, 1972.
Zander, M. *Cases and Materials on the English Legal System,* Weidenfeld, 1973.
These provide the essential background to English legal institutions and methods.

Evan, W.M. *Law and Sociology*—exploratory essays, New York Free Press, 1962.
Friedmann, W. *Law in a Changing Society*, Stevens, 1972.
Lloyd, D. *The Idea of Law*, Penguin Books, revised edition, 1973.
Lloyd, D. *Introduction to Jurisprudence*, Stevens, 1972.
Radzinewicz, L. and Wolfgang, M.E. *Crime and Justice*, Basic Books, 3 volumes, 1971.
Sawer, G. *Law in Society*, Oxford University Press, 1965.
Walker, N. *Crimes, Courts and Figures*, Penguin Books, 1972.
These place law in its social context.

INTRODUCTION

1. Thurman Arnold, *The Symbols of Government*, Yale U.P. 1935, p. 34.

Further reading
Lloyd, D. *Introduction to Jurisprudence* (see General sources), ch. 6.

CHAPTER I. LEGAL STRUCTURE AND SOCIAL STRUCTURE

References

1. P. Bohannan, 'The differing realms of the law', in Bohannan, ed., *Law and Warfare*, New York, Natural History Press, 1967, p. 47.
2. E. Durkheim, *The Division of Labour in Society* (trans. G. Simpson, 1933), New York, Free Press, 1964, p. 68.
3. M. Mead, 'Some anthropological considerations concerning natural law', *Natural Law Forum*, vol. 6, 1961, p. 51.
4. H.L.A. Hart, *The Concept of Law*, Oxford U.P., 1961, pp. 189–95.
5. Cf. W. Hurst, *Law and Economic Growth*, Harvard Univ. Press, 1964, p. 290.
6. Karl Renner, *Institutions of Private Law and Their Social Functions*: see the edition with Kahn-Freund's introduction, Routledge & Kegan Paul, 1949.
7. W. Friedmann, *Law in a Changing Society*, p. 19.
8. Friedman and Ladinsky, 'Social change and the law of industrial accidents', *Col. L.R.*, vol. 67, 1967, p. 50.
9. W.F. Ogburn, *Social Change with Respect to Culture and Original Nature*, new edn. Vintage Books, 1950, p. 236.
10. Friedman and Ladinsky, pp. 73, 74, 76.
11. Eugen Ehrlich, *Fundamental Principles of the Sociology of Law*, trans W.L. Moll, Harvard U.P., 1936. There is a sympathetic critique of Ehrlich's thought in Littlefield, *Maine L.R.* vol. 19, 1967, p. 1. Lloyd, *Introduction to Jurisprudence* prints an extract from Ehrlich at pp. 355–60.
12. A.V. Dicey, *Law and Public Opinion in England during the Nineteenth Century,* Macmillan, 1914, pp. 12–13.
13. Friedmann, p. 30.
14. Dicey, p. 34.
15. Roscoe Pound, *Harvard L.R.* vol. 53, 1940, pp. 366–7.
16. Dicey, p. 25.
17. Julius Cohen, Reginald A. Robson and Alan P. Bates, *Parental Authority : the community and the law*, Rutgers U.P., 1958.

18. See respectively Milner, *University of Pittsburgh L.R.* vol. 21, 1959, pp. 147, 149, and Cooperrider, *Michigan L.R.*, vol. 57, 1959, pp. 1123-4.
19. Friedmann, p. 25. Mandelker's comment is also pertinent: 'Effective judicial intervention in social controversy requires a consensus on the goals and objectives of social change at a time when it is our failure as a society to agree on the goals and objectives of social change that is one of the principal causes of social unrest' (*Osgood Hall Law Journal*, vol. 8, 1970, p. 355). Directed to North American society, this is apposite in a British context also.
20. W.G. Sumner, *Folkways*, 1907, p. 87. On Sumner see Ball, Simpson and Ikeda, *Journal of Legal Education*, vol. 14, 1962, p. 229.
21. Lester Ward, *Applied Sociology*, Boston, Atheneum Press, 1896, pp. 337-9.
22. See Lloyd, *Introduction to Jurisprudence*, p. 343.
23. See A. Sinclair, *Prohibition : the era of excess*, Atlantic-Little, Brown, 1962; also J. Gusfield, *Symbolic Crusade*, University of Illinois Press, 1963.
24. 347 U.S. 483 (1954).
25. Selznick, in *International Encyclopaedia of Social Sciences*, New York, Macmillan, 1968, vol. 9, p. 56; and see below, 126.
26. Pitts, in *ibid*, vol. 14, 381, at p. 388; and see below, 55 ff.
27. Race Relations Board, *First Annual Report*, 1967, H.C. 437, para 62; and see the book p. 55.
28. T. Duster, *The Legislation of Morality*, New York, Free Press, 1970, pp. 26-7. The importance of these variables underlies the dichotomy drawn in ch. 4 between enforcing conventional morality and changing social patterns.
29. Law Commission, *Field of Choice*, Cmnd 3123, HMSO, 1966, para 15.
30. In *Stockloser* v. *Johnson* [1954] 1 Q.B. 476, 495.
31. Friedmann, p. 131.
32. J.K. Galbraith, *American Capitalism*, Hamish Hamilton, 1952.
33. *M. and S. Drapers* v. *Reynolds* [1956] 3 All E.R. 814, 820.

But *cf Home Counties Dairies* v. *Skilton* [1970] 1 All E.R. 1227.

34. Baker, *Current Legal Problems,* vol. 24, p. 53 at p. 62.
35. [1966] 2 Q.B. 617.
36. This has now been done in the Supply of Goods (Implied Terms) Act 1973.
37. [1897] A.C. 22.
38. A.A. Berle and G.C. Means, *The Modern Corporation and Private Property*, 1932; revised edition, Harcourt, 1968.
39. K.W. Wedderburn, *Company Law Reform*, Fabian Tract no. 563, 1965, p. 12.
40. [1935], 2 K.B. 113.
41. Barbara Shenfield, *Company Boards; their responsibilities to shareholders, employees and the community*, Allen & Unwin, 1970, p. 12.
42. [1962] Ch. 927 at p. 963.
43. 98 A. 2d. 581, 586, (1953). See Blumberg, 'Corporate responsibilities and the social crisis', *Boston Univ. L.R.*, vol. 50, 1970, p. 157. It is interesting that Adolf Berle has noted the growth of 'corporate conscience', the realisation among large corporations of social responsibilities; see *The Twentieth Century Capitalist Revolution*, Harcourt, 1954.
44. On which see Friedmann, Part 4, esp. ch. 10.

Further reading

Aubert, V. *Sociology of Law* (see General sources), pp. 15–51, 69–99.

Borrie, G. and Diamond, A. *The Consumer, Society and the Law*, Penguin Books, 1973.

Dicey, A.V. *Law and Public Opinion during the Nineteenth Century*, Macmillan, 1914.

Eekelaar, J. *Family Security and Family Breakdown*, Penguin Books, 1971.

Finlay, H.A. *Divorce, Society and the Law*, Butterworths, 1969.

Freeman, M.D.A., 'Towards a Rational Reconstruction of Family Property Law', Current Legal Problems, vol. 25, 1972, p. 84.

Friedmann, W. *Law in a Changing Society* (see General sources), chs 1, 4, 7, 9, 10, 12.

Ginsberg, M. *Law and Opinion in England in the Twentieth Century*, Stevens, 1959.

Gower, L.D.B. *Modern Company Law*, Butterworths, 1969, pp. 57–64.

Hadden, T. *Company Law and Capitalism*, Weidenfeld & Nicolson, 1972.

Rheinstein, M. *Marriage Stability, Divorce, and the Law,* Univ. of Chicago Press, 1972.

Wedderburn, K.W. *The Worker and the Law*, Penguin Books, 1971.

CHAPTER 2.   LEGAL CONTROL AND SOCIAL CONTROL

References

1. E.A. Ross, *Social Control : a survey of the foundations of order*, Macmillan, 1901.

2. Maureen Cain, 'On the beat', in S. Cohen, ed. *Images of Deviance*, Penguin Books, 1971.

3. *The Sociology of Georg Simmel*, trans. Wolff, New York, Free Press, 1950, p. 102.

4. M. Banton, *The Policeman in the Community*, Tavistock, 1964, p. 2.

5. R.D. Schwartz, 'Social Factors in the development of Legal Control', *Yale Law Journal*, vol. 63, 1954, p. 471.

6. R.D. Schwartz and J.S. Miller, 'Legal evolution and societal complexity', *American Journal of Sociology*, vol. 70, 1964, p. 159.

7. E. Durkheim, *The Division of Labour in Society*, trans. Simpson, Macmillan, 1933, chs 2, 3.

8. S. Box, *Deviance, Reality and Society*, Holt, Rinehart & Winston 1971, p. 7.

9. S.K. Erikson, 'Notes on the Sociology of Deviance' *Social Problems,* vol. 9, 1962, pp. 307, 308.

10. For a recent example of this see D.J. West, ed. *Criminological Implications of Chromosome Abnormalities*, Cambridge Institute of Criminology, Cambridge, 1969.

11. Box, pp. 1–6.

12. R. Merton, 'Social structure and anomie', in *Social Theory and Social Structure*, New York, Free Press, 1957, p. 134.

13. Edwin Lemert, *Human Deviance, Social Problems and Social Control*, Prentice-Hall, 1967, p. 10.

14. Cohen, *Images of Deviance*, p. 10.

15. H.S. Becker, *Outsiders: studies in the sociology of deviance*, New York, Free Press, 1963, p. 9.

16. See respectively E.H. Sutherland, *White Collar Crime*, Holt, Rinehart & Winston, 1949, and W. G. Carson, 'Some Sociological aspects of strict liability and the enforcement of factory legislation', *Modern L.R.*, vol. 33, 1970, p. 396, and 'White Collar Crime and the enforcement of Factory Legislation', *British Journal of Criminology*, vol. 10, 1970, p. 383.

17. S. Cohen, *Folk Devils and Moral Panics*, MacGibbon & Kee, 1972.

18. E. Schur, 'Reactions to deviance', *American Journal of Sociology*, vol. 75, 1969, pp. 309, 313.

19. Ian Taylor, 'Soccer consciousness and soccer hooliganism', in Cohen, *Images of Deviance*, pp. 134, 160.

20. J. Pitts, 'Social control', in *International Encyclopaedia of Social Sciences*, Macmillan, 1968, vol. 14, pp. 381, 385.

21. Lemert, p. 17.

22. H.L. A. Hart, *The Concept of Law*, Oxford U.P., 1961, ch. 5.

23. *Ibid*, and Hans Kelsen, *The Pure Theory of Law*, California U.P., 1967, contain useful explications of this question. G. Marshall, *Constitutional Theory*, Oxford U.P., 1971, is a more general account.

24. *Max Weber on Law in Economy and Society*, ed. Max Rheinstein, Harvard U.P., 1954.

25. William J. Chambliss, 'A Sociological analysis of the law of Vagrancy' *Social Problems,* vol. 12, 1964, p. 67.

26. Jerome Hall, *Theft, Law and Society*, Bobbs-Merrill, 1952, ch. 1.

27. See Richard G. Salem and William J. Bowers, 'Severity of Formal Sanctions as a Deterrent to Deviant Behavior', *Law and Society Review*, vol. 5, 1970, p. 21.

28. But values change. See Criminal Law Revision Committee, *11th Report, Evidence*, Cmnd 4991, HMSO, 1972.

29. R.D. Schwartz and J.H. Skolnick, 'Two studies of legal stigma,' in H.S. Becker, ed., *The Other Side*, New York, Free Press, 1964, p. 103.

30. Herbert Packer, *The Limits of the Criminal Sanction*, Stanford U.P., 1968, p. 296.

31. L.T. Wilkins, *Social Policy, Action and Research*, Tavistock, 1964, p. 87.

32. Jock Young, *The Drugtakers*, MacGibbon & Kee, 1971.

33. S. Cohen, *Folk Devils and Moral Panics,* MacGibbon and Kee, 1972.

34. Wilkins, pp. 86–7.

35. Otto Kahn-Freund, 'The Shifting Frontiers of Law and Custom in Labour relations, *Current Legal Problems*, vol. 22, 1969, pp. 1, 24–5.

36. Stewart Macaulay, *Law and the Balance of Power, The Automobile Manufacturers and their Dealers,* Russell Sage Foundation, 1966.

37. Thomas Schelling, *Arms and Influence*, Yale U.P. 1966, p. 140.

38. Stewart Macaulay, 'Non-contractual relations in business: a preliminary study', *American Sociological Review*, vol. 28, 1963, pp. 55, 61.

39. V. Aubert, 'Competition and Dissension. Two Types of Conflict and of Conflict Resolution'. *Journal of Conflict Resolution* (Univ. of Michigan), vol. 7, 1963 (p. 26) at p. 34.

40. V. Aubert, 'Courts and Conflict resolution', *Journal of Conflict Resolution*, vol. 11, 1967 (p. 40). at pp. 45, 44.

41. Max Gluckman, *The Judicial Process among the Barotse of Northern Rhodesia*, rev. edn, Manchester U.P. 1967, pp. 20–1, 22.

42. K.N. Llewellyn and E. Adamson Hoebel, *The Cheyenne Way*, Univ. of Oklahoma Press, 1941.

43. Torstein Eckhoff, 'The mediator, the judge and the administrator in conflict resolution', in B–M Persson Blegvad, ed., *Contribution to the Sociology of Law*, Copenhagen, Munksgaard, pp. 148, 159; also in Aubert, ed. *Sociology of Law*, pp. 171, 172.
44. Race Relations Act 1968, s. 15(3)(b).
45. Bob Hepple, *Race, Jobs and Law in Britain* (Allen Lane, 1968), Penguin Books, 1970, p. 181.
46. T. Hetherington, *Race Today*, November 1971, p. 382.

Further reading

Abbott, S. *The Prevention of Racial Discrimination in Britain*, Oxford U.P., 1971.

Aubert, V. *Sociology of Law* (see General sources), pp. 151–209.

Banton, M. *The Policeman in the Community*, Tavistock, 1964, ch. 1.

Cohen, S. (ed), Images of Cranton, R.C. 'Driver Behavior and Legal Sanctions' *Michigan L.R.* vol. 67, 1969, p. 421.

Deviance, Penguin Books, 1971.

Frank, J. *Courts on Trial*, Princeton U.P., 1949.

Journal of Conflict Resolution, vol. 11, 1967, pp. 1–86: special number on law and conflict resolution.

Kahn-Freund, O. 'Trade unions, the law and society', *Modern L.R.* vol. 33, 1970, p. 241.

Kahn-Freund, O. *Labour and the Law*, Stevens, 1972.

Lester, A. and Bindman, G. *Race and Law*, Penguin Books, 1972.

Matza, D. *Becoming Deviant*, Prentice-Hall, 1969.

Parsons, T. 'The law and social control', in W.M. Evan, ed. *Law and Sociology*, 1962, pp. 56–72.

Pound, R. *Social Control Through Law*, Yale U.P., 1952.

Rock, Paul, *Deviant Behaviour,* Hutchinson, 1973.

Royal Commission on Trade Unions and Employers' Associations, *Report*, Cmnd 3623, HMSO, 1968.

Rubington, E. and Weinberg, M. *Deviance—and Interactionist Perspective*, Macmillan, 1968.

Salem, R.G. and Bowers, W.J., 'Severity of formal sanctions as a deterrent to deviant behaviour', *Law and Society Review*, vol. 5, 1970, p. 21.

Sawer, G. *Law in Society* (See General Sources) ch. 8.

Schwartz, R.D. and Skolnick, J.H., 'Two studies of social stigma', *Social Problems* vol. 10, 1962, pp. 133–42.

Stone, J. *Social Dimensions of Law and Justice*, Stevens, 1966, ch. 15.

Szasz, T.S. *The Manufacture of Madness*, Harper & Row, 1970.

Taylor, I. Walton, P, Young, J. *The New Criminology,* RKP. 1973.

Taylor, I. and Taylor, L. *The Politics of Deviance,* Penguin, 1973.

Zimring, F.E., and Hawkins, G.J. *Deterrence,* Univ. of Chicago Press, 1973.

CHAPTER 3.   LAW: BEHAVIOUR AND ATTITUDES

References

1. T. Duster, *The Legislation of Morality*, New York, Free Press, 1970, p. 24.

2. Svend Ranulf, *Moral Indignation and Middle Class Psychology*, Copenhagen, Munksgaard, 1938.

3. E.S. Turner, *Roads to Ruin*, Michael Joseph, 1950.

4. Herbert Spencer, *Social Statics,* 1851, Williams & Norgate ch. 28.

5. H.L.A. Hart, *Law, Liberty and Morality*, Oxford U.P., 1963, pp. 17–24.

6. John Stuart Mill, *On Liberty*, Everyman edn, Dent, p. 73. Ted Honderich, *Punishment: its supposed justifications*, Hutchinson, 1969, ch. 7, explains its philosophical context.

7. See Hart, *Law, Liberty and Morality*, p. 71; *The Concept of Law*, Oxford U.P. 1961, pp. 189–95; and 'Social solidarity and the enforcement of morality', *Univ. of Chicago Law Review*, vol. 35, 1967, pp. 10–11; and Patrick Devlin, *The Enforcement*

of Morals, Oxford U.P., 1965, chs 1, 5, 6, 7 and preface.

8. Good accounts are Basil Mitchell, *Law, Morality and Religion in a Secular Society*, Oxford U.P., 1967 (leaning towards Devlin), and Graham Hughes, 'Morals and the Geninal *Yale Law Journal*, vol. 71, 1962, p. 662. A useful contribution is C. Ten 'Crime and Immorality' *Modern L.R.*, vol, 32, 1969, p. 648.

9. [1969] 1 Q.B. 1.

10. An account is Tony Palmer, *The 'Oz' Trial*, Blond and Briggs, 1971. The convictions were upheld in *R.* v. *Anderson* [1971] 3 All E.R. 1152.

11. Duster, pp. 238, 21.

12. Cf. his preface to *The Enforcement of Morals*, pp. viii and 17.

13. P. Devlin, *Trial by Jury*, Stevens, 1956, p. 20. On the jury see this book, p. 131, particularly the discussion on the effect of the Criminal Justice Act 1972 at p. 132 and 135.

14. E. Schur, *Crimes Without Victims*, Prentice-Hall, 1965, p. 170.

15. See W.R. La Fave, *Arrest : the decision to take a suspect into custody*, Little, Brown, 1965; and for the attitude of the English courts, *R.* v. *M.P. Commissioner ex p. Blackburn* [1968] 2 Q.B. 118 and this book, p. 155 ff.

16. In Sami Zubaida, *Race and Racialism*, Tavistock, 1970, pp. 73, 78, 89–90; also this book, p. 150–151.

17. See *R.* v. *Birtles* [1969] 2 All E.R. 1131, and McClean 'Informers and Agents Provocateurs', *Criminal L.R.*, 1969, p. 527.

18. J.H. Skolnick, *Justice Without Trial*, Wiley, 1966, p. 215.

19. Lambert, in Zubaida, *op. cit.*, p. 79.

20. J.H. Skolnick and J.R. Woodworth, 'Morality enforcement and totalitarian potential,' in M. Levitt and B. Rubinstein, eds, *Orthopsychiatry and the Law*, Wayne State U.P., 1968, p. 176.

21. See Herbert Packer, *The Limit of Criminal Sanction*, Stanford U.P., 1969, pp. 277–82.

22. per W. Chambliss, 'Types of Deviance and the Effectiveness of Legal Sanctions', *Wisconsin L.R.* 1967, pp. 703, 708.

23. *Ibid*, pp. 707–8; cf. his study in *Crime and Delinquency*, vol.

12, 1966, p. 70, showing the impact of punishment on a typical instrumental offence, breach of parking regulations.

24. J. Skolnick, 'Coercion to Virtue', *Southern Californian L.R.* vol. 41, 1968, pp. 588, 625.

25. Packer, pp. 281–2.

26. Skolnick, *Southern Californian L.R.*, vol. 41, pp. 588, 626.

27. H.C. 437 (1967), para. 65. 1st Report of Race Relations Board

28. Harry V. Ball and Lawrence M. Friedman, 'The Use of Criminal Sanchous in the Enforcement of Economic Legislation: A Sociological View', *Stanford L.R.*, vol. 17, 1965, pp. 197, 220.

29. Leon Mayhew, *The Massachusetts Commission against Discrimination*, Harvard U.P., 1968, p. 260.

30. Olivecrona, *Law as Fact*, 1st edn, Copenhagen, Munksgaard, 1939; this emphasis is missing from the reworked edition of 1971; and Lundstedt, *Legal Thinking Revised*, Stockholm, Almquist & Wiksell, 1956.

31. Mildred A. Schwartz, *Trends in White Attitudes Towards Negroes*, Univ. of Chicago, Opinion Research Center, 1967, p. 116.

32. Olivecrona, *Law as Fact*, 1st edn, pp. 54–5.

33. Wahlke and Eulau, *Legislative Behaviour: a reader in theory and research*, New York, Free Press, 1959, p. 6.

34. Hodge, R.W. Siegel P.M. and P.H. Rossi 'Occupational Prestige in the United States, 1925–63', *American Journal of Sociology*, vol. 70, 1964, p. 286.

35. L. Berkowitz, and N. Walker 'Law and moral judgments', *Sociometry*, vol. 30, 1967, pp. 410, 415, 416, 418. The earlier experiment is reported in *British Journal of Criminology*, vol. 5, 1964, p. 570.

36. Evan, 'Law as an instrument of social change', in A.W. Gouldner and S.M. Miller, eds, *Applied Sociology*, New York, Free Press, 1965, pp. 285, 287.

37. Gunnar Myrdal, *The American Dilemma*, Harper & Row, 1944, pp. 1045–57.

38. Ray Marshall, *The Negro and Organized Labor*, Wiley, 1965.

39. Olivecrona, *Law as Fact*, 1st edn, p. 55; cf. *R. v. Metropolitan Police Commissioner ex. p. Blackburn.*

40. A. Larson, 'The New Law of Race Relations', *Wisconsin L.R.*, 1969, pp. 470, 522.

41. Morroe Berger, *Equality by Statute*, Columbia U.P., 1952, p. 168.

42. L.H. Mayhew, *Law and Equal Opportunity*, Harvard U.P., 1968, pp. 272–3; see also J. Greenberg *Race Relations and American Law*, Columbia U.P., 1959, pp. 20–5.

43. Quentin Hogg (now Lord Hailsham), H.C. Standing Committee B, 20 June 1968, col. 695, quoted in Hepple, *op. cit.*, p. 212.

44. Richard D. Schwartz, 'Law, violence and civil rights', *Law and Society Review*, vol. 2, 1967, p. 7.

45. See now Race Relations Board, *6th Report*, H.C. 296, paras 75–85.

46. H. Cantril, *Gauging Public Opinion*, Princeton U.P., 1951, p. 228.

47. Herbert H. Hyman and Paul B. Sheatsley, 'Attitudes toward Desegregation', *Scientific American*, vol. 211, no. 1, July 1964, pp. 16, 21.

48. Race Relations Board, *2nd Annual Report*, H.C. 262, 1968, para. 58.

49. Race Relations Board, *4th Annual Report*, H.C. 309, 1970, para. 95.

50. K. Lipstein, 'The Reception of Western Law in a country of Different Social and Economic Background: India *Revista del Institutio de Derecho Comparado* (1957–8), vol. 8–9, pp. 69, 213.

51. Y. Dror, 'Law and Social change', *Tulane L.R.*, vol. 33, 1959, p. 787 at pp. 800–1.

52. Jan Górecki, 'Divorce in Poland – A So Go – Legal Study' in B–M, Blegvad, ed., *Contributions to the Sociology of Law*, Copenhagen. Munksgaard, 1966, p. 68; and in Aubert, ed. *Sociology of Law*, pp. 78, 113.

53. V. Aubert *et al, Acta Sociologica*, vol. 1, 1955–6, p. 149; (also in Schwartz and Skolnick, *Society and the Legal Order*,

Basic Books, 1970, p. 559, to which references refer; and in Blegvad, ed. *op. cit.*, p. 98. (The last is also in Aubert, *Sociology of Law*, p. 116.)

54. Aubert *et al*, in Schwartz and Skolnick, p. 565.
55. *Ibid*, in Blegvad, ed., p. 104.
56. K.M. Dolbeare and P. Hammond, *The School Prayer Decisions*, Univ. of Chicago Press, 1971, pp. 23 and 7 respectively.
57. Aubert, in Blegvad, ed., p. 105.
58. George Break, 'Income Taxes and Incentres to work: An Emperial Study' *American Economic Review*, vol. 47, 1957, p. 529, and in Schwartz and Skolnick, p. 547.
59. J.H. Skolnick, *Justice without Trial,* Wiley, 1966, p. 219; cf this book, p. 151–2; and see also *Yale Law Journal*, vol. 76, 1967, p. 1519, and *Michigan L.R.*, vol. 66, 1968, p. 1347.
60. Morroe Berger, *Equality by Statute*, Columbia U.P., 1952, pp. viii and 187.
61. Hyman and Sheatsley, p. 20.
62. W.K. Muir, jr. *Prayer in the Public Schools : law and attitude change*, Univ. of Chicago Press, 1967.
63. J. Colombotos, 'Physicians and Medicare: a before-after study of the effect of Legislation on attitudes'. *American Sociological Review*, vol. 34, 1969, pp. 318, 326.

Further reading

Andenaes, J. 'The general preventive effects of punishment', *Univ. of Pennsylvania L.R.*, vol. 114, 1966, p. 949.

Andenaes, J. 'The Moral or educative influence of criminal law', *Journal of Social Issues*, vol. 27, 1971, p. 17.

Berger, M. *Equality by Statute*, Columbia U.P., pp. 170ff.

Berkowitz, L. and Walker, N., 'Law and moral judgments', *Sociometry*, vol. 30, 1967, p. 410.

Black, Donald J. 'The Mobilization of Law', Journal of Legal Studies, vol. 2, 1973, p. 125.

Chambliss, W.J. *Crime and the Legal Process* (see General sources) p. 360–420.

Colombotos, J. 'Physicians and medicare: a before-after study of
  the effect of legislation on attitudes', *American Sociological
  Review*, vol. 34, 1969, p. 318.
Duster, T. *The Legislation of Morality*, New York, Free Press,
  1970.
Friedmann, W. *Legal Theory*, 5th edn, Stevens, 1967, ch. 31.
Lambert, J.R. *Crime, Police and Race Relations*, Oxford U.P.,
  1970.
Lambert, J.R. 'Race Relations: the role of the police', in S.
  Zubaida, ed. *Race and Racialism*, Tavistock 1969, p. 73.
Levine, J.P., and Becker, T.L., 'Toward and Beyond a Theory
  of Supreme Court Impact', American Behavioral Scientist,
  vol. 13, 1970, p. 561.
Massell, Gregory J., 'Law as an Instrument of Revolutionary
  change in a Traditional Milieu: A Case of Soviet Central
  Asia', *Law and Society Review*, vol. 2, 1967, p. 179.
Mayhew, L. *Law and Equal Opportunity*, Harvard U.P., 1968.
Morris, N. and Hawkins, G. *The Honest Politician's Guide to Crime
  Control*, Univ. of Chicago Press, 1970, ch. 1.
Packer, H. *The Limits of the Criminal Sanction*, Oxford U.P.,
  1968.
Pound, R. *Introduction to the Philosophy of Law*, Yale U.P.,
  1954, ch. 2.
Rose, A.M. 'Sociological factors in the effectiveness of projected
  legal remedies, *Journal of Legal Education* (Duke University),
  vol. 11, 1959, pp. 470–81.
Schwartz, R.D. and Orleans, S. 'On legal sanctions', *Univ. of
  Chicago L.R.*, vol. 34, 1967.
Walker, N. and Argyle, M., 'Does the law affect moral judgements',
  British Journal of Criminology, 1964, p. 570.
Wasby, Stephen L. *The Impact of the United States Supreme
  Court,* Dorsey Press, 1970.
Zimring, F. and Hawkins, G., 'The legal threat as an instrument
  of social change', *Journal of Social Issues*, vol. 27, 1971, p. 33.

CHAPTER 4.   LAW: INTERESTS AND VALUES

References

1. Roscoe Pound, *An Introduction to the Philosophy of Law*, rev. edn, Yale U.P., 1954, p. 47.
2. See, for example, Julius Stone, 'The Golden Age of Pound', *Sydney L.R.*, vol. 4, 1962, p. 1.
3. John Dewey, *Human Nature and Conduct*, 1922, Pt. 11, secs. v and vi.
4. Lord Crowther, *Report of the Committee on Consumer Credit* Cmnd 4596, HMSO, 1971.
5. H.E. Francis, *Report of the Committee on the Rent Act,* Cmnd 4609, HMSO, 1971.
6. Mr. Justice Roskill, *Report of the Commission on Third London Airport*, HMSO, 1970.
7. Edwin W. Patterson, *Jurisprudence: men and ideas of the law*, Foundation Press, 1953, p. 518.
8. Sawer, *Law in Society*, p. 156.
9. [1971] 1 All E.R. 65, 77–78.
10. H.W.R. Wade, *Administrative Law*, Oxford U.P., 1971, p. 168.
11. *Home Office* v. *Dorset Yacht* [1970] A.C. 1004, 1067.
12. Roscoe Pound, *Jurisprudence*, vol. 3, p. 328ff, West Publishing Co. 1959.
13. [1966] 3 All E.R. 384, 390 (Thesiger J.)
14. Sawer, p. 152.
15. [1969] 1 Q.B. 349, 360, 363.
16. Cf. *Williams* v. *Settle* [1960] 1 W.L.R. 1072.
17. Cf. *Tolley* v. *Fry* [1931] A.C. 333.
18. *Argyll* v. *Argyll* [1967] Ch. 302.
19. M. Warner and M. Stone, *The Data Bank Society*, Allen & Unwin, 1970, p. 131.
20. (1931), 297 Pacific reports, p. 91.
21. See now *Report of Committee on Privacy*, Cmnd 5012, H.M.S.O., 1972, which concludes that there is no need for

a general law of privacy. The advantages of introducing a new tort are well phrased by Lyon in his minority report (pp. 210–12).

22. Friedmann, *Law in a Changing Society*, p. 94.

23. See Campbell, 'Seeking a foolproof business spy law', *The Times*, 8 December 1967.

24. [1956] 2 All E.R. 897.

25. Banks Committee on Patent System and Patent Law, Cmnd 4407, H.M.S.O., 1970.

26. [1970] 3 W.L.R. 713, 721.

27. Cyril Grunfeld, *Trade Unions and the Individual in English Law*, Institute of Personnel Management, 1963, p. 50.

28. See A. Buchan, *The Right to Work*, Calder and Boyars, 1972.

29. G. de N. Clark, 'Remedies for unfair dismissal', *International and Comparative Law Quarterly* (London), vol. 20, 1971, pp. 397, 402.

30. Charles Reich, 'The new property', *Yale Law Journal*, vol. 73, 1964, pp. 733, 785–6.

31. Margaret Wynn, *Fatherless Families*, Michael Joseph, 1954, and *Family Policy*, Michael Joseph, 1970, ch. 9.

32. Roscoe Pound, 'A Theory of Social Interests', *Papers and Proceedings of the American Sociological Society*, vol. 15, 1921, p. 16.

33. Friedmann, pp. 203, 207.

34. [1932] A.C. 562.

35. [1938] 4 All E.R. 631.

36. Cf. *Le Brocq* v. *Le Brocq* [1964] 3 All E.R. 464, 471.

37. *Ash* v. *Ash* [1972] 1 All E.R. 582, 586.

38. Sheldon Glueck and Eleanor Glueck, *Unraveling Juvenile Delinquency*, Harvard U.P., 1950, p. 91, Table VIII – 19.

39. 38 C.L.R. (1926)

40. Wade, pp. 306–7.

41. [1942] A.C. 624.

42. [1968] A.C. 910, particularly at p. 940 where Lord Reid contrasts two public interests involved; one that no harm

shall be done to the nation; the other, which prevailed, in the administration of justice.

43. Lord Radcliffe, *The Law and Its Compass*, Faber, 1961, ch. 1.
44. [1962] A.C. 220, 267; see now *Knuller* v. *D.P.P.* [1972] 2 All E.R. 898, on the offence of outraging public decency.
45. Roscoe Pound, *Social Control Through Law*, Yale U.P., 1942, pp. 112–16.
46. H.J. Laski, *The American Democracy*, Allen & Unwin, 1949, p. 443.
47. Sawer, p. 148.
48. B.M. Barry, *Political Argument*, Routledge, 1965, pp. 124–6.
49. R.W.M. Dias, *Jurisprudence*, 3rd edn, Butterworths, 1970, pp. 166–7.
50. On which see Hepple, 'Aliens and Administrative Justice: The Dutschke Case' *Modern L.R.* vol. 34, 1971, p. 501.
51. *Liversidge* v. Anderson [1942] A.C. 206.
52. [1968] 2 Q.B. 299.
53. De Smith, *Constitutional and Administrative Law*, Penguin Books, 1971, p. 460.
54. [1970] A.C. 1004, 1031.
55. [1963] Article 9.
56. (1772), *State Trials*, vol. 20, p. 1.
57. [1964] A.C. 413, 427.
58. [1940] A.C. 1014, 1026.
59. [1964] P. 67. But see how Family Law Reform Act 1969.
60. *Entick* v. *Carrington* (1765); *State Trials*, vol. 19, p. 1030.
61. [1920] A.C. 508.
62. [1965] A.C. 75.

Further reading

Dias, R.W.M., 'The value of a value-study of law', *Modern L.R.* vol. 28, 1965, p. 397.
Dias, R.W.M. *Jurisprudence*, 3rd edn, Butterworths, 1970, ch. 9.
Lloyd, D. *The Idea of Law* (see General sources), ch. 9.
Lloyd, D. *Introduction to Jurisprudence* (see General sources), ch. 6.

Pound, R. *Jurisprudence*, vol. 3, West Publishing Co., 1959.

Quinney, R., ed. *Crime and Justice in Society*, Little, Brown, 1969, pp. 1–30.

Sawer, G. *Law in Society* (see General sources), ch. 9.

Stone, J. *Social Dimensions of Law and Justice*, Stevens, 1966, chs 4–8.

CHAPTER 5.   THE LEGAL PROFESSION

References

1. P. Nonet and J. Carlin, 'Law: legal profession', in *International Encyclopaedia of the Social Sciences*, Macmillan, 1968, vol. 9, pp. 66–7.

2. B. Abel-Smith and R. Stevens, *Lawyers and the Courts*, pp. 1–2.

3. Michael Zander, *Lawyers and the Public Interest*, Weidenfeld & Nicolson, 1968, pp. 17–18.

4. J.H. Baker, *An Introduction to English Legal History*, Butterworths, 1971, p. 66.

5. B. Abel-Smith and R. Stevens, *In Search of Justice*, p. 13, commented on by Zander, p. 40.

6. Q. Johnstone and D. Hopson, *Lawyers and Their Work*, Bobbs-Merrill, 1967.

7. R.E. Megarry, *Lawyer and Litigant in England*, Stevens, 1962, p. 12.

8. But note solicitors' preference for conveyancing which in the nineteenth century left the fertile field of taxation to the new profession of accountants, where by and large it has remained.

9. Prices and Incomes Board, *Remuneration of Solicitors*, Cmnd 3529, HMSO, 1968, para. 48.

10. K. Llewellyn and E.A. Hoebel, *The Cheyenne Way*, p. 293.

11. D. Rueschemeyer, 'Doctors and lawyers: a comment on the theory of the professions', *Canadian Review of Sociology and Anthropology*, vol. 1, 1964, pp. 17, 21.

12. Johnstone and Hopson, p. 95.

13. *Ibid.*, p. 101.
14. *Ibid.*, p. 119.
15. *Ibid.*, p. 80.
16. Rueschemeyer, p. 19.
17. E.O. Smigel, *The Wall Street Lawyer*, rev. edn., New York, Free Press, 1969, p. 342; see also T. Parsons, 'The law and social control', in Evan, ed. *Law and Sociology*, pp. 64–70.
18. J.F. Handler, *The Lawyer and His Community*, Univ. of Wisconsin Press, 1967, p. 155.
19. Megarry, p. 51.
20. *Ibid.*, p. 53.
21. Lord Macmillan, *Law and Other Things*, Cambridge U.P., 1937, pp. 171, 181; see also Parsons's point in Evan, ed., p. 65, that 'no clearly "right" answers can be attained'.
22. Zander, p. 40.
23. William Plowden, 'Tomorrow's lawyers', in *What's Wrong with the Law?* BBC Publications, 1970, pp. 98, 124.
24. A small minority still do. The figures are undoubtedly less than those quoted in *New Law Journal*, 6 April 1967 (10 per cent in London and Manchester, for example). The PIB report on *Remuneration of Solicitors* (1968) para 12 reported only 5 per cent of solicitors requiring premiums.
25. Zander, p. 45.
26. Abel-Smith and Stevens, *In Search of Justice*, pp. 339–40.
27. *Report of Committee on Legal Education*, Cmnd 4595, HMSO 1971, paras 93–97, at para. 93.
28. Jerome Frank, *Courts on Trial*, Atheneum edition, 1949, p. 227.
29. *Max Weber on Law in Economy and Society*, ed. Rheinstein, 1954, ch. vii, pp. 198–203.
30. Johnstone and Hopson, p. 387.
31. Zander, p. 324. The case is put by Henry Cecil, *The English Judge*, Stevens, 1970, pp. 12–17.
32. Megarry, p. 11.
33. Smigel, *The Wall Street Lawyer*, New York, Free Press, 1969; and J.E. Carlin, *Lawyers on Their Own*, Rutgers U.P., 1962.

34. Ladinsky, 'Careers of lawyers, law practice and legal institutions', *American Sociological Review*, vol. 28, 1963, pp. 47, 54.
35. Nonet and Carlin, p. 70.
36. J.E. Carlin, *Lawyers' Ethics*, Russell Sage Foundation, 1966, p. 177.
37. Zander, p. 279.
38. Megarry, p. 26.
39. Johnstone and Hopson, p. 398.
40. *The Times*, 11 April 1972; *The Guardian* of the same date reports wide opposition to this move.
41. Goode: see e.g. 'Community within a Community: The Professions', *American Sociological Review vol.* 22, 1957, p. 194; 'Encroachment, Charlatanism and the Emergent Profession, psychology, medicine, and sociology', *ibid.*, vol. 25, 1960, p. 902.
42. Talcott Parsons, 'The professions and social structure', in *Essays in Sociological Structure*, New York, Free Press, 1949, pp. 185, 195.
43. Rueschemeyer, pp. 21, 22, 24.
44. Riesman, 'Toward an anthropological science of law and the legal profession', *American Journal of Sociology*, vol. 57, 1951, pp. 121, 128.
45. Cf. H.L.A. Hart, *The Concept of Law*, Oxford University Press, 1961, pp. 153–63.
46. Rueschemeyer, p. 24.

Further reading

Aubert, V. *Sociology of Law* (see General sources), pp. 265–350.
Elliott, P. *The Sociology of the Professions*, Macmillan, 1972, esp. pp. 118–24.
Ditchley Foundation. *Training for the Law*, Ditchley Paper no. 11, 1967.
Foster, K. 'The Location of Solicitors', *Modern Law Review,* vol. 36, 1973, p. 153.
Johnson, T.J. *Professions and Power,* Macmillan, 1972.

Johnstone, Q. and Hopson, D. *Lawyers and their Work*, Bobbs-Merrill, 1967.

Ladinsky, J. 'Careers of lawyers, law practice and legal institutions', *American Sociological Review*, vol. 28, 1963, pp. 47–54.

Llewellyn, K. *The Common Law Tradition*, Little, Brown, 1960.

Llewellyn, K.N. and Hoebel, E.A. *The Common Law Tradition*.

Megarry, R.E. *Lawyer and Litigant in England*, Stevens, 1962.

Monopolies Commission, *Professional Services*, Cmnd 4463, HMSO, 1970.

Parsons, T. 'The law and social control', in Evan, *Law and Sociology* (see General sources), pp. 56–72.

Prices and Incomes Board, Standing Reference on Remuneration of Solicitors, *First Report*, Cmnd 3529, Second Report, Cmnd 4217, HMSO 1969.

Report of the Committee on Legal Education, Cmnd 4595, HMSO, 1971.

Sawer, G. *Law in Society* (see General sources), ch. 7.

Stone, A.A. 'Legal education on the couch', *Harvard L.R.*, vol. 85 1971, p. 392.

Weyrauch, W.O. *The Personality of Lawyers*, Yale U.P., 1964.

Wilson, 'Survey of legal education in the United Kingdom', *Journal of the Society of Public Teachers of Law*, vol. 9, 1966.

Young Solicitors Group of the Law Society, *Tomorrow's Lawyers*, 1972.

Zander, M., 'Reforming the English legal profession', *Political Quarterly*, vol. 37, 1966, p. 33.

Zander, M., 'The English legal profession', in B. Crick, ed., *Essays on Reform*, Oxford University Press, 1967.

Zander, M. *Lawyers and the Public Interest*, Weidenfeld & Nicolson, 1968.

CHAPTER 6. JUDGES

References

1. See e.g. E. Moriondo, 'The value-system and professional

organisation of Italian judges', in Aubert, *Sociology of Law*, p. 310.

2. See D. Karlen, *Judicial Administration: the American Experience*, Butterworths, 1970, pp. 28–9.

3. The new attitude is exemplified by the Court of Appeal in *R. v. Metropolitan Police Commissioner ex p. Blackburn* (no. 2) [1968] 2 All E.R. 319.

4. J. Wisdom, 'Gods', *Proceedings of the Aristotelian Society*, 1944, in D. Lloyd, *Introduction to Jurisprudence*, p. 798–9.

5. From about 1890 to 1960.

6. Lord Pearson in *British Railways* v. *Herrington* [1972] 1 All E.R. 749, 785–6; cf. *Jones* v. *Secretary of State for Social Services* [1972] 1 All E.R. 145, and *Knuller* v. *D.P.P.* [1972] 2 All E.R. 898 per Lord Reid, pp. 902–3.

7. See *Cassells* v. *Broome* [1972] 2 W.L.R. 645, 652–4.

8. Weiler, 'Legal values and judicial decision-making', *Canadian Bar Review*, vol. 48, 1970, pp. 1, 33.

9. In *Jones* v. *Secretary of State for Social Services*, pp. 198–9; see also Lord Wilberforce in *Morgans* v. *Launchbury* [1972] 2 All E.R. 606 On the problem as a whole, see Friedmann, *Legal Theory*, Stevens, 1967, pp. 658–77.

10. See Lord Reid in *Saunders* v. *Anglia Building Society* [1970] 3 W.L.R. 1078, 1081; cf, however, Blom-Cooper and Drewry *Final Appeal*, Oxford U.P., 1972, pp. 90–5.

11. See the comparison drawn by L. Jaffe, *English and American Judges as Lawmakers*, Oxford U.P., 1969.

12. Assumed to be easy; cf. J. Frank, *Law and the Modern Mind*, New York, Brentano, 1930, and *Courts on Trial*, Princeton U.P., 1949. Note the reference to this problem in *Toohey* v. *Metropolitan Police Commissioner* [1965] A.C. 595, 608 (Lord Pearce) and see Blom-Cooper and Wegner, 'Psychological selectivity in the courtroom', *Medicine, Science and the Law*, vol. 8, 1968, p. 31, and D. Greer, 'Anything But the Truth? The Reliabilily of Testimony in Criminal Trials', British Journal of Criminology, vol. 11, 1971, p. 131.

13. See, for example, the attitude to actuarial evidence in *Mitchell*

v. *Mulholland* [1971] 2 All E.R. 1205, or to psychiatric evidence in the Court of Appeal decision in *Re W* [1970] 3 All E.R. 990.

14. 203 U.S. 412 (1908), and in Lloyd, *Introduction to Jurisprudence*, pp. 424–6.

15. [1968] 1 All E.R. 1140, 1144.

16. 'The Interpretation of Statutes,' Law Commission, 1969, p. 21. There was a lot of opposition, including that of the profession; see *Law Guardian* (London), December 1969, pp. 11–13.

17. Shapiro, 'Stability and change in judicial decision-making: incrementalism or state decision?', *Law in Transition Quarterly*, vol. 2, 1964, pp. 134, 140.

18. See Lloyd, *Introduction to Jurisprudence*, pp. 419–23; Julius Stone, *Social Dimensions of Law and Justice*, Stevens, 1966, pp. 687–95.

19. Dorothy James, 'Role theory and the Supreme Court', *Journal of Politics* (Univ. of Florida), vol. 30, 1968, p. 186.

20. Sawer, *Law in Society*, p. 101.

21. Blom-Cooper, 'The judiciary in an era of Law Reform', *Political Quarterly*, vol. 37, 1966, pp. 378, 380.

22. *R. v. Home Secretary ex p. Soblen* [1963] 1 Q.B. 829.

23. Brock, unpublished M. Phil. thesis (London); see appendix to Justice report on *The Judiciary,* Stevens 1972, p. 79; her methodology includes unusual assignments of class, and a further 15.3 per cent and 12.7 per cent of the judges are traditional landed upper-class and professional, commercial and administrative upper-class respectively.

24. *The Economist*, vol. 181, 15 December 1956, p. 946 at 947.

25. Henry Cecil, *The English Judge*, Stevens, 1970, pp. 26–31.

26. Goldstein Jackson, 'The Judicial Elite', *New Society* 14 May 1970.

27. C.H. Rolph, *The Trial of Lady Chatterley*, Penguin Books, 1961, p. 17.

28. [1966] 1 All E.R. 838.

29. [1970] 3 All E.R., 1008, 1009.

30. Abel-Smith and Stevens, *In Search of Justice*, p. 175.

31. See the works of Justice, paras 66–68, and Cecil, *The English Judge*, p. 81.

32. Cecil, *ibid*, p. 107–8.

33. Alfred Hinds, *Contempt of Court*.

34. Frank, *Courts on Trial*, Atheneum edn, 1963, p. 21.

35. *New Law Journal*, vol. 116, 1966, p. 928–9; the figure is for 1965. See R. Mark, in *The Listener*, vol. 76, 1965, p. 262, see now also S. McCabe and R. Purves, *The Jury at Work*, Blackwell, 1972.

36. *Report of the Departmental Committee on Jury Service*, Cmnd 2627, HMSO, 1965.

37. Bredemeier, 'Law as an integrative mechanism', in Evan, ed. *Law and Sociology*, pp. 78, 85.

38. Strodtbeck, James and Hawkins, 'Social status in jury deliberations', *American Sociological Review*, vol. 22, 1957, p. 718.

39. *Max Weber on Law in Economy and Society*, ed. Rheinstein, pp. 317, 318.

40. Kalven and Zeisel, *The American Jury*, Little, Brown, 1967, see also McCabe and Purves, *The Jury at Work,* Blackwell, 1972.

41. See Criminal Law Revision Committee, *11th Report*: Evidence, Cmnd 4991, HMSO, 1972, paras 47–101.

41a. 'Juries and the Rules of Evidence', (1973) Crim. L.R. 208.

42. Quoted in Abel-Smith and Stevens, *Lawyers and the Courts*, p. 30.

43. Roger Hood, *Sentencing in Magistrates' Courts*, Stevens, 1962.

44. *Report of the Royal Commission on Justices of the Peace*, Cmnd 7463, HMSO, 1948, para 214.

45. *The Training of Justices of the Peace in England and Wales*, Cmnd 2856, HMSO, 1965.

46. Hood, *Sentencing the Motoring Offender*, Heinemann, 1972, pp. 51–2. Cf Bartlett and Walker, New Society, 19 April 1973.

47. O.R. McGregor, L., Blom-Cooper, and C. Gibson, *Separated Spouses*, Duckworth, 1971; and see this book p. 189.

48. [1892] A.C. 25; [1901] A.C. 426; [1915] A.C. 120.

49. Abel-Smith and Stevens, *Lawyers and the Courts*, p. 117.

50. As exemplified by Dicey, *The Law of the Constitution*, Macmillan, 1885, or Lord Hewart, *The New Despotism*, Benn, 1929.
51. *Report of the Committee on Administrative Tribunals and Enquiries*, Cmnd 218, HMSO, 1957.
52. Kathleen Bell, *Tribunals in the Social Services*, Routledge, 1969, pp. 19–20.
53. McCorquodale, 'The Composition of Administrative Tribunals', *Public Law*, 1962, p. 298.
54. Harry Street, *Justice in the Welfare State*, Stevens, 1968, p. 3.
55. Bell, p. 36.
56. Carleton Allen, *Courts and Judgments*, University of Birmingham, Holdsworth Club, 1959, p. 36.
57. *Report of Committee on Administrative Tribunals and Enquiries*, Cmnd. 218, 1957 para 55.
58. Street, p. 13.
58a. Cf *McKenzie* v. *McKenzie* [1970] 3 All E.R. 1034.
59. Bell, p. 83.
60. *Ibid.*, p. 78.
61. Abel-Smith and Stevens, *Lawyers and the Courts*, p. 265.
62. In 1970 they heard at least 1,055,659 cases. This figure is computed from Council on Tribunals, *Annual Report* 1970–1, H.C. 26, Appendix 13, but only includes those tribunals superintended by the Council. This is the vast majority.

Further reading

Abel-Smith, B. and Stevens, R. *Lawyers and the Courts* (see General sources), ch. 5.

Abel-Smith, B. and Stevens, R. *In Search of Justice* (see General sources), ch. 6.

Becker, T. *Political Behavioralism and Modern Jurisprudence*, Rand McNally, 1964.

Bell, K. *Tribunals in the Social Services*, Routledge, 1969.

Blom-Cooper, L. and Drewry, G. *Final Appeal*, Oxford U.P., 1972.

Cardozo, B. *The Nature of the Judicial Process*, Yale U.P., 1921.

Cavenagh W.E. and Newton, D. 'The Membership of Two Administrative Tribunals', Public Administration, vol. 48, 1970, p. 449, and 'Administrative Tribunals: How People Become Members', vol. 49, 1971, p. 197.

Cornish, W. *The Jury*, Penguin Book, 1971.

Devlin, Patrick. *Trial by Jury*, Stevens, 1956.

Devons, E. 'Serving as a Juryman in Britain', *Modern L.R.* vol. 28, 1965, p. 561.

Freeman, M.D.A., 'Standards of Adjudication, Judicial Law making and Prospective Overruling', Current Legal Problems, vol. 26, 1973.

Griffith, J.A.G., 'The law of property', in M. Ginsberg, ed., *Law and Opinion in England in the Twentieth Century*, Stevens, 1959.

Jennings, W.I., 'Courts and administrative law—the experience of English housing legislation', *Harvard L.R.*, vol. 49, 1935–36, p. 426.

Justice. (Report of subcommittee) *The Judiciary*, Stevens, 1972.

King M. *Bail or Custody,* Cobden Trust, 1971.

McCabe, S. and Purves, R. *The Jury at Work*, Blackwell, 1972.

Schubert, G. *Judicial Behavior: a reader in theory and research,* Rand McNally, 1964.

Simon, R.J. 'Jurors' evaluation of expert psychiatric testimony', *Ohio State Law Journal*, vol. 21, 1960, p. 75.

Smith, A.B. and Blumberg, A.S., 'The Problem of objectivity in Judicial Decision-Making', Social Forces, vol. 46, 1967, p. 96.

Street, H. *Justice in the Welfare State*, Stevens, 1968.

Symposium. 'Social Science approaches to the judicial process', *Harvard L.R.*, vol. 79, 1966, p. 1551.

Tapper, C.F. 'Are the judges necessary?', *New Society*, 5 August 1965, p. 10.

Williams, G. *The Proof of Guilt*, Stevens, 1963, ch. 10.

CHAPTER 7.   THE POLICE

References

1. P. Laurie, *Scotland Yard*, Penguin Books, 1972, pp. 112–13.
2. T.A. Critchley, *A History of Police in England and Wales*. Constable, 1967, pp. 35, 54.
3. See Crown Proceedings Act 1947, s. 2(6); *Fisher* v. *Oldham Corporation* [1930] 2 K.B. 364 (police officer exercises original authority); Police Act 1964, s. 48.
4. See Mary Grigg, *The Challenor Case*, Penguin Books, 1965, ch. 17.
5. Ben Whitaker, *The Police*, Penguin Books, 1964, pp. 88–9.
6. [1968] All E.R. 763, 769. See also Williams, 'The Police and law enforcement', *Criminal L.R.*, 1968, p. 351.
7. *Report of the Royal Commission on the Police*, Cmnd 1728, HMSO, 1962.
8. De Smith, *Constitutional and Administrative Law*, Penguin Books, 1971, p. 385.
9. *Report of the Royal Commission on the Police*, para 117, quoting evidence of Inns of Court Conservative Society.
10. See John, in D. Humphry, *Police Power and Black People*, Panther, 1972, pp. 225–32; cf. *Select Committee on Police/Immigrant Relations*, HC 471/1, 1971–2, ch. 11.
11. Quoted in Whitaker, p. 19.
12. N. Morris and G. Hawkins, *The Honest Politician's Guide to Crime Control*, Univ. of Chicago Press, 1970, p. 94.
13. Brock, in C.H. Rolph, ed., *The Police and the Public*, Heinemann 1962, p. 119.
14. Maureen Cain, in Whitaker, ed., p. 109.
15. Skolnick, *Justice Without Trial*, Wiley 1966, esp. p. 45ff.
16. J. Lambert, *Crime, Police and Race Relations*, Oxford U.P., 1970, pp. 183–4.
17. Skolnick, p. 180.
18. Rolph, p. 183.

19. H.L. Packer, *The Limits of the Criminal Sanction*, Stanford U.P., 1969, pp. 149ff.
20. Skolnick p. 6.
21. M. Banton, *The Policeman in the Community*, Tavistock, 1964, p. 106.
22. Lambert, p. 170.
23. M. Zander, 'Access to a Solicitor in The Police Station', *Criminal L.R.*, 1972, p. 342.
24. See Criminal Law Revision Committee, *11th Report*: *Evidence*, Cmnd 4991, HMSO 1972, para 28–52.
25. Grigg, p. 44.
26. Whitaker, p. 84.
27. R.M. Jackson, *Enforcing the Law*, Penguin Books, 1971, p. 59, quotes an annual average of 11,474 for 1900–04 and 6,182 for 1960–64; cf. Humphry, p. 91.
28. Royal Commission on the Police, Appendix IV to *Minutes of Evidence*, Section ii.
29. Bordua and Tifft, 'Citizen Interviews, organizational Feedback, and Police Community Relations Decisions', *Law and Society Review*, vol. 6, 1971, p. 155, at 180–1.
30. W.F. Whyte, *Street Corner Society*, Univ. of Chicago Press, 1943, p. 136.
31. *The Times*, 24 April 1972.
32. R. Hood and R. Sparks, *Key Issues in Criminology*, Weidenfeld & Nicolson, 1970, p. 39.
33. Skolnick, p. 118.
34. La Fave, 'The Police and nonenforcement of the Law', *Wisconsin L.R.*, 1962, pp. 104, 188–238.
35. See examples given by D.J. Newman, *Conviction: the determination of guilt or innocence without trial*, Little, Brown, 1966, pp. 155–9.
36. F.H. McClintock and E. Gibson, *Robbery in London*, Macmillan, 1961, p. 5.
37. David Steer, *Police Cautions: a study in the exercise of police discretion*, Blackwell, 1970.
38. *Ibid.*, pp. 34–40. This is particularly surprising; see comment

of Wilcox, 'Police Cautions in Five Towns', *Criminal L.R.*, 1971, p. 515 at p. 517.

39. Piliavin and Briar, 'Police encounters with Juveniles' *American Journal of Sociology*, vol. 70, 1964, p. 206.

40. Goldman, *The Differential Selection of Juvenile Offenders for Court Appearance*, National Council on Crime and Delinquency, 1963.

41. Terry, 'Discrimination in the Handling of Juvenile Offenders by Social Control agencies' *Journal of Research in Crime and Delinquency*, vol. 4, 1967, p. 218.

42. Skolnick, p. 85.

43. Mack, 'Police juvenile liaison schemes', *British Journal of Criminology*, vol. 3, 1963, p. 361; see also his *Police Juvenile Liaison: practice and evaluation*; and further, Cain and Dearden, 'Initial reactions to a new juvenile liaison scheme', *British Journal of Criminology*, vol. 6, 1966, p. 421; James G. Somerville, 'A Study of the Preventive Aspect of Police Work with juveniles', *Criminal Law Review*, 1969, pp. 407, 472; and *Study of West Ham Scheme*, Home Office Research Study, HMSO, 1971.

44. K.C. Davis, *Discretionary Justice*, Louisiana State U.P., 1969, p. 223.

45. Justice, *The Prosecution Process in England and Wales*, Stevens, 1970; also in *Criminal Law Review*, 1970, p. 668.

46. *The Times*, 28 April 1972.

47. Paling, 'Police Act (Amendments) Bill 1973', (1973) *Crim. L.R.* 282.

Further reading

Banton, M. *The Policeman in the Community*, Tavistock, 1964.

Bayley, D.H. and Mendelsohn, H. *Minorities and the Police*, New York, Free Press, 1969.

Bordua, D., ed. *The Police*, Wiley, 1967.

Box, S. *Deviance, Reality and Society*, Holt Rinehart & Winston, 1971, ch. 6.

Cain, Maureen, *Society and the Policeman's Role*, Routledge, Kegan Paul, 1973.

Chambliss, W.J. *Crime and the Legal Process* (see General sources), pp. 84–206.

Chambliss, W.J. and Seidman, R.B. *Law, Order and Power*, Addison Wesley, 1971, chs 15–18.

Hood, R. and Sparks, R. *Key Issues in Criminology*, Weidenfeld & Nicolson, 1970, pp. 38–42, 70–9.

Justice, *The Prosecution Process in England and Wales*, Stevens, 1970.

Laurie, P. *Scotland Yard*, Bodley Head, 1970.

Law and Society Review, vol. 6, no. 2, 1971: special issue on the police.

Morris, N. and Hawkins, G. *The Honest Politician's Guide to Crime Control*, Univ. of Chicago Press, 1970, ch. 4.

Punch, M, and Naylor, T., 'The Police – a social service'. New Society, 17 May 1973, p. 358.

Reiss, A. *The Police and the Public*, Yale U.P., 1971.

Rock, P. *Deviant Behaviour,* Hutchinson, 1973, ch. 4.

Select Committee on Race Relations and Immigration, *Police/Immigrant Relations* (3 vols) Session 1971–2 H.C., 471

Skolnick, J.H. *Justice Without Trial*, Wiley 1966.

Westley, W.A. *Violence and the Police: a sociological study of law, custom and morality*, MIT Press, 1970.

Whitaker, B. *The Police*, Penguin Books, 1964.

Wilcox, A, *The Decision to Prosecute*, Butterworths, 1972.

CHAPTER 8.   LAW, LAWYERS AND THE PUBLIC

References

1. Abel-Smith and Stevens, *Lawyers and the Courts*, pp. 462–3.
2. M. Zander, 'Who goes to solicitors?', *Law Society's Gazette*, March 1969, p. 174. See now Abel-Smith, Zander and Brooke, *Legal Problems and the Citizen,* Heinemann, 1973.

3. This refers to the Registrar-General's categories. AB (13 per cent of population) includes professional and managerial classes; C1 (18 per cent of population) includes non-manual managerial and supervising grades, typists, owners of small retail shops; C2 (41 per cent of population) includes skilled workers; DE (28 per cent of population) includes labourers, farm workers, factory workers.

4. *Legal Aid and Advice*, Report of Law Society and Comments and Recommendations of Lord Chancellor's Advisory Committee, 1969–70, *20th Report*, H.C. 446, p. 37.

5. See Carlin and Howard, 'Legal representation and class justice', University of California at Los Angeles Law Review, vol. 12, 1965, p. 381. The five are studies by Lord and Thomas of California in 1940, the Iowa State Bar Association of Iowa in 1949, the Koos study of five cities in 1949, Belden's Texas study of 1952, and a Missouri State Bar Association sample of 1963.

6. J.E. Carlin, *Lawyers' Ethics*, Russell Sage Foundation, 1966, pp. 13–16.

7. Mayhew and Reiss, 'The social organization of legal contacts', *American Sociological Review*, vol. 34, 1969, pp. 311, 312.

8. A.F. Conrad, *et al*, eds *Automobile Accident Costs and Payments*, Univ. of Michigan Press, 1964, pp. 225–7.

9. M. Zander, 'The unused Rent Acts', *New Society*, 12 Sept. 1968.

10. *Report of the Committee on the Rent Acts*, Cmnd 4609, HMSO, 1971, pp. 14–15, 303–7; see also Milner Holland, *Report of the Committee on Housing in Greater London*, Cmnd 2605, HMSO, 1965.

11. See Harz, S.J., 'A Road Accident Survey', 118 *New Law Journal*, 22 May 1969, p. 492.

12. Carlin, Howard, and Messinger, 'Civil justice and the poor', *Law and Society Review*, vol. 1, 1966, pp. 9, 70.

13. See Friedman, 'The Idea of Right as a Social and Legal Concept', Journal of *Social Issues,* vol. 27, 1971, p. 189.

14. Research of Carlin in 1959 quoted in Carlin and Howard, p. 425.

15. Patterson, *Legal Aid as a Social Service*, Cobden Trust, 1970, pp. 26–7.
16. Statistics reproduced from Society of Labour Lawyers, *Justice for All* pp. 22–3. Cf. Foster, 36 M.L.R. 153.
17. M. Young and P. Wilmott, *Family and Kinship in East London*, Routledge, 1957.
18. Consumer Council, *Justice out of Reach*, HMSO, 1970, pp. 10–11.
19. Carlin and Howard, p. 428.
20. Friedman, 'Legal rules and the process of social change', *Stanford L.R.*, vol. 19, 1967, p. 806.
21. *New Society*, 27 April 1972, p. 166.
22. *The Times*, 22. February 1973: L.A.G. Bulletin (1973), p. 43.
23. *New Law Journal*, 30 April 1970, p. 414.
24. *Justice for All*, p. 24. A survey of Bradford's Citizens' Advice Bureaux in the autumn of 1971 showed that of an average of 57 enquiries a day no fewer than 40 raised some question of law; 48 per cent led to a legal reference, 29 per cent to solicitors, and 10 per cent to voluntary legal advice services; see *New Law Journal*, 18 May 1972, p. 349. See also Brooke, *Information and Advice Services*, Bell, 1972.
25. *Justice for All* p. 30.
26. See *The Times*, 18 July 1970, 10 August 1970, For more recent developments in other areas see Legal Action Group's Bulletins. For a good account of American neighbourhood law see *Harvard Law Review*, vol. 80, 1967, pp. 805–50. See also *Justice for All*, pp. 63–76.
27. Seebohm *Report*, Cmnd 3703, HMSO, 1968. The Report did not consider the problems of legal services, referring to them only cursorily in para. 391. It suggested that local authorities should set up centres for housing advice and guidance, but did not discuss the role, if any, of lawyers in this.
28. See North Kensington Local Legal Centre, 1st *Annual Report*, February 1972: 33 percent concern housing, 25 per cent criminal matters, 10 per cent family problems, 8 per cent employment matters, 8 per cent consumer cases.

29. Quoted in *The Times*, 10 August 1970.

30. *Justice for All*, p. 39.

31. Smigel, *Wall Street Lawyer*, New York, Free Press, 1969, pp. 367–8.

32. A Bill to set up a Local Legal Centres Corporation which would establish centres in poor neighbourhoods was introduced in the House of Commons on 1 December 1971 by Michael Meacher, MP (Bill 36), but it made no progress.

33. But not, of course, by divorce. Only half those who obtain magistrates' court orders go on to the divorce courts, see (McGregor) Blom-Cooper and Gibson, *Separated Spouses*, Duckworth, 1970, ch. 9.

34. See Abel-Smith and Stevens, *Lawyers and the Courts*, pp. 32–4.

35. Figures available from the Lord Chancellor's department.

36. Consumer Council, *Justice Out of Reach*, pp. 13–16.

37. There is a note to this effect in *New Law Journal*, 20 August 1970.

38. *Justice Out of Reach*, pp. 30–4; see also *New Law Journal*, 20 August 1970, p. 783. On American experience see *Stanford L.R.* vol. 21, 1969, p. 1657.

39. Ison, 'Small claims', *Modern L.R.*, vol. 35, 1972, pp. 16, 24–7, 29.

40. See *The Guardian*, 6 July 1971. A fuller description is Foster, 'The Manchester Arbitration Scheme', *Solicitors' Journal*, vol. 116, 1973, p. 502. Westminster is also to have one. See LAG Bulletin (1973), p. 87.

41. Recent American history is replete with examples of intimidation of activist Negroes. The Talbert case is often cited, see, e.g. Charles V. Hamilton, 'Southern Judges and Negro Voting Rights', *Wisconsin L.R.*, 1965, pp. 72, 91–6.

42. Macaulay, 'Non-contractual relations in business: a prelimary study' *American Sociological Review*, vol. 28, 1963, p. 55.

43. T.C. Willett in *Criminal on the Road*, Tavistock, 1964, refers to police animosity towards juries because of their over-readiness to acquit.

44. See Hoffman and Brodey, 'Jurors on Trial', *Missouri L.R.*, vol. 17, 1952, p. 235; and Harry Kalven and Hans Zeisel, *The American Jury*, Little, Brown, 1966, ch. 28.

45. Cornish, *The Jury*, Penguin Books (Pelican), 1971, pp. 135–7.

46. *Shaw* v. *D.P.P.* [1962] A.C. 220; cf. now *Knuller* v. *D.P.P.* [1972] 2 All E.R. 898, 904.

47. A. de Tocqueville, *Democracy in America*, trans. Phillips Bradley, Vintage Books, 1960, vol. 1, pp. 291–7, as reproduced in Richard D. Schwartz and Jerome H. Skolnick, *Society and the Legal Order*, Basic Books 1970, p. 317.

48. In *Home Office* v *Dorset Yacht.* [1970] A.C. 1004.

49. In *Dutton* v *Bognor Regis Building Co.* [1972] All E.R. 462.

50. In *Chorlton* v. *Lings* (1868), L.R. 4 C.P. 374, 383.

51. *The Judiciary*, report of a Justice subcommittee, 1972, gives comparative figures. England has 8 per million, as compared with France (82) or Switzerland (121) or Scotland (15). But nearly all criminal cases in England are tried by lay magistrates.

52. See M. Gluckman, *The Judicial Process among the Barotse*, Manchester U.P., 1967, pp. 21, 429.

53. Goitein, *Primitive Ordeal and the Modern Laws*, Macmillan, 1923.

54. Macaulay and Walster, 'Legal structures and restoring equity', *Journal of Social Issues*, vol. 27, 1971, p. 184.

55. G. Drewry, 'Language and the law', *New Law Journal*, 16 April 1972, p.367.

56. Bredemeier, 'Law as an integrative mechanism', in Evan, *Law and Sociology* (see General sources), p. 87.

57. *Ibid.*, p. 84.

58. Rosenberg, 'Court congestion: status, causes and proposed remedies', in H.W. Jones ed. *The Courts, the Public and the Law Explosion*, Prentice-Hall, 1965, pp. 29, 32.

59. See Jackson, *The Machinery of Justice*, Cambridge U.P., 1972, pp. 69–76.

60. Rosenberg and Sovern, 'Delay and the Dynamics of Personal

Injury Litigation', *Columbia L.R.*, vol. 59, 1959, pp. 1115, 1127–39.
61. McGregor et al, *Separated Spouses*, ch. 8; the quotation is from p. 122.
62. *Criminal Law Review*, 1971, p. 132ff, esp. pp. 154–64.

Further reading

Abel-Smith, B. Zander, M. and Brooke, R. *Legal Problems and the Citizen,* Hutchinson, 1973.
Brooke, R. *Information and Advice Services,* Bell, 1972.
Carlin, J. and Howard, J. 'Legal representation and class justice', *UCLA* Law Rev. vol. 12, 1965, p. 381.
Carlin, J., Howard, J. and Messinger, S. 'Civil justice and the poor', *Law and Society Review*, vol. 1, 1966, p. 9.
Conservative Political Centre, *Rough Justice*, 1968.
Fabian Society, *Justice for All*, 1968.
Ison, T. 'Small claims', *Modern L.R.* vol. 35, 1972, p. 18.
Journal of Social Issues, vol. 27, no. 2, 1971, 'Socialization, the law and society', contains valuable contributions by, *inter alia,* Tapp and Kohlberg, Torney, Rokeach et al, Macaulay and Walster, Friedman, Kadish and Kadish, and Kalven.
Law Society of Scotland, *Report on Public Attitudes to Legal Profession in Scotland* by Campbell, C.M. and Wilson, R.J. 1973.
Legal Action Group, *Bulletins*, 1, 1972.
Lord Chancellor's Office. *Legal Aid and Advice*, Annual Reports of Law Society and Comments and Recommendations of Lord Chancellor's Advisory Committee.
Morris, P., White R., and Lewis, P. *Social Needs and Legal Action,* Robertson, 1973.
Patterson, A. *Legal Aid as a Social Service*, Cobden Trust, 1970.
Podgorecki, A. et al, *Knowledge and Opinion About Law*, Robertson, 1973.
Report of Advisory Committee on Better Provision of Legal Advice and Assistance, Cmnd 4249, HMSO, 1970.

Widgery Committee: *Report of Departmental Committee on Legal Aid in Criminal Proceedings*, Cmnd 2934, HMSO, 1966.

Zander, M. 'Unrepresented defendants in the criminal courts', *Criminal L.R.*, 1969, p. 632.

Zander, M. and Glasser, C. 'A study on representation', *New Law Journal*, 27 July 1967, p. 815.

Table of Cases

Table of statutes

Index